We Are Fighting the World

NEW AFRICAN HISTORIES SERIES

Series editors: Jean Allman and Allen Isaacman

David William Cohen and E. S. Atieno Odhiambo, *The Risks of Knowledge: Investigations into the Death of the Hon. Minister John Robert Ouko in Kenya, 1990*

Belinda Bozzoli, *Theatres of Struggle and the End of Apartheid*

Gary Kynoch, *We Are Fighting the World: A History of the Marashea Gangs in South Africa, 1947–1999*

We Are Fighting the World

A History of the Marashea Gangs in
South Africa, 1947–1999

∾

Gary Kynoch

OHIO UNIVERSITY PRESS
ATHENS

UNIVERSITY OF KWAZULU-NATAL PRESS
PIETERMARITZBURG, SOUTH AFRICA

Ohio University Press
The Ridges, Building 19
Athens, Ohio 45701
www.ohio.edu/oupress

University of KwaZulu-Natal Press
Private Bag X01, Scottsville, 3209
South Africa
Email: books@ukzn.ac.za
www.ukznpress.co.za

12 11 10 09 08 07 06 05   5 4 3 2 1

Maps by Wendy Job

Part of chapter 1 appeared as "From the Ninevites to the Hard Livings Gang: Township Gangsters and Urban Violence in Twentieth-Century South Africa" in *African Studies* 58, no. 1 (1999): 55–85 and is reprinted by permission.

Part of chapter 3 appeared in "A Man among Men: Gender, Identity, and Power in South Africa's Marashea Gangs" in *Gender and History* 13, no. 2 (2001): 249–72 and is reprinted by permission.

Part of chapter 4 appeared in "Politics and Violence in the Russian Zone: Conflict in Newclare South, 1950–1957" in *Journal of African History* 41, no. 2 (2000): 267–90 and is reprinted by permission.

Part of chapter 5 appeared in "Marashea on the Mines: Economic, Social and Criminal Networks on the South African Gold Fields, 1947-1999" in *Journal of Southern African Studies* 26, no. 1 (2000): 79–103 and is reprinted by permission.

Library of Congress Cataloging-in-Publication Data

Kynoch, Gary.
We are fighting the world : a history of the Marashea gangs in South Africa, 1947–1999 / Gary Kynoch.
  p. cm. — (New African histories series)
Includes bibliographical references and index.
ISBN 0-8214-1615-4 (cloth : alk. paper) — ISBN 0-8214-1616-2 (pbk. : alk. paper) 1.
Gangs — South Africa — History. I. Title. II. Series.
HV6439.S6K96 2005
364.1'06'60973 — dc22

                                                        2004021754

University of KwaZulu-Natal Press ISBN 1-86914-072-9

Contents

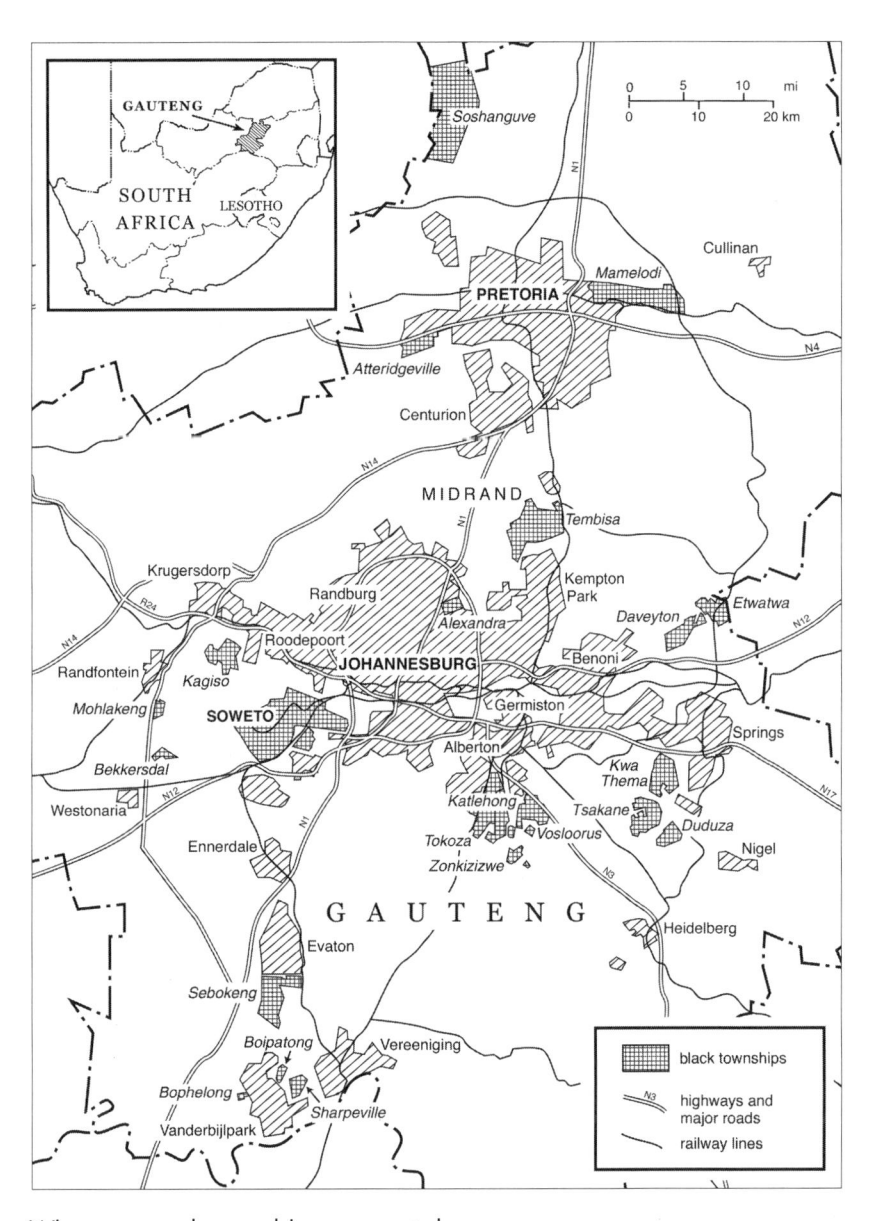

Witwatersrand townships, present day

Preface

THIS BOOK IS THE FIRST attempt to write a comprehensive history of an African criminal society known as the Marashea, or "Russians," from its inception in the 1940s to the present.[1] It covers the formation of the association in the townships and mining compounds of the Witwatersrand, the massive street battles of the 1950s, and the government's forced removal schemes that dispersed the Russians from some of their urban strongholds during this same period.[2] These original groups of Marashea drew their strength from Basotho migrants who worked and lived on the Johannesburg area mines, as well as those who resided in the townships and were employed in the city.[3] The gold-mining industry's expansion into the far West Rand and Free State during the 1950s and 1960s, coupled with the Aliens Control Act of 1963 (which made it illegal for the vast majority of Basotho migrants to work in South Africa outside the agricultural and mining sectors), resulted in a Marashea migration that shifted Russian power from the Rand to the townships and informal settlements surrounding the emerging gold mines. The Marashea remains a powerful force in many of South Africa's gold mining areas.

Newspapers and archival documents proved to be valuable source materials but are limited in the range of issues they address. Police, mining, and township officials tended to focus on the disruption to order that Russian activities caused, and the Marashea came to public notice almost exclusively as a result of their involvement in violence. Newspapers intended for white readership rarely mentioned Marashea because, except for the most spectacular instances of violence, their activities did not impinge on the white world. African newspapers reported on collective violence, robberies, and court appearances and typically condemned the gangs as primitive tribal thugs. This was the public face of the Marashea.

Archival sources were useful in providing government and mining officials' views of the Marashea, as well as supplying dates, casualty figures, and arrest records for specific events. In the archival records, the Marashea appear

as a nuisance in the townships and mines—because of their involvement in street battles, faction fights, murders, and robberies—but not as a political threat to the state. Instead, they are depicted as tribal Africans untainted by communist or other revolutionary ideology, with no grievances against whites and no political agenda. Mining officials expressed occasional concern over Russian violence that threatened to disrupt mining operations, but the gangs did not challenge white authority on the mines. White commentators sometimes characterized the Marashea as murderous thugs but not as political subversives. These sources of evidence provide little information on the inner workings of the Marashea but are particularly valuable in situating the Russian gangs in a political context. Documentary evidence clearly indicates that the apartheid regime not only discounted the Marashea as a threat to white rule but that the police made common cause with gangster and vigilante groups as early as the 1950s in their campaigns to undermine the ANC and its affiliates. In this way the state was directly responsible for sponsoring episodes of conflict in the townships long before the politicized violence of the 1980s and 1990s.

Gathering oral testimony from current and former Marashea was the only way to probe into issues of culture and gender relations, to better understand how the gangs fit into their environment and how they perceived of and represented themselves. The major limitation to this approach is that one does not get an outsider's view of the society. I interviewed a handful of mineworkers, police, and mining officials, but, for the most part, outsiders' perceptions are examined only through the claims of Marashea themselves.

Between April 1998 and June 1999, seventy-nine Marashea (sixty-three men, sixteen women) were interviewed in Lesotho, in the townships and informal settlements of Gauteng province, and in Marashea settlements surrounding the mining towns of Klerksdorp, Virginia, Carletonville, and Welkom.[4] These seventy-nine individuals span six decades of experience as Marashea. Some respondents spent the majority of their adult lives as Marashea while others were members for only a year or two. The ages of those informants who knew their birth dates ranged from twenty-eight to eighty-four. With the exception of two respondents who spoke very good English, all interviews were conducted in Sesotho.

The foremost difficulties involved gaining access to active members and women. Meetings with current Marashea visiting Lesotho led to trips to Russian settlements in South Africa, where additional interviews were conducted, including one with BM, the leader of the Matsieng faction in the Free State. In the end my research assistants and I spent time in four different Marashea settlements, and a total of nine active Marashea participated in in-

terviews. Moreover, informal conversations yielded information about protection arrangements, rental agreements with white farmers, the demographics of the camps, business ventures, living conditions, social practices, and relations with mineworkers.

BM refused our request to interview women, saying that women did not know history and would say silly things. The same experience was repeated in the other Marashea settlements. As a result, only one active woman, a relation of an intermediary, was interviewed. Marashea women in general were difficult to identify, especially in Lesotho. Former Marashea women who have returned to Lesotho tend not to advertise their status and, despite exhaustive efforts, female informants made up just under 20 percent of the total interview pool.

Interviewing people who had experience with Marashea was often problematic. It would have been valuable to consult with more police officers, but I decided against this because of the extensive connections Marashea groups have with police. If it was discovered that I was asking the police about the Marashea it is possible that avenues would have been closed off. Consequently, I did not pursue any police contacts in South Africa until near the end of my fieldwork, although I discussed the Marashea with a few police officers in Lesotho. Several mineworkers were also interviewed during the initial stages of fieldwork in Lesotho. Although a number of South African mining officials refused to discuss the Marashea, staff at Harmony Mine in the Free State were very helpful. An NUM representative enthusiastically participated in an interview, as did a former liaison division employee of the Employment Bureau of Africa. In the 1950s Johannesburg gangs attracted a great deal of public attention, primarily because of the massive street battles in which they engaged. Unfortunately, many of the lawyers and township officials who came into contact with the Johannesburg Russians are deceased. With the exception of one advocate who represented Russians in the 1960s and 1970s, I was unable to track down any members of the legal profession or government service who had done business with the Marashea.

Not surprisingly, some Marashea informants were evasive or refused to discuss certain topics. Questions concerning relationships with the police, criminal activities, conflicts with ANC supporters, and links with political parties in Lesotho were the most likely to elicit such responses. The political turmoil stemming from the May 1998 national elections in Lesotho, which eventually led to military intervention and occupation by a South African–led force in September 1998, made discussions of political affairs extremely sensitive.

Problems of accuracy and reliability are two central issues that oral historians continually confront. This study was no different and gathering testimony

from respondents who were involved in a range of criminal activities rendered these concerns even more salient. The formulation of collective memory in oral testimony has been commented on by many practitioners. Discussing the testimony of Holocaust survivors, Deborah Lipstadt observes that "lots of survivors who arrived at Auschwitz will tell you they were examined by [Dr. Josef] Mengele. Then you ask them the date of their arrival and you say, 'Well, Mengele wasn't in Auschwitz yet at that point.' There were lots of doctors . . . somehow they all became Mengele."[5] In this instance it seems that larger societal perceptions influenced how people remembered and related their stories. Mengele became a symbol of evil, representing the horror of the concentration camps, so some survivors appropriated his presence to make sense of their own horror and to perhaps better express it to others, including the interviewer. This raises the issue of the construction of memory, or as Alistair Thomson suggests, the composure of memory. "In one sense we 'compose' or construct memories using the public language and meanings of our culture. In another sense we 'compose' memories which help us feel relatively comfortable with our lives, which gives us a feeling of composure. We remake or repress memories of experiences which are still painful and 'unsafe' because their inherent traumas or tensions have not been resolved. . . . Our memories are risky and painful if they do not conform to the public norms or versions of the past."[6]

Marashea informants recited careful constructions of particular events and personalities. One of the defining events for Marashea active on the Rand in the 1950s and 1960s was a series of battles between combined Marashea forces and Zulu hostel dwellers that took place in 1957. The fighting raged for days between hundreds, if not thousands, of combatants, and the Dube Hostel Riots, as the conflicts came to be known in official parlance, were the subject of a government inquiry and extensive media attention. Virtually all the men interviewed who were members during this era claim to have taken part in these battles and recite details that have obviously become embedded in popular lore. It is extremely doubtful that all these informants actually participated in the fighting. For example, some men date their arrival on the Rand after 1957. Given the confusion with dates this is not absolute proof they were not present, but the likelihood that they all were is extremely remote. The Marashea's image as defenders of the Basotho resonates very strongly among these men, and the Dube Hostel conflicts provide the foremost example of the Marashea rallying to the defense of fellow Basotho during this era. It was also a great victory for the Russians, and informants wished to be associated with an event that reinforced their identity as champions of the Basotho and successful warriors. Philip Bonner notes a similar development in discussions

of a 1940s clash between Basotho and Zulu in Benoni: "A host of other informants claim to have witnessed this latter episode. I am almost certain that for a number it was hearsay."[7]

The collective memory phenomenon also emerges in the strikingly similar accounts of the Dube Hostel conflicts. Informants' recitations of the beginning of the conflict in which a Russian named Malefane was castrated by Zulu men in the hostel's shebeen has the feel of a story that has been many times in the telling. The same sort of mythologizing surfaced in testimony surrounding the famous leader Tseule Tsilo. Again, it is unlikely that all the men who claimed to have witnessed Tsilo's feats and interacted with him could have done so. Rather than invalidating such testimony, these responses speak to the power of the myth of Tsilo. Once such developments are recognized, they can be used as windows to interpret the ideals and worldviews of informants instead of simply dismissing suspect statements and stories as falsehoods. As Allesandro Portelli argues, "Oral sources tell us not just what people did but what they wanted to do, what they believed they were doing, and what they now think they did."[8]

Kathleen Blee's experience gathering testimonies from former members of the Ku Klux Klan led her to consider how people from groups that have been publicly maligned consciously attempt to rehabilitate the group's (and their individual) reputation during the interview process: "Meanings are created in social and political contexts; memory is not a solitary act. Thus it is not simply that narratives constructed by former Klan members to explain their role in one of history's most vicious campaigns of intolerance and hatred are biased by their own political agendas and their desire to appear acceptable to an oral historian but also that informants' memories have been shaped by subsequent public censure of this and later Klans."[9]

Marashea informants are well aware of their public reputation as thugs and assassins, and some men went to great lengths to portray the Marashea, or at least their particular group, as a benign force that fought crime and dispensed justice in the townships and informal settlements. This was especially evident among active informants, who dismissed Marashea of the past as violent criminals. These men depicted the current Marashea as a business and mutual-aid association for migrant Basotho, denying that they or their fellow members engaged in criminal or other antisocial activities. To cite one example, despite overwhelming evidence to the contrary, Russian leader BM denied that his group participated in the violent conflicts between Marashea and union supporters that took place in and around Harmony Gold Mine in 1990. When questioned, BM insisted that his followers had no stake in the conflict and that any Marashea who joined the fighting did so in their capacity as miners,

not as Marashea.[10] The testimony of active informants, who were unlikely to incriminate themselves and who had a more direct interest in the well-being and reputation of the current Marashea, has to be considered in this light. Sensitive information about the modern Marashea was more readily supplied by recently retired veterans who were active in the 1980s and 1990s. These men and women tended to be more candid and discussed aspects of their experiences that active Marashea were reluctant to divulge.

Retired informants' reflections on their lives as Marashea differed. While a few women emphasized the excitement of being associated with the Russians, most spoke of the hardships and violence they endured. Some men expressed regret for the crimes they committed while others were boastful and unrepentant. The diversity of responses on many issues leads me to believe that the informants comprise a fairly representative cross-section of the Marashea, despite the underrepresentation of women and young, active male members.

Gathering oral testimonies from gang members who were regularly involved in criminal activities presented particular difficulties, the foremost being identifying informants and persuading them to participate in an interview. Second, because of the nature of their activities and the climate of repression that characterized their lives in South Africa, some informants were evasive or refused to discuss certain topics. I labor under no illusion that I have uncovered the definitive history of the Marashea. Many aspects of people's lives as Marashea remain obscured for a host of reasons. The archival record is extremely limited in the scope and range of issues commented on and the collected testimony cannot possibly relate the entire story of the many thousands of people who have comprised the Marashea over the years. Perhaps most important, respondents revealed mere fractions of their experiences. Bearing these qualifications in mind, I believe this work provides an insight into the lives led by the women and men of the Marashea; the coping strategies they employed; the impact the association had in the townships, informal settlements, and mining hostels; and the autonomy that groups like the Marashea exercised within the structural constraints established by the apartheid state.

Acknowledgments

THIS BOOK WOULD NOT have materialized without the efforts of Tsepang Cekwane and Booi Mohapi. Along with conducting and transcribing interviews, Tsepang proved particularly adept at finding Marashea throughout Lesotho and in South African townships and informal settlements. His navigational skills saved me from getting lost more times than I can remember, and his enthusiasm for this project made him a pleasure to work with. We learned much about the Marashea together. Booi, assisted by his wife, Mampolokeng, completed a number of superb interviews. Teke Tseane lent valuable assistance at a time when interviews were hard to come by. Litabe Majoro, who studied the Marashea as a student at the National University of Lesotho, was kind enough to direct me to one of his informants and conduct an interview. The stories told by the men and women who related their lives as Marashea provide the foundation of this study.

Philip Bonner's work inspired my research and, despite an extraordinarily demanding schedule, Phil generously gave his time, advice, and copies of interview transcripts. David Coplan also offered encouragement. I owe a special debt to Rosemary Burke, the Employment Bureau of Africa's archivist. Rosemary helped me sift through files and took it upon herself to contact several people in the mining industry on my behalf. Kent McNamara graciously passed along numerous materials and discussed the Russians' activities on the mines. I would like to express my appreciation to various staff at Harmony Gold Mine who took the time to speak with me. Thanks are due to Puseletso Salae, Raymond de Boiz, and Don Mattera, who all shared their experiences with the Marashea.

The research for this book was conducted while I was a visiting fellow at the University of the Witwatersrand's now-defunct Institute for Advanced Social Research. I am grateful to Charles van Onselen and the IASR staff for hosting me at Wits. Barb and Herb Anstadt provided a home away from home in Johannesburg and have become our South African family.

At Dalhousie University, Jane Parpart and Phil Zachernuk nurtured the thesis that has eventually become a book. Their support, guidance, and friendship sustained me throughout my tenure as a graduate student. I thank them both.

Jean Allman's patience in steering the manuscript through to publication is also greatly appreciated. I gratefully acknowledge funding from the Social Sciences and Humanities Research Council of Canada for research in South Africa.

Finally, this book is dedicated, with all my love, to Theresa Ulicki.

Abbreviations

ANC—African National Congress
BCP—Basotho (Basutoland) Congress Party
BNP—Basotho (Basutoland) National Party
BOSS—Bureau of State Security
EPTC—Evaton People's Transport Council
IFP—Inkatha Freedom Party
LLA—Lesotho Liberation Army
NP—National Party
NUM—National Union of Mineworkers
SAP—South African Police
SAPS—South African Police Service (after 1995)
UDF—United Democratic Front

Marashea posing for a photograph, 1960s. Collection of the author.

1 ～ Urban Violence in South Africa

SOUTH AFRICA IS ONE OF the most crime-ridden societies in the world.[1]
In a country where unemployment runs between 30 and 50 percent and the
majority of the population struggles on the economic margins, high crime
rates are not surprising. It is the violence associated with so much of the crime
that has created a climate of fear. Carjacking, rape, murder, armed robbery,
gang conflicts, taxi wars, vigilantism, and police shootings dominate the headlines and the national consciousness. This culture of violence has become
one of the defining features of contemporary South African life.

Although segregation and apartheid nurtured hostility and conflict among
all population groups in South Africa, surprisingly little effort has been made
to investigate the historical roots of the current crisis. To the extent that historical factors are considered, the epidemic of violent crime is most often attributed to the civil conflicts of the 1980s and 1990s. These conflicts — usually
referred to as political violence — raged throughout many of South Africa's
urban townships as well as some rural areas. In 1985 the African National
Congress (ANC) called on its supporters to make the townships ungovernable
and urban violence escalated as thousands of activists heeded that call. The
National Party (NP) government responded predictably, ordering the police
and military to crush political dissent. Government security forces also encouraged various elements within the black population to take up arms against
ANC militants, known as comrades. Once the ANC was unbanned in 1990
and elections loomed on the horizon, the violence intensified. Agents within
the security apparatus sponsored and directly assisted the Inkatha Freedom
Party (IFP), a "moderate," ethnically Zulu political movement, in its war against

1

the ANC and supported conservative black groups that refused to acknowledge the authority of the comrades. The South African Police (SAP) allowed criminal gangs to operate with impunity in return for their services as informants and assassins. All the warring parties recruited criminal gangs to some extent and were unable to exercise full control over the elements that fought in their name. Large parts of KwaZulu-Natal, along with many townships and informal settlements in other areas of the country, became war zones.

In conventional accounts this anarchic violence created a residuum of men, inured to killing, who have pursued purely criminal endeavors following the cessation of politically motivated hostilities.[2] The youth who engaged in these conflicts are often referred to as the lost generation, partially because they sacrificed their education for the liberation struggle. Comrades who had been valorized for their role in the struggle felt betrayed by an ANC government that discarded them once it was voted into power. These men, and other combatants who had exploited the violence to achieve positions of power, continued with and expanded their predatory activities while shedding any pretense of political motivation. The current generation of South African youth has grown up with this legacy and embraced a criminal lifestyle. In this interpretation, the civil conflicts gave birth to a culture of violence and lawlessness that continues to haunt South Africa long after the political struggle was effectively settled by the ANC's 1994 election victory.

This explanation is limited by its failure to consider the longer-term historical dimensions of the prevailing crisis. The fighting between government forces, the ANC, Inkatha, and their various proxies infused localized disputes with a political veneer and significantly escalated the scale of violence. However, these conflicts did not create a culture of violence in the townships. A historically grounded analysis clearly demonstrates that political rivalries degenerated into bloody conflicts partially because a culture of violence was already ingrained in township society. South Africa's endemic violence, in other words, is not a post-conflict affair but rather a continuation of preexisting conditions.

This book explores the nature of power and violence in the apartheid era through the history of the Marashea. In particular, this study counters the notion of apartheid as a systematic program of social engineering that regulated virtually every aspect of black urban life. The failure of the colonial state to control urban townships and informal settlements and to provide effective civil policing created the space and incentive for the emergence of various criminal and vigilante groups that proliferated during the turbulent decades of apartheid. Despite the battery of legislation introduced by the apartheid regime to further restrict the lives of black urbanites, the activities and inter-

actions of criminal gangs and vigilantes were, in many respects, more instrumental than government policy in shaping the day-to-day lives of township residents. Gangster and vigilante violence, often exacerbated by a police force primarily concerned with enforcing racial legislation and suppressing political dissent, became a normative feature of life in many townships and a driving force behind the culture of violence that developed in South Africa. The shifting character of urban violence indicates the need to move beyond the resistance-collaboration binary that still defines much of South African social history. Organizations like the Marashea established, protected, and expanded spheres of influence independent of larger political and ideological concerns. Their actions were guided by immediate local interests that at certain times led to clashes with state forces and at others resulted in alliances with police and government officials. The resistance-collaboration dyad makes no allowances for this complexity and an approach that is sensitive to—yet not defined by—the struggle for liberation provides an improved understanding of the range of social relationships that developed under apartheid.

The title of this book, "We Are Fighting the World," reflects Marashea members' conviction that a range of forces were arrayed against them in the urban and mining environs of apartheid South Africa. Their collective story of survival reveals much about how Africans constructed their worlds within the structural constraints imposed by the white-ruled state. The relative autonomy of these gangs of migrant Basotho highlights the limitations of apartheid hegemony. The state simply never possessed the resources to effectively govern and control the urban areas designated for black settlement. At any given time the government could concentrate its forces and occupy a township or group of townships, but it was unable to maintain a constant presence. The Marashea was one of hundreds of African organizations that filled this void and shaped the experiences of township, mining hostel, and informal settlement residents. Apartheid, no less than other forms of colonial governance, was mediated by the Africans it was designed to subjugate and control. A system that denied black South Africans protective policing and access to an equitable justice system inevitably produced a variety of groups that attempted to fulfill these functions as well as those that capitalized on the opportunities these conditions presented.

The central aim of this study is to account for the Marashea's ability to survive throughout the apartheid era. To this end, I explore the ways in which identity formation, gender relations, economic opportunism, collective violence, and political maneuvering contributed to the long-term integrity of the gangs. There were four pillars to the Marashea's success: its economic relationship with mineworkers, its nonadversarial stance toward the apartheid state,

the control of migrant women, and ethnic mobilization. The following summary of the history and historiography of urban violence provides a context within which these strategies and the Marashea gangs themselves can be better situated.

A HISTORICAL OVERVIEW OF CRIME, POLICING, AND VIOLENCE

We have a reasonably good understanding of the development of different criminal organizations and patterns of collective violence in twentieth-century South African townships. The discovery of massive gold deposits in the area that was to become Johannesburg attracted fortune seekers of European descent from all over the world. The corresponding demand for cheap labor brought Africans from throughout the subcontinent to work in the mines and associated industries. Between 1887 and 1899 Johannesburg was transformed from a mining camp with a population of three thousand into a metropolis with over one hundred thousand inhabitants.[3] In a rough environment where criminals of all population groups plied their trades, successive white governments worked to bring white society under control. Legislation designed to eradicate organized criminal activity was introduced and hundreds of white gangsters were imprisoned and deported between 1898 and 1910.[4] In contrast, the densely populated, impoverished, and ethnically diverse black settlements that had mushroomed on the fringes of mine properties and white neighborhoods enjoyed no such protection. As long as violent crime was contained within the townships and posed no threat to whites, it was not a police priority.

In the first half of the twentieth century, a succession of migrant gangs, most with close ties to the mining industry, dominated the criminal landscape.[5] The Zulu-based Ninevites on the turn-of-the-century Witwatersrand terrorized the inhabitants of urban black locations.[6] In early-twentieth-century Durban, attacks on unsuspecting individuals by gangs of migrant "kitchen boys" known as Amalaita "remained a ubiquitous feature of suburban labouring life."[7] The Rand mining compounds of the 1920s and 1930s were plagued by the Mpondo Isitshozi gangs, which "established a reign of terror on the paths leading to and from the mines."[8] A resident of Johannesburg's Western Native Township, reflecting back on the early 1930s, recalled, "The most dreaded gang in those days were the [Pedi-dominated] Amalaitas. . . . They used to beat up people mercilessly."[9] After its emergence in the late 1940s the Marashea soon became the dominant migrant gang on the Rand.

Young thugs, known as *tsotsis*, formed street corner gangs in the 1940s and 1950s, following the waves of massive black immigration to urban centers that occurred during the Second World War. The tsotsi phenomenon took root as large sections of the rapidly growing population of urbanized youth turned to violent crime. Indeed, Clive Glaser claims that by the 1950s "the majority of permanently urbanized black youths in South Africa's key urban conglomerate, the Witwatersrand, was involved, to a greater or lesser extent, in tsotsi gangs."[10] In Cape Town's District Six, before the population removals of the 1960s and 1970s, extended family gangs "ordered the ghetto through their connections, intermarriages, agreements, 'respect' and ultimately, their force and access to violence."[11] Tsotsi gangs such as the Black Swines and the Pirates established a strong presence in Soweto in the 1960s, while the Hazels reigned supreme in the 1970s.[12] And although it seems that many Soweto gangs were thrown on the defensive by politicized students following the 1976 uprising, they reemerged in the form of the "jackrollers" of the 1980s and 1990s. In the Cape Peninsula, the relocation of Coloured communities to the Cape Flats spawned several different types of criminal syndicates that have survived to the present day. Many gangsters and their gangs, like Rashied Staggie of the Hard Livings Gang, have become household names.[13]

The impact of policing designed to serve white needs can be traced to the early days of the Rand. The Ninevites dispensed their own rough brand of justice in Johannesburg because for Africans it was "a town without law."[14] John Brewer summarizes township policing in the 1950s: "Passes and documents were checked, raids for illicit liquor conducted and illegal squatters evicted, all while murder, rape and gangsterism flourished."[15] A 1955 report on youth crime on the Rand recorded that gang members boasted openly that police were so intent on liquor and pass offenses that tsotsis had little to fear from them.[16] The police campaign against township youth during the 1976 Soweto uprising marked a turning point in community-police relations as increasing numbers of township residents turned against the SAP.[17] With protest against the apartheid regime mounting throughout the 1980s, the police focused almost exclusively on political offenders. Hence, the Diepkloof Parents' Association's 1989 complaint: "There is a growing feeling in the community that the SAP is quick to act against anti-apartheid activists and their organisations but they do nothing to stop the criminals presently terrorising us."[18] During the final decade of apartheid, the SAP was deeply implicated in the violence that engulfed so many townships across the country.

Just as the absence of adequate policing and social control provided an incentive for township gangsters, the lack of state protection necessitated the

formation of vigilante movements as communities organized to protect themselves and punish suspected offenders. Neighborhood policing initiatives known as Civilian Guards were formed in the 1930s on the Rand, and township residents consistently supported such movements for the next fifty years. ANC supporters established street committees and people's courts in the 1980s and 1990s and vigilantism and popular courts continue to play a prominent role in many townships.

A HISTORIOGRAPHY OF VIOLENCE

Within the sizable South African literature dealing with violence, only the more recent episodes of civil conflict have inspired integrated analyses that investigate the manner in which various police forces, criminal gangs, vigilantes, political groups, and localized struggles interconnected to fuel the cycle of conflict.[19] Despite widespread recognition that endemic violence is almost always the product of a combination of circumstances and forces, South African historical accounts tend to treat criminal gangs, vigilantism, and policing as separate phenomena. Furthermore, very few analyses explore township violence over a protracted period to identify trends and turning points.[20] Thus, the historical literature focusing on urban crime and violence constitutes a collection of isolated case studies that are still largely mired in the resistance-collaboration framework.[21]

Tim Nuttal and John Wright recently observed that South African historians have long been "in one way or another, to a greater or lesser degree, caught up in the deep and narrow groove of 'struggle history.'"[22] Many leading South Africanists came of age in apartheid South Africa and identified with the struggle against racist oppression. Not only did this result in the categorization of a multitude of different acts and behavior as resistance, but groups that cooperated with the authorities or who came into conflict with liberation movements have typically been classified as collaborators. Attempts to provide more subtle and nuanced interpretations of the struggle still tend to view resistance as the definitive South African story. For example, in their call to expand the category of resistance, Bonner, Peter Delius, and Deborah Posel argue that "the resistance and opposition which confronted the governing authorities was far more wide ranging and amorphous than has been revealed by the conventional focus on national political organisations. Countless individual or small-scale acts of non-compliance proved more pervasive, elusive, persistent and difficult to control than more formal or organised political struggle."[23]

Here we have the tendency to conflate survival with resistance and to imbue a wide range of prosaic activities with subversive dimensions. Frederick Cooper explains the allure of this approach: "Scholars have their reasons for taking an expansive view. Little actions can add up to something big: desertion from labor contracts, petty acts of defiance of white officials or their African subalterns, illegal enterprises in colonial cities, alternative religious communities—all these may subvert a regime that proclaimed both its power and its righteousness, raise the confidence of people in the idea that colonial power can be countered, and forge a general spirit conducive to mobilisation across a variety of social differences." However, as Cooper points out, such a sweeping interpretation of resistance undermines an appreciation of the complexities of colonial societies and reduces the lives of the colonized to participants in the struggle against colonial oppression. As a result, "the texture of people's lives is lost; and complex strategies of coping, of seizing niches within changing economies, of multi-sided engagement with forces inside and outside the community, are narrowed into a single framework."[24] Following Cooper's lead, Africanist scholars have increasingly abandoned the basic oppressor-resistor axis in favor of a more multilayered understanding of the relationships that comprised the colonial process. Nancy Rose Hunt argues, "Social action in colonial and postcolonial Africa cannot be reduced to such polarities as metropole/colony or colonizer/colonized or to balanced narrative plots of imposition and response or hegemony and resistance."[25]

Some historians of settler states, which suffered more oppressive forms of colonial rule and experienced bloodier trajectories to independence, have had a difficult time abandoning these polarities. Teresa Barnes claims that while local struggles and misunderstandings existed in colonial Zimbabwe, a larger struggle was operative. Most settlers acted like racist overlords and most Africans resisted colonial rule. She warns, "Lilting along in deconstructionist mode . . . can lead scholars to miss the forest for the trees."[26] However, one can accept that most white South Africans were racist and that most black South Africans were opposed to white rule in general and apartheid in particular without narrowly defining the lives of the colonized according to their relationships with the forces of apartheid, however such relationships were perceived.

Resistance needs to be distinguished from the strategies of avoidance, manipulation, circumvention, and adaptation regularly employed by black South Africans. Negotiation and navigation are more useful labels for these coping strategies. Most people living under colonial rule navigated the spaces available to them and created new spaces in which to realize their aspirations. The colonized were forced to deal with constraints imposed by oppressive regimes and

usually chose to quietly subvert rather than openly challenge those conditions. Specifically because colonial states suppressed groups and individuals that posed a direct threat, navigation and negotiation were generally more prudent and popular options. They allowed colonial subjects more latitude to achieve their immediate objectives and the daily business of survival ensured that most people prioritized these immediate needs rather than focusing on resistance. Accepting these concepts as the most common strategies of engagement with colonial rule does not signify a belief in the essential passivity of black South Africans or any other colonial subjects. Instead, this approach recognizes that people coped with repressive conditions in an almost infinite variety of ways.

The study of criminal gangs has proved particularly susceptible to the resistance-collaboration dyad. Analysts have tended to depict black South African gangsters as social bandits battling the repressive state on behalf of the oppressed masses,[27] or less commonly, as destructive predators victimizing fellow blacks and undermining progress.[28] To privilege a gang's relationship to the government and its agents as the defining characteristic of that gang (whether the gang is classified as antistate, apolitical, or allied with the government) overlooks the complex manner in which gangs fit into their communities and the variety of roles they played in the townships.[29] This approach also obscures the issue of identity. Gang identities were forged as a result of numerous factors—relations with rival gangs, the methods by which gang members supported themselves, political affiliation, specific rituals and cultural idioms, gender relations, ethnicity, age, territorialism, and so on—designed to contextualize the world of the townships, an environment in which the white-ruled state was an important but by no means the only, or even the dominant, influence. Group identities, which shaped activities and community relations, developed to meet the needs and correspond with the worldviews of gang members struggling to survive in hostile surroundings. Gangs tended to be preoccupied with rival groups within the townships rather than with larger political issues. This is not to argue that gangs defined themselves exclusively through relationships with competitors or did not consciously resist the agents of the state, only that a host of influences contributed to gang identity and determined gang activities. In other words, it is unlikely that gangs defined themselves, or were regarded by different groups in the community, primarily according to their place on the resistance continuum.

Focusing exclusively on the destructive impact of gangs obscures the multifaceted roles these groups performed within the townships. Without discounting the mayhem gangs inflicted on urban residents, it is important to recognize that the communities that harbored criminal groups did not view

them solely as a destructive force. It is unlikely that gangs could have flourished in South Africa without a significant degree of support from segments of urban communities. This support shifted in emphasis, from mere tolerance to outright alliances, and different gangs drew support from different sections of the community at different times, contingent on a variety of social, economic, and political factors.

Gang-community relationships merit much closer scrutiny than they have typically received. Resentment toward the authorities that regulated township dwellers' movements, rights of residence, and access to jobs and subjected townspeople to constant harassment through liquor and pass raids meant that gang violence directed at the police was likely to be celebrated by many community members. A former tsotsi highlights the ambivalent relationship between gangs and their neighbors. "The gangs were a great paradox. People couldn't understand why they would rob them, stab them and then fight the police. So there was this love-hate relationship."[30] Other than battling the police, gangs engaged in activities that met with varying degrees of popular approval, including the victimization of white-, Indian-, and Chinese-owned businesses, brawls with white gangs, and participation in political initiatives. Moreover, many gangs conducted their criminal activities away from their home areas and thus probably did not earn the enmity of the people among whom they lived.

Some township residents shared in the spoils of the gangs' criminal exploits, especially through the distribution of heavily discounted stolen goods.[31] Poverty and the brutally high rates of unemployment in the townships ensured that many families appreciated any source of income, including proceeds from criminal activity, and in certain areas gangs provided crucial economic inputs. Cape Flats gangs seem particularly influential in this regard: "They are popular figures providing income for an estimated 100,000 people through the illicit economy they control, sometimes paying the water and electricity bills of entire neighbourhoods."[32] Such developments fostered an economic interdependence between gangs and local residents and entrenched an acceptance of criminal culture within large sections of the affected communities. Although the vast majority of gangs were predatory in some respect, they often engaged in activities or represented ideals that were approved by substantial numbers of township residents.

THE MARASHEA

Readers familiar with South African urban and gang literature will have come across the Russians in articles by Bonner, Jeff Guy, and Motlatsi Thabane and,

more recently, some of my own work.[33] Despite the gangs' widespread reputation for violence and the fact that the association has operated in South Africa for more than fifty years, these articles are the sole publications whose primary focus is the Marashea.[34] Bonner, much like Guy and Thabane, presents the Marashea as a fighting association of Basotho migrants who banded together on the Rand in the 1940s and 1950s for protection from urban criminals and ethnic rivals, to obtain control over migrant Basotho women, and to celebrate their identity as Basotho by engaging in exhilarating internecine battles. Both articles deal with the Russian gangs in their formative years on the Rand and pay special attention to the violence that seems to have defined the gangs. Indeed, Bonner states, "The Russians on the Reef were, above all, a fighting machine."[35] Neither study extends its focus beyond the Witwatersrand of the 1950s, although Bonner claims that increasingly heavier prison sentences imposed on regular offenders, combined with more stringent influx controls, significantly weakened the Russians by the mid-1960s.[36]

While the Russians retained a presence in Johannesburg and neighboring towns, the strength of the association shifted to informal settlements and townships surrounding the newly established gold mines. Members not employed on the mines were forced to seek alternative sources of income, and the gangs became increasingly commercially oriented. In particular, they established large-scale liquor distribution and prostitution rackets that catered to the needs of African mineworkers housed in single-sex hostels. The patronage of mineworkers became the economic backbone of the Marashea, and different gangs operated throughout the mining areas. Their close ties with miners ensured that the groups became involved in the often violent politics of the mining industry. As mining groups expanded, the remaining urban Marashea struggled to survive. With diminishing numbers and a shrinking economic base, these groups competed fiercely for resources and became central players in a series of taxi wars that raged throughout the 1980s. However, despite efforts to maintain connections with their colleagues in the mining areas, the Johannesburg gangs were never able to regain their former stature.

The politicized conflicts of the 1980s and 1990s drew in the Marashea, along with many other combatants. A number of mining groups fought with supporters of the newly formed National Union of Mineworkers (NUM), which had close, albeit informal, links with the ANC. Marashea networks of influence and patronage were threatened by this new force, and the gangs defended their interests, sometimes in collusion with mine management and security. Following bloody and protracted fighting, the NUM emerged victorious and the Marashea had to adapt to a new political dispensation on the mines. The Russians were not as active in the violence on the Rand, which

was dominated by conflicts between ANC supporters and IFP-aligned hostel dwellers. The few incidents of conflict seem to have been fought largely along generational lines when older members of the urban Marashea groups refused to recognize the authority of the youthful comrades. These disputes, while bloody, were overshadowed by ANC-Inkatha hostilities. The Marashea continues to operate in South Africa, although its livelihood is threatened by retrenchments in the mining sector and the AIDS pandemic that is taking a particularly heavy toll among mining populations.

2 ↬ The Anatomy of the Marashea

THE MARASHEA WAS FOUNDED by adult male Basotho migrants working in South African cities and mines. Age, gender, and ethnicity have remained defining features of the Russian gangs to the present day. The stability associated with adult members who do not graduate out of a youth gang lifestyle has been important to the organizational coherence of the Marashea. Men control the various Marashea groups, and the exploitation of female members, combined with a militaristic masculine identity, has shaped the history of the society. A Sesotho identity remains at the very core of Borashea, for the gangs exist to meet the needs of Basotho migrants operating in an alienating and often hostile South African environment. Over the past fifty years the Marashea has undergone many changes and in many ways has stayed the same. In any case its existence reinforces the argument that, despite the constraints imposed by apartheid, Africans constructed influential organizations that often had a greater degree of localized power than various government agencies.

FORMATION

Any study of the Marashea must begin by acknowledging Philip Bonner's pioneering work on the origin and first decade of Russian existence on the Reef in the late 1940s to 1950s. Bonner argues that Basotho differed from other migrant groups on the Rand in this period because of their tendency to permanently settle in the urban areas and that "it was the scale and rapidity of this transition from migrant to immigrant status that was responsible for the Rus-

sians' development."[1] Basutoland was in deep distress in the 1930s. Population growth, land shortages, and soil exhaustion were exacerbated by severe drought. At the same time bridewealth prices were higher than elsewhere in South Africa. As a result of these circumstances, increasing numbers of men left Basutoland for longer periods of time. Desertion of wives became more frequent and thousands of impoverished women migrated to the Rand to scrape out a living, often as beer brewers and prostitutes. Many of these migrant men and women formed liaisons that eroded family commitments at home and mitigated against their return to Lesotho. At the same time, burgeoning employment opportunities and the higher wages available in secondary industries meant that Basotho men were leaving their jobs on the mines and moving into the urban areas. As a result, Basotho migrants began dominating many of the squatter movements and established an increasing presence in the townships. This process, Bonner believes, resulted in battles over territory, housing, and women and eventually gave birth to the Marashea, the bulk of whom lived and worked in the townships.

The movement of Basotho workers from the mines to secondary industry during the 1940s, combined with the fact that the majority of his informants followed that trajectory, led Bonner to conclude that "the preponderance of Russian leaders were working in secondary industry (much of it heavy), with the balance self-employed, mainly in tailoring. Their membership, while being regularly replenished and reinforced from the mines, was likewise employed for the most part in secondary industry."[2]

My research indicates different work and settlement patterns. The Russian gangs on the Rand in the 1950s were led by men who lived in the locations, and while there is no doubt that many Marashea moved out of the compounds during this period, oral and documentary evidence suggests that mineworkers still comprised the majority in most Russian groups on the Rand.[3] Alarmed by the weekend rampages of visiting mineworkers, township representatives urged the authorities to place tighter restrictions on miners' movements. Following a series of weekend robberies in 1965 in which Russians were implicated, a member of Phiri's (Soweto) Joint Advisory Board insisted, "These men are not local, but come from compounds in the East Rand. . . . It is clear that after drinking all their money . . . they tend to go out and hunt for innocent prey in the streets."[4] The African press highlighted the activities of marauding Russians on numerous occasions, and the report of an attack on Naledi (Soweto), announcing that "Blanketed 'Russians' from the mines hit the township at dawn," was typical of such coverage.[5] Township officials in areas regularly visited by Russian mineworkers complained vociferously—"Basutos employed in the gold mining industry habitually visit Pimville at weekends

and terrorise the respectable and law abiding residents of the location. This it may be mentioned is a typical pattern of behaviour of the Basutos employed on the Reef."[6] The involvement of Basotho mineworkers in the 1950s New-clare violence was deemed sufficiently serious for the director of native labor for the Witwatersrand to request that compound managers prevent Basotho employees from visiting the township.[7] While some Russians, including the leaders, resided in the townships, it was widely perceived that the gangs drew their strength from the compounds.

Moreover, a more urbanized Basotho populace did not necessarily signal a migrant-to-immigrant shift for the circumstances of most Basotho workers during this period were not so sharply defined. Marashea veterans interviewed for this study almost all maintained close ties with relations and friends in Lesotho and moved frequently between South Africa and Lesotho. Some settled permanently on the Rand and lost contact with families, but most regarded Lesotho as home and returned when their working lives were finished. Others migrated between Lesotho and South Africa on a more or less continual basis, depending on work opportunities, family circumstances, and the need to escape criminal prosecution in South Africa. Borashea was a survival and coping mechanism for its members but it did not arise from a migrant-to-immigrant transition. Bonner's period, when large numbers of Russians worked in secondary industry, was an aberration. If the Marashea had largely cut their ties with the mines, one might expect that the Basotho gangs, like the Isitshozi mining gangs before them, would have become indistinguishable from the numerous urbanized gangster organizations on the Rand. A wider temporal and geographical focus on the Marashea demonstrates that nothing could be further from the truth.

As for the timing of the formation of the Marashea, an additional factor might well be of consequence. A number of early Marashea, including several of the men I interviewed, were veterans of the Second World War. Some accounts credit these veterans with being the founding members of the society. BH, a prominent Matsekha leader in the 1950s East Rand who arrived in Johannesburg in 1946, recalls that "Marashea began at the time of men like Ntate [term of address for an adult male] Mapiloko, Ntate Likhetla, and Ntate Matsarapane when they arrived from the world war. . . . . There were many men from the world war and they were the ones that began the groups of Marashea."

Before the Second World War, Basotho migrants who fought with *melamu* (traditional fighting sticks) were known as *liakhela*, a label that distinguished them from "respectable," law-abiding Basotho (multiple interviews).[8] These early groups of fighters sometimes organized according to regional divisions in Lesotho, as was the case in a series of disputes in Vereeniging in the mid-

1940s. However, the Marashea proper seem to have been born in Benoni, on the East Rand, in 1947 or 1948.[9] The name Marashea surfaced in the late 1940s and was taken from the Russians, who were understood to have been fierce and successful fighters in the recent world war. At first no regional distinctions were made, but by 1950 a bitter rivalry had emerged. One faction referred to themselves as Marashea, while their rivals took the name Majapane, after the Japanese. "It is like naming a football team. The new team might be named after one that is already famous. Marashea were those from Matsieng [southern Lesotho] and Majapane were from Leribe [northern Lesotho]. Those from Matsieng named themselves after Russia while Molapo named themselves after Japan. These two countries were known to be strong in war. That's why those two groups chose those names. But within no time the name of Majapane died away and even those of Molapo were called Marashea" (MK).[10] The two main factions have since identified themselves as Matsieng (sometimes referred to as Makaota), from the south of Lesotho, and Molapo/ Masupha (collectively known as Matsekha), from the north.

COMPOSITION

Membership was open to all Basotho men (most came from Lesotho, but Basotho from the Eastern Free State and the ethnic homeland of QwaQwa were also readily accepted); however, people from other ethnic groups were generally allowed to join as long as they spoke Sesotho. For example, Hlubi from the Matatiele area on Lesotho's southern border (who speak both Xhosa and Sesotho) made up a portion of some Marashea groups. The typical trajectory for male youth was to herd their families' animals, attend initiation school to learn the customs and rituals associated with manhood, and then migrate to the cities and mining areas to find work. Female members left Lesotho and the more impoverished rural areas of South Africa to escape desperate economic and social circumstances. The overwhelming majority of Marashea, both male and female, came from backgrounds of rural poverty and few had any significant formal education. Men labored in the mines and secondary industry while women most often took positions as domestic servants, brewed beer, and engaged in sex work.

Occupational divisions among male Marashea will be discussed in detail later; it is enough to note here that groups were composed of employed members and those known as *malofa* (loafers), who relied on various, often illegal, means to support themselves. None of the retired members interviewed in Lesotho could be considered well off and many live in poverty. Marashea still

active in South Africa typically live in informal settlements, although a select few men in the upper echelons of the organization display such trappings of wealth as private vehicles and cell phones.

As Bonner has noted, "Unlike other urban gangs on the Rand, the Russians were overwhelmingly adult in composition. No age cohort dominated, certainly not the youth."[11] Men usually joined in their youth but senior positions were generally reserved for long-serving veterans, and *marena* (chiefs or leaders; sing., *morena*) were required to be men of stature and experience. Given their perilous lifestyle, Marashea valued members who had proven themselves in difficult situations. A 1950s Matsekha commander, Maliehe Khoeli, explained that when a killing was planned he depended on seasoned veterans. Even if they were arrested these men would not divulge information to the police, whereas a youth would probably inform on his comrades if tortured.[12]

Elderly Marashea usually returned to Lesotho when they left the gangs. In such circumstances veterans received transport money and perhaps a little extra. "There is no big sum—at his farewell he gets something, but not enough for him to live on at home. However, we are responsible for his funeral like any other Lerashea" (KI). BM explains that "The old Lerashea is advised to go home, but if he does not want to go back home we do not force him, especially those Marashea who joined a long time ago who abandoned their families in Lesotho and do not have a home to go to." Those who stayed were not expected to contribute as warriors. "He is not required to go to the fights because he would get killed" (DS). Instead, they acted as advisors for fights and for dealings with the authorities. Retired fighters also fulfilled other functions: "When Lerashea is old he stays looking after the women. He is given a simple job and he must make sure the [kidnapped] women do not escape" (DG). Probably more women than men remained in South Africa, because Marashea women are considered outcasts and prostitutes by many people in Lesotho. Men typically maintained families in Lesotho and returned to them when they retired. Fewer women enjoyed that option and many became estranged from their families. "If a woman is old she stays until she dies or her man dies—the old women are always selling *joala* [beer]. Others become *lingaka* [traditional doctors; sing., *ngaka*] giving *moriana* [traditional medicine], to Marashea. When the men go to fights and meetings she prepares her moriana to make them strong" ('Mè RB).

GEOGRAPHY

The Marashea has settled in a variety of areas and environments during its fifty years of existence. Since the formation of the gangs, members have

resided in the mining compounds. On the Rand in the 1950s, "Marashea groups tended to congregate in the less regulated parts of urban locations,"[13] like Newclare and the "Asiatic" (Indian) section of Benoni as well as various informal settlements. As Soweto was divided into different ethnic enclaves, Marashea became concentrated in the "Sotho" sections—Phiri, Naledi, Tladi, Molapo, and Moletsane. On the East Rand, Benoni, Springs, and Germiston were Matsekha areas. At least one faction of Marashea lived in a white area, sharing the servants' quarters inhabited by their *linyatsi* (lovers or concubines; sing., *nyatsi*). In the 1960s PL, along with a number of men from his group, operated out of the Johannesburg suburb of Booysens. "We were living in the whites' houses. Our linyatsi were working in the whites' homes, so we were living there. When the owner of the house asked the woman when I go to work, she told him that I work at night, whereas really I did not work at all" (Lesotho, 24 May 1998). This group of Matsieng drew the majority of its members from nearby Crown Mines and held its meetings in a forest that separated the town from the mine or traveled to Phiri for larger gatherings. Veterans' reports, along with documentary evidence, indicate that Russian gangs operated in and around both Bloemfontein and Pretoria in the late 1940s and 1950s, but these groups were not sustained. The Bloemfontein gangs are said to have consisted largely of railway workers, while the Russians operating in the Pretoria area worked in industry and were directly connected to some of the Johannesburg gangs.[14]

With the opening of mines in the far West Rand and Free State, Marashea groups established informal settlements adjacent to the mines and resided in townships such as Khutsong and Thabong.[15] Squatter groups typically rented land from white farmers and formed independent settlements. Although these camps might occasionally be raided by the police, there was less police pressure than in urban areas and fewer pass problems for illegal migrants. Some Marashea groups leased the land, some paid per dwelling, and others worked out liquor kickback and protection agreements with the farmers. In 1998 and 1999, I visited three camps in the Free State and one near Carletonville in which the Marashea constituted the ultimate authority.

As foreign migrants, Marashea who lacked the proper documents were vulnerable to deportation. The adoption of harsher pass control measures, particularly the imposition of a single standard reference book, the "dompass," in 1952, caused considerable hardship for some Marashea groups on the Rand. Johannes Rantoa reported, "At the time of Jan Smuts we had no problems but when the dompass was introduced we had a difficult time. We had to fix the whole thing in Lesotho; as such we had our number reduced. Some of us were arrested and others could not return to South Africa. . . . this was one of the reasons the group disintegrated" (21 May 1987, Bonner transcript). The

1963 Aliens Control Act was a further blow to the urban-based gangs. However, some Marashea men, by virtue of their birth in South Africa or their duration of employment on the Rand, retained the right to reside in Johannesburg. This cohort, along with the continuing trickle of Basotho who migrated to the Rand and eluded the authorities, ensured the survival of the urban Marashea into the 1990s.

For Marashea in the mining areas, pass and border controls became simply one more obstacle with which to contend and did not significantly weaken the organization. 'Mè TF, who was active in the Free State in the 1970s and 1980s, was deported several times but always returned. "We were arrested at Christmas because the South African government wanted everyone to go back to their home, so they would deport us to the border posts. But we would not stay in Lesotho, we would just go back again by trespassing." Active Marashea illegally residing in South Africa experience no real difficulties. A Free State informal settlement resident explains: 'Sometimes the police come here and deport us to Lesotho. At Christmas in 1997 they came and I was one of those deported. They dropped us at Ficksburg bridge and we crossed and then came back. A taxi took us here the same day" (TC). CN takes advantage of lax border controls to avoid the inconvenience of deportation: "I renew my temporary permit every month because I go home [to Lesotho] almost every month. If I do not go home, I give my passport to a taxi driver I know to renew it."

Lesotho is considered neutral territory by Marashea, and instances of conflict between rival groups have been rare. "We don't fight in Lesotho. It only happens here [South Africa] where Marashea belongs. If I went to Thabong [Free State Township] now they would kill me, but if we meet in Lesotho, nothing will happen" (CN). The Marashea's original purpose was to protect migrant Basotho, so the gangs filled a need that did not exist in Lesotho. Much of the internecine fighting in the mining areas was caused by competition over territory and markets. There are no mines in Lesotho and little if any money to be made, so the Marashea have operated exclusively in South Africa. Many veterans echoed TT's claim that "Borashea was a thing of South Africa; there was no need for such a group in Lesotho." For many years now Marashea groups have returned to Lesotho for funerals, feasts, and meetings. The Malunga Hotel on the outskirts of Maseru was a popular meeting place for the Russians.

Other than occasional skirmishes between rival groups on holiday or at a funeral, Marashea are active in Lesotho only in the sense that they can be hired to intimidate people and resolve disputes. Interested parties travel to South Africa and contract men to do this type of work for them. "The Marashea are doing nothing [in Lesotho], but if I want to attack someone in

Lesotho I can go to South Africa and hire Marashea who will come back and kill him. There are no Marashea in Lesotho but you can invite them if there is a problem" (SM). A detective in the Royal Lesotho Mounted Police confirmed that Marashea are sometimes hired for the purposes of intimidation and assassination. According to him, Marashea are most visible at their funerals, where they invariably display and discharge illegal firearms. The police choose to overlook these activities rather than confront large groups of well-armed Marashea (Detective M, Maseru, 20 April 1998). Although some prominent veterans who retire to Lesotho maintain contact with their former groups, act as mediators and advisors, and still consider themselves Marashea, the bulk of retired members seem to share KI's assessment of their status: "Those who live in Lesotho after leaving Marashea are no longer regarded as Marashea. Like in my case, I don't regard myself as Lerashea. . . . my being Lerashea ended when I left South Africa."

JOINING THE MARASHEA

Like virtually every aspect of Borashea, the process of joining the group was profoundly gendered. Men chose to join and, although there were no elaborate induction ceremonies, were usually informed of the responsibilities and expectations that accompanied group membership. SO's account of joining Matsieng in 1972 is typical of the process: "When I joined I was surrounded by all the members and the morena told me all the rules. He asked me whether I was ready to fight any rival and I said yes. Will you kill anyone who tries to kill you, he asked. When you are arrested you must not inform on others, he told me. You must keep all our information secret from the police. They said, this is what we need you to do. And they told me not to tell the other miners our secrets. Even in Lesotho you were not supposed to tell anything concerning Marashea."

There were no qualifications for membership other than the ability to speak Sesotho. Men simply presented themselves to the group, expressed their desire to join, agreed to abide by the rules, and paid an initial fee. Different groups constantly sought new members as there was strength, both military and financial, in numbers. Most often, potential members were introduced to the group by established Marashea who were "homeboys," workmates, or relatives. BM joined in 1968 after he was invited by fellow mineworkers: "When I started working on the mine I found men in my compound room who stayed outside the mine compound on weekends. . . . There were five Marashea in my room and this influenced me to follow them on weekends. I

asked them, what was this Marashea? They explained to me and I became interested."

Some male Marashea were introduced to the group through family connections, often an uncle or a cousin. I am also aware of several instances of brothers belonging to the same group and sons following fathers into the Marashea. However, there has never been an established pattern of generational succession in the Marashea. Indeed, some informants report that groups discouraged close relatives from joining because of the dangerous lives led by Marashea. "People from the same family were not allowed to join. That was done so that when my brother dies I would support his family and also to prevent the death of two people in the same family" (DG).[16] Most veterans we spoke with, male and female, regard Borashea as a harsh life and hope for something better for their children. I have not learned of any parents encouraging their children to become Marashea, and several informants indicated that they had forbidden their children to join. However, some young men became Marashea against their fathers' wishes. As DB replied when asked whether it was common for the sons or brothers of Marashea to join the group, "It happened because when you are here, your son goes to the mines somewhere and one day you see him holding *molamu* [fighting stick] and there is nothing you can do." Certainly sons did not succeed fathers as leaders, and there was no core of family at the heart of the organization as with the Cape Town area "mafia" gangs.[17]

The most common reasons cited by male informants for becoming Marashea were physical security and access to women.[18] Urban locations could be dangerous environments, especially for migrants, and group membership provided a measure of safety. In the 1940s and 1950s the Mpondo in particular are remembered for preying on Basotho: "I joined Marashea to protect Basotho who were ill-treated by Mapondo. Some were even killed in the bush when they walked from one mine to another. The Mapondo gathered at the railway stations to rob and kill Basotho" (MK). WL echoes these sentiments: "Mapondo used to beat us. Therefore I joined in order to be safe. I started enjoying life when I became a member." Additionally, Basotho from southern Lesotho were sometimes targeted for intimidation and assault by Matsekha groups, as were northerners by Matsieng. Consequently, men joined their homeboys for protection. Joining a fighting association for safety is not without irony. However, even though collective violence was a staple of life in the Marashea, members judged that group security was preferable to the vulnerability of isolation.

Male veterans acknowledge that the gangs led harsh and often brutal lives. Most were arrested and all saw comrades die. However, male respondents

reminisced fondly about the access to women that their status as Marashea afforded. Nonmembers had to pay to enjoy the company of women under Russian control. Former miner TL remembers:

> If one of the miners who was not a member had maybe a woman
> outside, say a girlfriend or so, the Marashea would say that since
> that person is not a member he should pay something like a protec-
> tion fee . . . because they are protecting all women outside. So these
> guys had to pay such fees, and if they didn't pay, they take the woman
> away and she's not going to be yours anymore. It was not like there
> were some negotiations, they would do what they wanted to do be-
> cause they were a large group and they could force people into
> whatever idea they wanted.[19]

Russians were frequently given a woman and had free access to unattached women affiliated with the group. GK reports that his life improved significantly once he joined the Marashea. "What made me join was my love for women. I found that I was spending a lot of money to pay for women and this made me join in order to get them for free and without intimidation. I lived a happy life as Lerashea because I got what I always wanted." "Mako" Thabane, a Matsieng commander in the 1950s and 1960s, declared, "There were many women to be had as Lerashea. There is no other reason why I became Lerashea except it meant entertainment" (Molefi Thabane, 15 June 1987, Bonner transcript). Others were motivated by an attachment to a particular woman. "I joined Marashea because the woman I loved lived in a squatter camp next to the mine and I was not free to see that woman unless I paid a fee to the Marashea. I joined because as a member it was easy for me to live with her" (KB). CN, who worked on a Free State mine in the 1970s, rated access to women as the primary benefit of Borashea, "because in the mine compound life is difficult and very lonely."

Of course, men joined the group for a combination of reasons. WL, as stated above, joined for personal security, but also "because I was attracted to their life. They lived a bold life in Gauteng. When I saw Basotho putting on their blankets I became attracted and decided to join them in order to be like them." Pride caused TC to become Lerashea: "I was working at Buffel [Buffelsfontein mine] and Marashea from Gauteng were coming here for *stokvels*. They would sometimes provoke me, saying that I was not a man, so I joined to show them that I was also a man like themselves. I had been to initiation school and I had learned molamu and I did not want to be mocked by other men." A long-serving Matsieng veteran viewed membership as an effective

strategy to thwart personal enemies: "When I worked [at St. Helena] as a miner there was a troublesome supervisor who undermined me. He even demanded bribes from people. And there was a Shangaan cook at the kitchen who gave me bones instead of meat, and I decided to join Marashea because of those two people so that I could get revenge against them" (PK). For LT, affiliation with the Marashea offered the best prospect of survival. "I was forced to join because I lost my job. I had no money to return home and there was nobody to assist me to get home." The Marashea became more commercially oriented as the numbers of malofa increased over the years and many members joined for primarily economic reasons. KI, on the contrary, viewed membership as the fulfillment of a long-standing dream: "When I came out of initiation school I was interested in the people called Marashea in South Africa. I wanted to go to the mines so that I could join them. When I arrived there I visited Thabong, where I met Marashea. Since I was already interested I decided to join immediately. . . . I told myself when I was growing up that I would undergo initiation and thereafter go to the mines and join the Marashea." Mineworkers sometimes commented on the social life available as a result of membership. "The good things about being Lerashea were to have security and a place where one can enjoy himself because on the mines life is too lonely for those who stay in the compound" (KI).

Large numbers of Basotho women have migrated to the urban and mining centers of South Africa since at least the early 1900s. Bonner, Tshidiso Maloka, and Judy Gay all assert that widows and abandoned wives made up the largest proportion of female migrants from the early years of the century to the 1970s.[20] These women left Lesotho for a variety of reasons, including ill treatment by in-laws, the search for husbands who failed to send remittances, and desperate economic circumstances. Oral evidence indicates that these motivations, especially the economic imperative, continue to be the prime factors driving women to leave Lesotho. While it has become more difficult for Basotho women to migrate legally to South Africa since 1963, large numbers have continued to undertake the journey.[21] Farm areas near the mines have long been the destination of homeland women whose options were severely constrained by influx regulations. Since the relaxation and eventual abolition of influx control in the 1980s, former homeland residents have poured into informal settlements throughout South Africa.

Female migrants seeking formal-sector employment generally lacked the qualifications to compete for the more prestigious positions open to women, such as nursing and teaching, and were largely confined to factory and cleaning work, but even these positions were closed to foreign migrants after 1963. Consequently, seasonal agricultural labor was virtually the only legal employ-

ment available to Basotho women in South Africa.[22] Bonner states that by the late 1920s Basotho women dominated the brewing business on the Rand,[23] and the opening of the Free State mines in the 1950s ensured that large numbers of female migrants continued to rely on brewing for their livelihood. Many of these women fell under the dominion of the Marashea.

Some women did not choose to become Marashea, rather they were kidnapped and coerced into becoming members. Perhaps the majority of women joined voluntarily, but for reasons that often differed from those of male Marashea. These women usually linked up with men who were Lerashea and automatically became part of the group. "My cousin was Lerashea and he stayed with us in the house and I became a friend of Marashea. My cousin was from the Matsieng group. They were dancing in the third house from this one and I met Tsotsi—he proposed and I agreed" ('Mè RW). Others joined out of desperation: "You are just there [with the Marashea] because you do not have anywhere to stay and you are not even allowed to stay in South Africa. So you just stay there and sell joala" ('Mè TF). Some women accepted proposals without knowing the man was Lerashea. Once they discovered his identity it was too late to leave the group ('Mè FD).[24] Marashea men frequented the railway stations and taxi ranks to scout for women who had just arrived in the locations. These women often had no place to stay and were susceptible to offers of accommodation (DG).

Women who joined without being attached to a particular man most often cited the need for protection from criminals and the law as their primary motivation. Independent women were vulnerable to criminal predation, police harassment, and deportation, and association with the Marashea afforded a degree of protection. For example, the men of Marashea ensured that customers honored their debts and women were not robbed, a significant benefit in the crime-plagued townships and informal settlements. Newspaper reports from the Rand confirm oral evidence that criminals and even African municipal police who interfered with Marashea women were subject to retribution. In Dobsonville (Soweto) a gang of seven tsotsis who allegedly molested a female Lerashea was chased into a house by avenging Marashea. "When the gang of seven ignored a challenge to fight it out, the raiders removed the iron roofing, poured petrol inside, and set the house alight. Overcome by smoke, the gang ran out to be thrashed by the Russians. All of them landed in hospital."[25] On the East Rand in 1967 four African police also ended up in hospital following a fight with the Russians resulting from their arrest of female Marashea.[26] The hazards of life as an illegal migrant convinced 'Mè ID to join the Marashea in Carletonville in the 1980s. "In South Africa we were staying illegally because we did not have work permits or residence permits,

so I felt afraid. That's why I joined the Marashea, because Marashea were not deported at all." Additionally, the group usually paid the fines of women arrested for brewing and other minor offenses.

Although some women were impressed with the reputation of Marashea, admired their fine clothing, and enjoyed the dances and concerts, it seems that most joined simply because their male partner was Lerashea or as a measure of last resort. 'Mè ID summarizes the plight of the latter group: "Women still leave Lesotho but it is unusual for a woman to leave knowing or intending to join Marashea. I think for most it is like it was for me. They intend to find jobs but it is very difficult, and then the easiest thing to do is to join the Marashea."

ORGANIZATIONAL STRUCTURES

The Marashea has consisted of dozens of separate groups in the course of its history. These groups have operated largely independently of each other and have been differentiated by composition, leadership, relations with white authorities, size, and the environments in which they carved out a niche. A 1950s group in the urban township of Newclare would necessarily be quite different from a 1990s gang presiding over an informal settlement in the rural Free State. The Marashea has never been a monolithic entity; however, it remains a society linked by national origin, a distinct culture, and a common history. Borashea continues to be recognized as a Sesotho organization. Sesotho culture has played a key role in the identity of the Marashea—language, dress, and some social customs emanated from Lesotho, as did the divide that separated the two main factions. Marashea groups dispersed throughout the Free State and Gauteng have come together for general meetings, celebrations, and funerals and have assisted each other in times of conflict, both with rival factions and outsiders. And, while each group had its own particular character, oral testimony indicates that there was (and remains) a common organizational culture governing hierarchies, rules, and discipline, albeit one that adapted to circumstances and change over time.

The different groups of Marashea have varied widely in size. A cohort of at least twenty to thirty men was required for a group to be formed, but groups have been much larger and Marashea battles on the Rand sometimes involved several hundred combatants. The key determinants seem to have been the number of Basotho in a given area and proximity to the mines that sustained the groups. An influential morena could attract followers from a large area and establish control over several smaller groups. Solomon Hlalele was

one such leader. He commanded the allegiance of most, if not all, Matsieng groups on the Rand in the early 1950s before he was jailed and deported to Lesotho. Other famous marena from both Matsieng and Molapo have established powerful networks in the years since. BM estimates that he rules approximately two hundred male Marashea and more than a thousand women. According to KB, the size and strength of each group was largely dependent on the quality of the morena. Without proper leadership, groups disintegrated. "The strength of Marashea differs from place to place depending on how they organize themselves, especially the morena's ability to organize them. Another factor is their number, which is also determined by the number of Basotho in the area. If the morena is good many Marashea will join, but if he is not favored many will run away or resign."

With a single exception, all informants reported that leaders were elected by the male Marashea. BM is the exception to the electoral rule. He claims he was appointed by his predecessor, who was preparing to retire.

> I was called to Klerksdorp by Ntate Mokhemele, who was morena of the Klerksdorp region, which covers the Free State and Orkney and Klerksdorp. He said he looked all over the area but he could not find a leader among his people who could take his position as he was old and intended to retire. He found me to be the only one who could take his position. He called all marena under him and asked them to elect someone to take his position, but he rejected all their candidates and chose me as the general morena. He called me to Klerksdorp to take his position. He called me together with sixteen men—I was the seventeenth—to take his position as morena of the whole Free State and Klerksdorp. These men became my council and advisors.

In most cases it seems as if the morena was elected by all the men in the group. In larger groups, senior members sometimes arrived at a decision among themselves, but their decision needed to be confirmed by popular consensus. When Lenkoane, a powerful Matsieng leader in 1960s Soweto, was assassinated in 1963, PL reports that he was chosen morena of the group by the senior strata. "We had lost our brave leader. We had big men like 'Mako' Thabane, Menchele, and Nape and an old man whose name I forget. We sat down to discuss who was going to be morena and they appointed me and all Marashea approved this appointment." The morena usually designated a committee of advisors, including a secretary, a treasurer, and a

second-in-command. Each group also had whistle blowers who functioned as sentries and directed fights through different whistle signals. Marena were selected from these senior positions. KI explains: "Morena appoints wise men whom he trusts to work with him as his advisors. When morena dies we call them and put them in front and say, 'Which one can we put on the seat of morena?' If the majority agrees on one man, we install him as morena. We make a big feast, we eat and drink joala and dance all sorts of dances."

Leaders were elected wholly on the basis of merit. Accomplished strategists and powerful fighters became commanders; royal connections and noble bloodlines in Lesotho carried no weight in the Marashea. HL discusses the qualities that groups looked for and the manner in which marena were expected to rule: "You cannot be morena if you are careless; you must have the qualities to rule people and you must speak in a way that you can convince people. You must be a good leader because you are not going to fight alone, you are fighting along with the people under your control. We sit at a meeting for every issue. You discuss with the members about how you can trap your rivals. You must investigate how many people they have so that you do not get your people into trouble."

The safety of the group depended on the morena, and his leadership was under scrutiny, especially in the beginning of his term. "Morena is elected by the members who consider his qualities and experience. But if he is shit, we remove him and put another as morena. We might even kill him" (KI). PM concurs: "We wanted a person who is brave, who can look after people. If he is careless we could kill him. That's why we want a good person, we tell him that he must be very careful." Successful marena wielded a considerable amount of power but had to be sensitive to popular opinion. For example, BM was not pleased when he discovered his eldest son had joined one of the groups under his control. "I advised my son to leave the Marashea but I failed because my members asked me where that rule comes from. I didn't stand a chance. They said that if a man has joined, he has joined. He cannot all of a sudden leave because he already knows the secrets."

Marena performed a variety of functions with the assistance of the committee. They dispensed group funds to pay bail and legal fees and negotiated all sorts of arrangements with the police. Group discipline was the responsibility of the morena, who decided on punishments and arbitrated disputes. Marena decided when, whom, and how to fight and, in larger groups spread throughout several areas, controlled the actions of their subchiefs. For example, in October 1998, BM summoned his lieutenants from settlements throughout the Free State to a meeting in Virginia to discuss rumors that some of them were participating in taxi conflicts without his permission (BM). SAPS Inspector K reports a similar hierarchy among the group he worked with in

the 1970s and 1980s, initially headed by Mokhemele: "It worked like this—MoKimbelele [Mokhemele] was in charge first and he had a lot of lieutenants under him. At that time it was Buffels, Harties, Stil, Jouberton, Canana [mining areas]. He was in charge of them—anything they do, they must first discuss it with him" (Potchefstroom, 7 June 1999).

Once marena were solidly entrenched, coups were uncommon. One of BM's assistants, when discussing the matters of electing and removing marena, stated that "[BM] is morena for life. He is more than morena now. He is the father of us and he is above these conditions" (CN). Long-serving marena usually died on the job, although a few retired, ended up in jail, or were deported. BM plans to retire shortly, partly because he feels he is losing control. "I am retiring next year if I am still alive, because I am aware that I will end up killed by these youngsters because they do not like to be corrected. I should point out that Kloof, Khutsong, and Bekkersdal were under my rule, but because they were not prepared to accept my control, we parted."

Many of the most famous marena died violent deaths. Matsarapane was hanged for his part in the killing of a white police officer; Lenkoane was assassinated by a fellow Matsieng; Bifa was killed by Mamalinyane, who was in turn slain by Bifa's compatriots; Tsilo was stabbed to death under mysterious circumstances; Maseko was killed by the police; and Tsotsi Raliemere was killed by a rival faction.

Matsieng leader Tsotsi Raliemere's funeral in Lesotho, 1985. Collection of the author.

Life was precarious for all Marashea and the gangs adopted strict rules to in-
still order and maintain male control. Although there have been minor varia-
tions between groups there seem to be some general rules that have applied
to the Marashea as a whole. Regulations were designed to maintain group integrity, specifically to minimize conflict within each group, to maximize the
financial and human resources of the group, and to prevent betrayal. Members were expected to follow instructions issued from the morena and the
committee. "You have to take orders from the top. . . . When you are ordered
to go somewhere, maybe to collect money, you have to obey" (MM). Members were required to settle quarrels through arbitration and to accept the
judgment of the *lekhotla* (council). To take matters into one's own hands invited severe punishment.

> If maybe you beat someone [another member] who has taken your
> *nyatsi* instead of taking him to the lekhotla then you would be con-
> victed and the fine was maybe R600 for such offences. And you had
> to pay that fine immediately. If you failed to pay immediately you
> would be beaten. They beat you severely and then they would take
> you to the hospital. They would break your bones and after the hos-
> pital you would come back to the group. You were required to re-
> spect the members in the group. (SO)

The linyatsi of group members were introduced to the group and it was an offense to covet another man's nyatsi. "You should not propose to the woman of
another member in the group. When you have nyatsi you have to report it to
the group so that she would be known and an investigation would be made to
ensure that she is not involved with another man within the group" (DG). For
serious matters such as infidelity or attempting to escape, women were judged
and punished by men. Some groups allowed women to deal with minor offenses such as personal quarrels. "We have a women's council composed of
elderly women that looks into the matter of rule-breaking. They can fine her
some money or corporal punishment may apply depending on the nature of
the case" (BM).

All male group members paid a regular contribution to the group treasury.
In some groups this levy was collected monthly and in others it was paid weekly.
These funds were used for the benefit of the group—to pay bail and legal fees,
to hire traditional doctors and pay for *moriana*, to bribe police, and to pay for
transport and funerals. When larger sums were needed—for example, to cover

legal expenses when several members faced serious charges—both men and women Marashea were required to pay extra.

Once a man committed to the Marashea he was not free to leave the group. "It is not easy to leave because you are like a soldier, so you cannot leave while the fight is on" (DS). The old, the badly injured, and the sick were typically given a choice between returning home to Lesotho or staying with the group as advisors. For the young and active it was more problematic. "If you are healthy and young we cannot let you go—you are like an ox in a yoke plowing—we cannot let you go especially when you are young" (HL). This condition applied equally to men and women. "No one in Marashea is allowed to leave the group except for those who are old and useless" ('Mè ID). Along with the determination to retain men of fighting age and younger women, who could attract mineworkers, there was a concern that absconders would reveal secrets to rivals and place the group in jeopardy. "You are not allowed to leave because you have seen our secrets; you have even seen our doctors and how they give moriana to us" (BH). "If you leave without our permission, then we consider you a traitor because you can inform on us to our rivals and the police, who can kill and arrest us" (HL). Healthy members could secure their release in select circumstances. Employed men who lost their jobs were often permitted to leave provided they returned to Lesotho— thus posing no danger. KI was forced to retire from the mines in 1985 and obtained permission to leave the group. He explains that "it is not easy to leave Marashea. But for those who work on the mines, if the job is finished, as in my case, one has to go home. . . . If one leaves the group because he was working and then lost his job, that is a valid reason and they let him go. But if he just decides to step aside while still living in South Africa, it might be like a decision to die." It appears that some groups allowed members to purchase their release. "When you want to leave you must pay money for going out, and if you do not have money we do not permit you to leave" (MM).

Those who betrayed the group were sentenced to death and great effort was expended in tracking them down. "The most serious offence that a member can commit is treason, and he is killed instantly like a dog when he is discovered" (KI). Treason could encompass informing on colleagues to the police, defecting to a rival group or even leaving the group without permission. After being shot and wounded by the police during a skirmish, ML testifies that he was tired of life as Lerashea: "After that I wanted to leave the group but it was difficult to leave because after committing yourself there is no way to go back, as they will call you a traitor and chase you until they kill you."

The most common method of discipline was corporal punishment. "In most cases the punishment will be melamu. We are Marashea here, not a

church society—he must pay with his flesh" (CN). Beatings were usually administered in front of the group and there was a definite element of humiliation. "You are beaten like a child—but with melamu. You are stripped naked and beaten" (GL). Furthermore, offenders were expected to admit their culpability. "The one who broke the rules is surrounded by others and beaten with melamu. If he is ready to stop breaking the rules, it ends with a severe beating, but if he is stubborn, he might be killed" (WL). For lesser offences, transgressors were sometimes fined. If members were unable to pay the fine, their valuables were impounded and released upon payment.

Marashea arrested on group business were entitled to legal counsel funded from the treasury. However, those who participated in criminal acts that were not sanctioned by the group were not afforded this protection. "When you were arrested we would pay for your bail or fine if you were arrested for a group fight. If you were arrested for robbery we would not pay any fine for you because that was not for the group's purpose, it was for your own needs" (PL, Lesotho, 23–24 May 1998). Some marena forbade their members to take part in certain criminal activities and not only withheld financial assistance but punished transgressors. BM declares that there should be "no rape, robbery, or assassinations. If a member is found guilty of any of these he is severely beaten. If he is arrested by the police we do not bother ourselves about him. We let him go to jail. . . . I should point out that one morena under me in Klerksdorp is now on trial because of a taxi conflict. He broke my rule by accepting payment to engage in that conflict and we will not pay for his lawyer because he broke that rule." These efforts to maintain discipline within each group did not apply to the association as a whole; the Marashea have a long history of infighting.

INTERNECINE CONFLICT

Russian gangs fought with other ethnically organized migrant groups; urbanized criminal youth, known as tsotsis; and the police. But above all, the rival factions battled each other. The rivalries that distinguished the different Marashea groups reflected regional animosities rooted in Lesotho's history of succession disputes. "The factions of Matsieng and Ha-Molapo/Masupha reproduced and reignited the historical antagonism between the royalists of south Lesotho, follower of Moshoeshoe's [founding king of Lesotho] heir, Letsie I, with his capital at Matsieng, and the restive collateral nobility of north Lesotho led by Moshoeshoe's second and third sons, Molapo and Masupha, whom he installed at Peka and Thaba Bosiu, and who consistently defied or rebelled against the paramountcy."[27]

There are numerous stories as to why the split took place, ranging from fights over women to disputes over money, but it is evident that Basotho migrants carried a keen awareness of their homeland's historical divisions. "We fought with the people of Molapo because they wanted to rule us. . . . We know that the king of Lesotho is living at Matsieng and we would not allow people from Ha-Molapo to rule us, so our quarrel started there" (DG). Oral evidence is consistent, however, that in the beginning Marashea were united: "Marashea began at Benoni. People from Lesotho were friends—there was brotherhood from Leribe to Matsieng, but we ended up separating because of women. The people from Matsieng killed a man named Lehloailane because of a woman, and the people of Molapo were furious" (BF).[28] As Bonner observed, "Once this factional polarisation had taken place it quickly spread to other areas where Basotho migrants and immigrants were congregated and where the same latent rivalries were present. By the early 1950s there was scarcely a Reef township untouched by the fighting, which very often reached extraordinary intensity, involving up to a thousand combatants at any one time."[29]

These conflicts were a defining feature of Borashea, and the rivalry between Matsieng and Matsekha persists to this day. The Russian gangs in the Johannesburg area gained much notoriety in both the African and the white press because of the battles they waged across the length and breadth of the Rand from the 1950s to the 1970s. Colorful descriptions of hordes of blanketed warriors engaging in bloody disputes regularly made the headlines. Reports of train station crowds fleeing as Russian gangs joined in combat, officials and spectators scrambling to safety as opposing gangs continued their fights in the courtroom, and trials in which dozens of Russians were charged with public violence were all a result of internal rivalries.[30] Russian disputes in mining districts attracted less attention because they took place in more isolated areas, away from official scrutiny, and tended to be less of a spectacle than the Rand battles. Still, fights in the Free State appeared in newspapers as well as police reports and mining correspondence.[31]

A variation of the conventional rivalry seems to have existed in the early years, when conflict sometimes occurred between Russian mineworkers and township Russians, based on this occupational and spatial division, rather than strictly adhering to the Matsieng-Matsekha divide. In fact, one report traces the formal establishment of the Marashea to conflict between mineworkers and residents of Benoni location. According to this account, Basotho living in Benoni formed the original Russian gang in 1947 to prevent Basotho miners from visiting resident women.[32] The testimony of a Molapo member active in Johannesburg during the 1950s indicates that in some groups little love was lost between location residents and mineworkers. PG1, who worked in the Johannesburg general post office and lived in Moroka, explains that the

relationship between Russian mineworkers and township Russians "was not friendly because those people living in the mines, they were after the women. Now they have to be fucked up by [township Russians]." Presumably because of this antipathy, there were "not more than ten" mineworkers in PG1's group, which, he reports, numbered in the hundreds. Before a 1960 battle between resident Russians and invading mineworkers, the Russians from the mines visited Naledi and left a note declaring, "Their home-boy Basothos of the township were women,"[33] and vowed to return the following day. Forewarned, the local Marashea repelled the attack, killing at least two of the invaders. It is likely that such conflicts erupted on the Rand before the mid-1960s because township Russians could more readily find employment and were not as financially dependent on their mining compatriots. It is also possible that it was relatively easy for mineworkers, who had access to numerous locations throughout the Rand, to find women who were not resident in Russian-controlled areas and thus had less of a need for formal links with township Marashea. However, even in this environment, internecine conflict was characterized by clashes between Matsieng and Matsekha groups that incorporated both township dwellers and mineworkers.

In spite of the ferocity of the fighting between rival Marashea factions, veterans draw a clear distinction between these conflicts and the battles Marashea fought with outsiders. There was a definite recreational aspect to early internecine battles as groups fought for bragging rights as Basotho. When veterans recount fights with rival groups, they describe rousing encounters. Before the battle the women would encourage the men by singing their praises and celebrations followed victories. During the week when Matsekha and Matsieng worked side by side in the mines and factories they would discuss previous battles, speak admiringly of brave and accomplished fighters, and predict victory in upcoming conflicts. "The fighting was good," claims DB, a Matsieng veteran of the 1950s. "Although it was tough, we did not regret it because it was our choice and we enjoyed fighting." NT, who also fought as a member of Matsieng in the 1950s, reminisced, "We were happy to fight because it was a sort of play; at that time we were not killing. When we beat you with melamu and you fell, we would leave you and chase your friends. We fought on Saturdays and Sundays; during the week we went to work because all of us were working. It was nice because it was like when Basotho boys play melamu at home."

Guy and Thabane have discussed this phenomenon as it applied to the Rand conflicts of the 1950s:

> Internecine fighting amongst the *Ma-Rashea* could possibly so
> weaken them that they could no longer effectively fulfill their
> function as defenders of the Basotho. It might leave them open to

destruction by other groups—criminal or ethnic—or by the coercive arm of the state. Thus, deadly and violent as these confrontations were, there were certain devices that the Basotho factions adopted which limited the ultimate outcome—devices which they could use because there were certain assumptions that they as Basotho, could share, and which they could not share with other groups.[34]

Thus, in the course of a battle when a man was wounded and helpless, his opponent might stand over him to ensure he was not killed. On some occasions defeated opponents were released after being beaten and forced to relinquish their valuables. HM, a 1950s veteran, explains: "We even showed mercy to other Marashea in a fight. We would just take your clothes and send you to your morena; we would not kill you." ML, a 1970s veteran, describes much the same practice: "When we chase one and catch him, we kill him. But if he is well dressed in smart clothes, wearing a blanket like this one, we take the blanket and send him away and say, 'Go!' so that tomorrow when one of us is caught during a fight, his clothing will be taken but he will not be killed."

In the heat of battle men were sometimes struck down and mercilessly killed—there were no guarantees of protection. However, in the early years the different groups generally adhered to a moral code that when violated could result in severe consequences. Mamalinyane, who led a 1950s group of Marashea, mainly composed of Hlubi, was targeted for assassination by a combined Matsieng-Molapo force precisely because he broke the rules of the time. "In those days marena were not supposed to be killed. If morena was captured he would be taken to lekhotla and asked about his group. When he answered those questions, he was supposed to be released, not killed, and then his group would go and fight back. But Mamalinyane killed morena Bifa from QwaQwa in Masakeng. He stabbed him with a spear, and Marashea from Molapo and Matsieng joined to attack Mamalinyane" (NT). Mamalinyane was killed in his house in 1956, reportedly stabbed in the same way he killed Bifa (multiple interviews).

When the Marashea began in the 1940s and 1950s, most combatants used melamu, battle axes, or swords and it was relatively easy to limit hand-to-hand conflicts. As firearms became more prevalent, it was difficult to control the fights and the practice of sparing fallen enemies, as well as the tendency to prearrange battles, gradually died out. BM, who has more than thirty years of experience as Lerashea, gives his perspective on these changes:

> The fight between Marashea started a long time ago, around the
> 1940s. I do not know how it started but we are told many stories

about it. It was like a game when one person hits another—the rule was that if he falls down he should not be hit again, rather you would just take his blanket. After the blanket is taken the owner would want to claim it back by fighting. It would be an ongoing fight. There were notices from the attacking group to the other group in order to make them prepared for the fight. Somebody would be given a letter telling morena of the other group that on such and such a day we will come and fight over our blankets, which you captured last time. He would be given a drink as we are drinking now and they would reply and say, okay, we shall be waiting for you, or we will not be in a position to fight because of a funeral or stokvel or anything. But these days things have changed. If there is a fight, it is a fight, not a game. If we were to send someone to Thabong now, they would kill him; he would never come back.

The proliferation of firearms was partially responsible for eroding the practice of ritualistic combat governed by a recognizable set of rules. A second factor has been the increasing commercialization of the Marashea. Instead of fighting for recreation and bragging rights, Marashea in the last thirty years have battled for control of lucrative transport routes and liquor distribution networks. Rather than the prearranged, set-piece battles of former days, hit-and-run raids using taxis are the method of choice in recent years. However, battles between Marashea groups are still viewed in a different light than fights with non-Basotho, as truces and agreements are more easily negotiated.

As transport became more readily available in the 1970s and 1980s, Marashea groups began to accompany the bodies of fallen members to their home villages in Lesotho, where they conducted funeral ceremonies. Before this practice, funerals in South Africa often erupted in violence when groups attempted to prevent rivals from burying their dead.[35] "It was difficult to bury Lerashea because when we were taking the body to the cemetery the other group would come and start a fight at the funeral. If they defeated us, before they buried the body they would break the coffin and sometimes even pour petrol on the body and burn it" (HM). Funeral conflicts could also be prearranged. NN, a Matsekha veteran, explains, "If Lerashea died in a fight, before he was buried we would invite the Matsieng group and fight with melamu before the burial began" (20 May 1998). Less often, fights have occurred at funerals in Lesotho when one group follows a rival back home to disrupt the proceedings. In 1996 members of a rogue Matsieng group attacked

Matsekha during a funeral service near the university town of Roma, killing several people.[36]

Impromptu battles also took place, especially on trains, when groups met on the way to dances and other celebrations. With a near constant state of warfare between rivals, spontaneous fights erupted for the most trivial reasons. Molefi Thabane was at a loss to explain these internecine conflicts: "Really there is no reason why Marashea fight each other. I still remember at times in court when we were asked why we fought. The answer was puzzling, and only fit to be given by an insane person—'These Masupha people despise us'" (Bonner transcript). KP remembers, "The cause of those fights was when Molapo people called us girls and we had to prove that we were not girls." DS was wounded because "someone from the Molapo group said that we were farting and we had to go outside. The fight started and my head was injured by a sword."

Not all fights were so whimsical; groups fought for material gain and to increase their power. Raids to abduct women and revenge attacks to reclaim stolen women featured prominently. The 1940s clashes in Vereeniging were reportedly due to "the abduction by a member of the Matsieng clan of a woman of the Molapo clan."[37] In 1957 the *World* (Johannesburg) carried an editorial on Marashea clashes that were plaguing the Sotho zones of what was to become Soweto: "We learn that one of the causes of fights between these factions is the indecent habit of woman-grabbing."[38] As the Marashea extended into the Free State so did the internecine battles that often revolved around women. A 1960 clash in Thabong was said to have begun when "a member of one of the two groups was accused of having an affair with the wife of one of the members of the other group."[39]

Fighting was also precipitated by the desertion of members to a rival group, and assaults on individual members sometimes instigated large-scale revenge attacks. Raids on rival settlements had an economic rationale because of the prospects of booty. "When they defeat the other group, they take away watches, clothes, everything a person has" ('Mè TF). Thus an attack to avenge the abduction of a female member was also potentially lucrative. Marena attempting to extend their power over neighboring groups occasionally initiated confrontations. "Sometimes they fight for power, as when one leader wants to rule over another. He attacks and tries to defeat him in order to rule over him, as in politics" (KK).

The men and women interviewed supplied dozens of accounts of fights between different Marashea gangs. Three specific incidents demonstrate some of the conditions and consequences of these conflicts. SC was Lerashea with

a Matsekha group on the East Rand in the 1950s, where he worked as a miner. He attended meetings and dances and fought alongside his colleagues on weekends. His experience illustrates how membership in the Marashea could put individuals at considerable risk even when they were not engaged in group fights.

> One Sunday morning I was with two friends and we jumped the fence to the location. At that time I didn't drink joala. We went to where the women hid joala by burying the cans and we saw some of the containers above the ground. We took all the joala . . . to an isolated place and hid in the grass because we were afraid of the police. I was the one who poured the joala until I decided to drink it myself, and that was my first time. We were busy drinking and then we saw a crowd of men coming toward us. They were Matsieng. . . . My friends ran away but I was not able and they beat me. I tried to fight but it was useless because the Matsieng were many. . . . I was beaten unconscious and when I regained consciousness my head was covered in blood and my hand was badly injured. I felt the grass on my back and realized I had no clothes—they left me with only my trousers. When a person is badly beaten we say *limohatile* [trampled by horses or cattle]. I tried until I managed to stand. I didn't know where I was because I was afraid and drunk. I walked until. . . . I saw another crowd of men and gave up because I thought they were Matsieng, but they were Molapo. . . . My group went in front of a car driven by a white woman, forced her to stop, and ordered her to take me to the hospital at the mine where I worked. (7 June 1998)

The original group of an abducted or runaway woman was honor bound to attempt her reclamation. 'Mè ID, who belonged to a Carletonville group in the 1980s and early 1990s, explains the outcome of one such fight:

> Most of the fights between Marashea are caused by women. Although I cannot recall all the details, I remember a fight over a woman called Ntsoaki from Qacha's Nek [Lesotho], next to White Hill. She had been staying with Lerashea at Kloof [informal settlement near Kloof Gold Mine] when I was at Bekkersdal. Ntsoaki had run away from Kloof to stay at Phiri, where she was discovered two months after her escape. Marashea from Khutsong, Kloof, and Bekkersdal came together to go to Phiri and return with Ntsoaki.

They left in the afternoon with six taxis and one van. They came back with her around nine the next morning. She was badly wounded, stabbed in many places. They did not tell us the exact number of those from Phiri who died, but for us three died and two were badly injured.

Revenge attacks were also commonplace and LG, Matsieng Lerashea under Tsotsi Raliemere in the 1980s, describes how his leader engineered revenge after LG suffered at the hands of a rival group:

I was beaten by Matsekha at Carletonville. I went to the hospital at Deep Level [mine]. Marashea of Matsieng went to Phiri and told them I was beaten by Matsekha. Raliemere told them they would come to see me. I was beaten and went to the hospital on Saturday. On Sunday members of my group arrived at the hospital and Raliemere gave me R40. He told me I must go to the dance next Saturday and did not care whether I was discharged or not. I was badly injured but I had to go to the dance at Phiri. On Wednesday I was discharged and on Saturday I took the train to Phiri. My head was aching but I could not refuse. At twelve o'clock the whistle was blown and Marashea came and formed a group. At two o'clock we all bathed with moriana. I didn't know where we were going. At eight o'clock three vehicles arrived, two taxis and Raliemere's private car. Some entered the taxis and I was with Sanki, Bothlenyane, Mohlomi, and Raliemere in the private car. We left, going straight for Carletonville. Before we entered the location, the vehicles stopped and they locked me inside a taxi and they attacked that location. I heard many gunshots. When they came back I didn't know what had happened, but they took me to the scene of the fight and there were fifteen people dead.

As Marashea became established in the Free State from the 1950s, some of the groups ignored the Matsieng-Matsekha divide that had caused so much fighting on the Rand. Given time, however, this split was replicated in the Free State. BM recounts how his group was torn apart:

There was a fight between Marashea that caused a division between us. We were united as Basotho. The fight was caused by a woman named Mantoa who was staying with Ntate Sootho. This led to the groups of Ha-Molapo and Matsieng that did not exist in the Free

State, only in Gauteng and some other places. In the Free State we had only one group that did not belong to either Molapo or Matsieng. A young man from Leribe called Maseko happened to fall in love with Sootho's woman. People from Matsieng did not like this because they thought that this young man was being unfair to the old man. Those from Leribe supported Maseko when he took Sootho's woman. This led to a serious dispute between the two parties. That's why we fought each other. The fight began in the morning around five. . . . Our men left Virginia to go to Thabong early and surround their area before they realized we were there. We started throwing stones at their houses and it seemed as if they were expecting us. The fighting continued until around ten [a.m.] and nobody died but many were injured. Since that day we have never been together with the people of Molapo.

By the 1970s, the Free State factions were as divided as their compatriots in Gauteng. Alliances between Free State and Rand groups reflected this division, as a Matsieng faction from Virginia would call on Matsieng from Soweto for assistance and vice versa. Matsieng established strongholds in the Virginia and Klerksdorp areas, while Matsekha enjoyed supremacy in the vicinity of Welkom.

The Matsieng-Matsekha rivalry was not responsible for all internecine fighting within Marashea. Disputes over leadership sometimes led to fighting and the proliferation of splinter groups. Commonly recited examples include the cases of Mashai and Lenkoane. A renegade Matsieng group based in Carletonville led by Mashai fought many battles with Matsieng from Soweto in the 1980s and continues to defy the authority of the leader of Matsieng in the Free State. Lenkoane was assassinated by a man who aspired to his position. This led to fighting between those who had supported Lenkoane and the followers of his assassin, Teboho Majoro.[40]

SOCIAL PRACTICES

Relations between groups of Marashea were cemented at dances, concerts, stokvels, and funerals, and these social affairs also acted as fundraisers. For example, BM has an annual feast and celebration for all the members in each one of the settlements under his control. Additionally, Matsieng from the Free State maintained relations with Matsieng on the Rand by means of feasts and funerals. Some activities, especially funeral rites, were Marashea inven-

tions that distinguished members from other migrant Basotho. The following description of a ceremony and the answer to a research assistant's question reveal the distinct nature of the organization.

> At the vigil for the dead we do not pray or sing hymns; rather we talk a lot of nonsense about this man. We tell him to go and tell Satan about his deeds on earth because he killed people. We jump over his coffin. There is no singing of hymns but the accordion is played the whole night, just like at stokvels. His blanket and molamu and other weapons are placed on top of him. When we proceed to the cemetery the coffin is shot three times, or it is hit with melamu. The coffin is swung up and down as we walk toward the graveyard while the women are marching and yelling.
>
> QUESTION: But are you Christians?
>
> Yes, I am Catholic, but in Marashea one forgets all those things. ('Mè LW)

Since advances in transport made it feasible for the Russians to bury their dead in Lesotho, the groups guarantee male members a funeral in their home area and financial compensation for relatives. PL explains that in the old days, "we did not bring them home, we buried them in South Africa, but now they are brought home to their relatives. . . . We buy an ox for food and everything is bought by Marashea. We give R1,000 to his relatives" (Welkom, 21 May 1999). Other interviews confirm that this has been standard practice for many years now. Retired members and their families are accorded the same privilege by some groups. "We tell them to make their families aware that when they die we must be notified so that we can come and bury them—it is our obligation. For their funeral we buy two sheep, one cow, a coffin, some groceries, and we give the family of the deceased R1,000" (CN).

Marashea women on the Rand in the 1950s and 1960s were famous for their enticing displays when they performed the *famo*, a dance in which the buttocks and sometimes even the genitals were displayed to cheering men. One of David Coplan's informants provides a detailed description:

> A famo is like a [church] "tea-meeting" with an accordion [laughter]. The women are there. And the men are naked under their blankets, and we are in a circle, and there is a command: *Likepi!* [steel pick—euphemism for penis] Then we lay our pricks on the table. And the women are not wearing any panties under their

skirts. It's a stokvel, for money. When the famo dance is done, there shouldn't be any laughter; it's quite serious. They display themselves to the men. They even shave their vulvas, and put some lipstick, called "stoplight," around them. The man who is the good dancer and a good stick fighter is the one who the women want, and he gets whatever woman he wants.[41]

The famo seems to have been a particularly effective recruiting device, as it convinced visiting miners and other nonmembers of the benefits of membership. "Women make a living making famos, they show their naked buttocks and the men feel very attracted and want to take them to bed" (PL, Lesotho, 23–24 May 1998). The famo, as far as I can ascertain, was a Marashea creation that was never practiced in Lesotho, and it seems to have died out in recent years. 'Mè OW reports, "In the past there was a dance called famo—this dance was so dirty I could not enjoy watching it. Women would pull up their dresses to expose their private parts to men who were sitting down in front of them watching." The demise of the famo might be related to the proliferation of firearms, which increased the costs of fights between group members. "These dances caused great jealousy among the men because it provoked them so much."

Normative sexual mores, as they were understood in Lesotho, were largely abandoned. For example, several women reported that sexual behavior in the Marashea deviated from accepted practice in Lesotho in that intercourse was not kept private. These accounts stress that women in Lesotho were accorded a degree of respect noticeably absent in Borashea. "There were no moral standards. More than ten men and women were sleeping together in one room. Sex was just like eating papa [maize meal, the staple food of Basotho], there was no respect at all" ('Mè OW). There are several possible reasons for changes in sexual behavior. Many Marashea women worked as prostitutes and had already abandoned conventional notions of appropriate behavior. Others traded sexual services for protection. In such an environment an aggressive assertion of sexuality could reap dividends. Most men had several linyatsi and this was seen as one of the most coveted aspects of membership. Finally, group survival was dependent on the economic support of mineworkers. To attract miners the groups actively marketed the sexual services of Marashea women. Given these conditions, it is not surprising that the Marashea deviated from traditional Sesotho concepts of acceptable sexual mores.

Most Marashea men maintained families in Lesotho and kept linyatsi in South Africa. Since the mines opened in the Free State and bus and taxi services between the mines and Lesotho have become more affordable and

dependable, it has become easier for Marashea (and mineworkers) to visit home more frequently. KI, who was Lerashea from 1975 to 1985 in the Welkom area, explains that "most Marashea have real families in Lesotho that they visit at least monthly. Just like myself, I used to visit my family every month." Additionally, KI had a steady nyatsi in South Africa with whom he operated a business selling *dagga* (marijuana).

A large majority of the men consulted for this study indicated that their "real" families were in Lesotho. "Most Marashea still have families in Lesotho. The women in South Africa are just on a temporary basis" (ML). Some men assumed responsibility for the children conceived with their linyatsi, but many did not. It was more common for male veterans to retire to Lesotho and sever connections with their female companions. "We have two families," explains PL. "When we leave Lesotho and go to work in South Africa we find another woman who will help us in South Africa. When we come back the wives at home are here looking after families and agriculture." CN, who resides in a squatter camp adjacent to Vaal Reefs Mine, summarizes the relationships between male and female Marashea: "They are linyatsi—*masehlalisane* [let's stay together]. We part when we go home [Lesotho]."

Very few Marashea women had husbands and stable families back in Lesotho. Children born in South Africa were often sent back to Lesotho to stay with relatives and, if possible, to attend school. It was difficult for women to travel back and forth between Lesotho and South Africa for visits. The stigma of being Marashea mitigated against their return, as did their illegal status in South Africa, which rendered border crossings risky or expensive (due to bribes). Additionally, women did not have the same freedom of movement as men. "Most women have abandoned their families. It is difficult for women because men will not allow them to go home, fearing they will not come back" ('Mè ID). Despite these obstacles, some Marashea women achieved a measure of familial stability with their linyatsi. More likely, a woman was only one of several linyatsi kept by a male Lerashea.

GENDER RELATIONS

South Africa has long been one of the most violent societies in the world and currently lays claim to the world's highest reported incidence of rape. Various analysts contend that the ubiquity of violence against women in South Africa is largely a function of the apartheid system, which emasculated black men. After studying the gendered nature of violence during the recent conflict in KwaZulu-Natal, Catherine Campbell concludes, "The ability of men to control

women, or keep them in line, and the use of violence to ensure this control, is one area where the power of working-class men has not been threatened by a racial capitalist society."[42] Glaser's exploration of gender relations within the tsotsi gangs on the Rand reveals, "As black, working-class youths, *tsotsis* were structurally subordinate in terms of race, class and generation. But, as males, tsotsis were structurally *dominant*. Gender was the one sphere in which they found themselves 'naturally' in the ascendant. Hence the need to assert their masculinity and sexual difference. They defended their one area of privilege vigorously."[43]

Male subcultures, especially gangs, often assert and define their masculinity at least partially through the violent domination of girls and women. Thus, "A tsotsi was a man but his masculinity was unconvincing if he did not have a woman to dominate."[44] In the South African context, various studies of different gangs have uncovered the centrality of gender violence. This is true of rural gangs such as the Mpondo *indlavini* of the 1930s through the 1950s, the tsotsi subculture that pervaded urban South Africa from the 1940s, and the more recent "jackroller" gangs in Soweto, for whom rape is an organized group activity.[45] In environments where females were not readily available, some gangs used violence to control male sexuality.[46]

Forced sex, abduction, sexual exploitation, and the concept of women as trophies have been common elements in gangs' gender relations. Glaser argues that within gangs, "Women tend to be the rewards, the trophies for male successes. Apart from providing sexual and domestic services to males they are the symbols of status to be won or lost in the male exclusive spheres such as fighting."[47] Gender relations within the Marashea fit this general typology but also exhibit specific characteristics. The control of women has been crucial to the economic survival of the gangs, and the abduction of women became common practice between competing factions. Furthermore, women have been fully integrated members of Marashea society, as opposed to many gangs where females were confined to the periphery.

The status of women and gender relations within the Marashea has never been examined in detail. Bonner discusses the importance of women to recruiting and the gangs' determination to control independent Basotho women on the Rand in the 1940s and 1950s. Guy and Thabane note Rantoa's insistence that women precipitated some of the major conflicts between groups and warn, "The role of women in the history of *Ma-Rashea* needs careful treatment."[48] A careful treatment of the subject reveals that although some men and women forged strong bonds, Coplan's assertion that "Russians and their women were mutually supportive and independent counterparts" needs to be rethought.[49]

From its inception, Marashea has been a male-dominated organization, founded and run by men. Men made the major decisions, negotiated with police and lawyers, dictated and dispensed discipline, and engaged in the violence that publicly defined Borashea. Many veterans refer to Borashea as a *koma*, a secret male society, and view it as an extension of the practice of skirmishing between boys from neighboring villages in Lesotho.[50] "We learned to fight when we were young boys and this grew in our hearts" (PL, Lesotho, 23–24 May 1998). There was an overt martial character to Borashea, and men frequently refer to themselves as *marabele* (fighters) and *masole* (soldiers). Perhaps the best illustration of the militaristic identity of Marashea is provided by a glimpse of their funeral ceremonies. "The funerals of Marashea are no different from the soldiers. We take the corpse to the grave, where we don't sing hymns but songs of war" (KB). Staged fights between group members were common at funerals because "blood had to be shed before the man could be buried. . . . the intention was not to kill anybody but at least a wound must be seen as an honour to that man who was a soldier" (BM). During a 1965 funeral at Doornkop Cemetery in Johannesburg, three hundred Marashea allowed a minister to perform a Christian service but then conducted their own ritual, smashing the coffin and insulting the dead man. One of the mourners explained, "There is absolutely no ill-feeling against the dead man. This is just our way of bidding a comrade goodbye. . . . When you attend a soldier's funeral you see that he is honored by being given a full military funeral, so it goes with us."[51] ML adds, "When we bury Lerashea, as the coffin descends into the grave we shoot it, saying, 'You were a man,' and we put the weapons in the grave so he may fight beyond the grave."

Robert Morrell's discussion of hegemonic masculine identities is useful to an understanding of Marashea masculinity. "The concept of hegemonic masculinity provides a way of explaining that though a number of masculinities coexist, a particular version of masculinity holds sway, bestowing power and privilege on men who espouse it and claim it as their own."[52] The Marashea's dominant, or "hegemonic," masculine identity celebrates fighting prowess and the domination of women. The Marashea began as a fighting association and has always used violence to protect and advance its interests. Demonstrations of bravery and fighting ability earn the respect and admiration of one's colleagues and one cannot hope to assume a leadership position without such qualities. The economic foundation of the Marashea is based on the control of women, and violence has been a key element in acquiring and maintaining that control. There are secondary masculine ideals within the Marashea— many miners, for example, take pride in the arduous and demanding nature of work underground. Aspects of what Morrell terms "African masculinity,"

stemming from the rural experience and based on the authority of elders and respect for custom, resonate strongly within the Marashea.[53] However, given the nature and activities of the association, the construction of a warrior identity was inevitable.

The differing reflections of male and female respondents are indicative of their status within the Marashea. The Marashea evoke fear but also a degree of admiration among some Basotho. Leslie Bank, who researched taxi violence in 1980s QwaQwa, observed that the taxi drivers "were enamoured by the mystique of the Russians; they admired their tradition of resistance and survival and spoke proudly of their relationships with individual gangsters."[54] It was a hard life but there are aspects of their struggle as Marashea to which male veterans cling proudly, including their reputation as fighters. "There were no benefits in Marashea. If you are a soldier you don't expect any return. When you are Lerashea you are not paid but you are proud to say, I defeated someone in the fight, or to say, I won the fight; someone is afraid of me—you become proud of that. What I can be proud of is that people of Ha-Molapo were afraid of me . . . that's the only benefit I got" (HG). They also boast about their sexual exploits and gleefully recount old battlefield and courtroom victories. Some female informants have fond memories of their days as Marashea. "We went to dances at Benoni, Springs, and other places. We rode the trains and I enjoyed it very much. I was a singer and I even recorded a cassette—it was nice to be there" ('Mè SP). However, for the most part women's recollections tend to be more negative.

In Basotho society the women of Marashea benefit from none of the positive imagery commonly associated with the group. They are not regarded with awe, they are not feared, and they are not glamorized. Rather, the women of Marashea, when acknowledged, are typically dismissed as prostitutes and considered outcasts. Group pride is a much less relevant concept to women who do not bask in the reflected glory. Their marginalized status, within both Marashea and Basotho society, ensures that women have little stake in the Marashea's reputation and thus accrue no benefits from the creation of an idealized masculine version of the history and values of the association.

Women were regarded as Marashea, as full members of the group who enjoyed many of the rights of men. Women were given ceremonial burials; they had their legal expenses paid when arrested on group business; and they were protected from assault and robbery by outsiders. Men and women celebrated at feasts and stokvels, and many couples worked together in productive economic unions. Women sang men's praises before battles and even fought alongside them on occasion. By virtue of special skills, physical beauty, relationships with powerful men, and seniority within the group, a small minority of women assumed elevated status and wielded authority over other women.

At the same time, women as a group were regarded as property to be exploited both materially and as spoils of war. Women's sexual lives and freedoms were closely regulated, as were their personal relationships with male partners. Whereas men frequently had multiple lovers, each woman belonged to a certain man, or if no man wanted her, she was expected to prostitute herself for the group.

Women were clearly at the bottom of the power structure within the Marashea, but the position of individuals varied depending on mode of entry, relationships with male partners, seniority, and the ability to enhance the prestige or security of the group. There were three basic categories of women: kidnap victims, women without a male partner, and linyatsi, the lovers of specific men. Kidnapped women were treated as captives with virtually no rights until they were integrated. During the initial period of captivity they were especially vulnerable to abuse. "Those like myself who are kidnapped are available to any man who is interested" ('Mè KW). Women who joined the group but did not have a recognized relationship with a male member were also available to all and were sometimes forced into prostitution. "If a woman does not have nyatsi she is given to any man and told to sleep with him. She has no choice about that" ('Mè OW). 'Mè TF explains the finances of prostitution: "They send you to attract men at the mines. . . . At the mine you are proposed to by a man and you are allowed to bring him back to the *mekhukhu* [informal settlement], but after his departure you have to give money. . . . Marashea are moving all around on the weekends and that is the time to have sex with other men. . . . There are old women staying there and if you try to keep that money for yourself, they will tell Marashea that the man was there, so then they want the money, and if you do not give it, they beat you."

Unattached women also lacked a male partner who could speak on their behalf and from whom they might reap some economic benefits, from the proceeds of robberies, for example. While the marena and their committees made financial decisions for the group, the extent of earnings that individual women were allowed to keep depended on their relationships with male partners. Some men appropriated virtually all the earnings of their linyatsi, while others shared more equitably. 'Mè OW split her earnings with her man: "One week I brewed joala and sold it for him, the next week the money comes to me." Fully integrated women with an established male partner, especially those attached to powerful men, had some standing in the group and a degree of protection that unattached and kidnapped women did not enjoy.

Women valued for their beauty or singing ability were prized by all Marashea, and groups had a vested interest in treating them well to prevent them from absconding to rival factions. Female traditional doctors contributed essential services and seem to have commanded respect as long as they were

seen to be effective. Senior women, who had been with the group for long periods of time and had proven themselves trustworthy, were put in charge of kidnapped women and sometimes given the authority to resolve disputes between their junior colleagues. Women were neither elected nor appointed to leadership positions, but the nyatsi or wife of the morena was often acknowledged as a senior figure among female members. "We only respect the wife of morena. She is our leader—but we only respect her if she respects us" ('Mè MG). Regardless of their position in the female hierarchy, all women were subject to varying degrees of male control.

The women who reflect positively on their experience as Marashea tend to have had either a caring partner or a morena who treated the women in the group fairly. 'Mè MD and 'Mè TW evaluated their lives as Marashea at least partially through the lenses of their relationships. 'Mè MD explains: "I lived a nice life because my husband was honest with me. I was not beaten or arrested." Although she was once tortured by the police for refusing to divulge Tsotsi's whereabouts, one of his linyatsi reports, "I lived a good life because of the man I lived with" ('Mè TW). Tsotsi was lauded by the women from his group. "He was a good morena. If a woman went to him and asked for money, he would go to the man and ask why his wife was looking for money. He was the father of all. If I quarreled with my husband I would report to him." ('Mè MD). The various marena treated their female members differently. Some are remembered as benign, while others are condemned for their cruelty. 'Mè LW, who was Lerashea in Phiri after the death of Tsotsi, envied the women in another group who fared much better. "In Phiri, women live a different life. In CNC [squatter camp in the Free State] I learned that women were happier and freer than women in Phiri. Most of them I heard were able to come home with money and clothes for their children. But at Phiri most of us were just used by these men to satisfy their needs; they never cared for us."

Female informants emphasized their lack of power in relation to the men who controlled virtually all aspects of Marashea society. 'Mè ID reported that "[Women] are full members but in some cases it is just like they are used by Marashea to work for them because women do not have a say in decision making; only men take part in making decisions." When asked about the role of men within Marashea, 'Mè KW responded, "Men are the ones who protect us. They are the ones who fight when there is fighting to be done. The management of the group is run by men." 'Mè LW summarized the status of women: "Women are just like babies or animals, they have no say, no choice—they are not free." Perceptions of gender roles indicate the extent to which male violence was an integral element of Borashea. Men identified with their role as warriors and considered the use of violence to obtain and control women to be norma-

tive. 'Mè LW's response to the question, "How do men contribute to the group?"—"Their role is to kill, commit robberies, and kidnap women"—reflects a common understanding of the male function in Borashea.

Although women did not collectively challenge male dominance within the Marashea, individual women resisted particularly oppressive conditions, most often by fleeing, but sometimes more directly. DS kidnapped a woman who took her revenge by attempting to tip a burning coal stove on him while he was sleeping. Such incidents were exceptional, no doubt because of the danger involved in active resistance. For the most part, female members have accepted gender relations within Marashea as an unjust but fundamentally immutable reality. An example of this fatalism is the role of fully integrated women as the primary guards preventing the escape of female kidnap victims. This argument mirrors Campbell's conclusion regarding female attitudes to violence and subordination in KwaZulu-Natal: "So entrenched were these patriarchal norms in the lives of these young women that avoidance or tolerance were the only two options mentioned for dealing with male violence. None of them mentioned the possibility of redefining gender relations."[55]

The degree of women's subjugation within the Marashea is perhaps best illustrated by exploring issues of personal autonomy and control over sexuality, movement, and material resources. Women, once they joined, belonged to the group in the most fundamental sense. When asked what happens to a female Lerashea if her man dies or goes to prison for an extended period of time, 'Mè ID replied, "A woman is taken by another man in the group or by the morena. She is not allowed to go home or to join another group—she belongs to the group, not individual Lerashea." This theme appears time and again in oral testimony. 'Mè FD states simply, "They tell you that you have to be nyatsi of another Lerashea." If for some reason, a woman did leave the group, compensation was expected. 'Mè EW's nyatsi retired and went back to Lesotho and she moved in with a man who was not affiliated with the Marashea. This caused her great difficulty. "After I started living with a man who was not Lerashea I had to pay a lot of money. My man had to pay R1,000 so they would let him stay with me. They also beat him. I ended up hating them because of what they did to me. They came to collect from the man I lived with every time they had a funeral."

When women first joined the group, unless they were claimed by a specific man, they were allocated out to members by the morena. If no man was interested she was considered communal property. KI explains: "If a woman arrives, she reports to morena and he will announce that a new woman has come and asks who wants her. Then if someone wants her, he takes her. If

nobody volunteers to take her, she will be accepted into the group, and when miners come for drinking she will be told that if a certain man wants her, '*Hei uena* [you]! Take this man and sleep with him.' She has to accept that order without hesitation."

Chiefly privileges were sometimes invoked when new women were brought into the group. "When these women arrive at our place morena chooses first, and when he is satisfied he gives some to us" (WL). HM's perception of women as possessions emerges in his discussion of internecine conflicts. "When we were fighting with people if they ran away we were supposed to take their blankets. If we stole blankets then that group would come back for revenge, just like with women."

Women were closely monitored to ensure that male Marashea maintained control over their sexuality. To take a lover or even sleep with a man other than one's official nyatsi was to invite harsh retribution. This was probably the one offense for which women were most commonly punished. Men usually had more than one woman, often under the same roof, an arrangement bitterly resented by some women but one over which they had very little control. "The man can stay with two women. We are not supposed to complain; if we complain we are punished until we do what he wants" ('Mè RB). LG provides the male perspective: "A man chooses where to sleep among three women; none of those women can refuse to sleep with me because I would beat her and force her to go to bed with me."

A woman could not choose to renounce her nyatsi. "Only men can decide to leave a woman and take another one, or have both of them" ('Mè SP). If she was unfaithful she could be made an example of in a chilling public spectacle. Men were not penalized for sleeping with other women, only for transgressing with a woman of a fellow group member—even then the punishment was not nearly as severe. "I was told that a woman should not sleep with a man other than her own and if found guilty of this crime a woman was beaten to death—they call it *kola*—that means the woman is beaten by everyone around. It is not just the man who stays with her that beats her, but every Marashea, including the Lerashea you slept with. As for the man who sleeps with another Lerashea's woman, he is fined maybe R100" ('Mè LW).

A few female informants reported a particularly horrible punishment for infidelity. "Sometimes they even push molamu into her vagina as a torture, because sleeping with another man is the most terrible crime a woman can commit" ('Mè KW). Mere suspicion could lead to beatings. 'Mè TW's group in Phiri was being visited by a group from Welkom and the men from Phiri watched their women very closely. "I went to the store after we had been told not to leave the house. They all beat me—they thought I went to meet a man.

Marashea women parade during festivities at Buffelsfontein in the Free State, late 1990s. Collection of the author.

We were not allowed to talk to the men from Welkom because our men were jealous." Exceptions were made with male consent if the act was remunerative. "They do not want any man to come close to you unless they agreed that man could use you as his wife—that man must then pay money for being with you" ('Mè RB). The worst excesses of gender violence were directed at kidnapped women.

A tradition of elopement and abduction in Lesotho is traceable to the precipitous rise in *bohali* (bridewealth) prices in the early twentieth century. By the 1920s and 1930s *chobeliso*—eloping with a man while appearing to offer resistance—"became almost commonplace as *bohali* spiraled out of the reach of most men."[56] Chobeliso was transformed by Marashea men, who did not require a woman's acquiescence to abduct her. In some instances, especially when a woman was stolen from one group by another, the act was prearranged with her consent, but this seems to have made up a minority of such cases.[57] Women were occasionally abducted from Lesotho and taken back to South Africa by Marashea groups that had returned to bury their dead (Detective M, Lesotho, July 1998), but migrant women already in South Africa were the usual victims. One of Bonner's informants explained that these women were chosen for their vulnerability as they lacked the protection of a chief or male kin in the urban setting.[58] However, even attached women were not safe from Marashea, as a single man was easily overpowered by a group of armed Russians.

African newspapers in the 1950s and 1960s featured several accounts of women abducted by Marashea. A 1958 story that chronicled a kidnapping, declared that the woman "was a victim of the Russian habit of simply taking a woman if they want her whether she is married or not." The kidnappers reportedly told the victim's mother, "If a Russian liked a woman he took her, even if she was married. If her husband interfered, they would kill him."[59] Informants expressed similar sentiments. SM, active in the 1940s and 1950s, remembers, "Maybe a woman from Lesotho is visiting her husband and we would kidnap her at the train station. . . . [If] we find you with your wife, you were given the choice of being killed or giving up that woman. We would take her to our place and give her to one of our members to marry." Especially sensational were those occasions when armed bands of Russians surrounded and broke into houses to carry away the women they wanted.[60]

Although newspaper coverage of such events was limited to the early days of the Marashea on the Rand, kidnapping has remained an integral part of Borashea. A veteran from Thabong, who retired in 1989, reflects fondly, "It was nice because if I loved a woman from another place I just invited my friends and we would go there and kidnap that woman" (KF). And just as in earlier years, OB's more recent account of acquiring a woman illustrates that men were often helpless to protect their women from Marashea. "One of the best things was that I was given a woman to marry. I took her from another man who was not Lerashea. I was at Vaal Reefs, under the control of Mokhemele, and they told that woman that I am her husband and she is my wife. . . . Her husband did not have a chance to fight for her because he was not Lerashea and I was with a group of people."

Rather than preying exclusively on vulnerable women, Marashea groups often specifically targeted women from rival factions. Such activities inevitably led to violence and were the cause of much internecine fighting within the Marashea. Oral evidence indicates that kidnapping continues to generate conflict between rival groups.

During the days of prearranged battles, women were sometimes the reward for victory. "We had our women but if one of our members did not have one we would write a letter to Matsieng challenging them to a fight, and if we defeated them we would take their wives, and that was how those who did not have wives obtained them" (NN, 13 May). The symbolic importance of women to the Marashea rivalries is explained by a veteran of the fighting on the Rand in the 1950s: "Women are the cause of fighting in Marashea. One group of Marashea will see a beautiful woman and they will want her or their morena will want her. Then they will have to fight that group to get that woman. And if they are successful the group that lost her will want her back,

so the fight will continue until one group decides to stop or is defeated entirely" (MR). The trophy aspect is emphasized by the fact that groups often kidnapped women renowned for their beauty or singing talent.[61] Other favorite targets were the women of faction leaders. Such acts were deliberate provocations designed to demonstrate contempt for a rival group. "Marashea of Molapo came to our place and kidnapped our morena's nyatsi. They took her to the mountain and bound her for three days. On Friday we rode in the taxis and attacked those people in order to rescue the nyatsi of our morena. We found her on the mountain bound and unable to speak but we managed to come back with her. . . . she had not been given food or water for three days" (DG).

The enduring nature of disputes over women is captured by the following two accounts. The description of a raid and counterraid for a woman on the 1950s Rand is remarkably similar to a 1990s battle near Carletonville. 'Mè OW joined the Marashea in the late 1940s and vividly recalls a kidnapping-related battle:

> The alarm was raised and when we came out we saw a large lorry
> full of household equipment. We were told those things belonged to
> a woman who had been kidnapped from Germiston. She had been
> brutally beaten. She had come all the way through Johannesburg
> naked and beaten. Guards were posted and also spies in Germiston
> because they expected those people to follow them. . . . She arrived
> at night. In the morning we were worried that something was going
> to happen. In the afternoon I heard whistles blowing from the bush
> at the back of our place. We scattered and ran as we heard gunshots
> from that side. The men tried to drive away with her in the lorry but
> they were stopped and had to run away. When we came back we
> found that five of the Marashea from Germiston had been killed, but
> they managed to take back that woman as well as all her belongings.

A woman, who was herself kidnapped and held captive in a squatter camp near Khutsong in the early 1990s, describes a raid in which an aggrieved group sought revenge against rivals who had kidnapped one of their woman—Moelo:

> One day I heard a whistle blowing far away. I did not know what it
> meant because I was still new to Marashea, but then somebody
> raised the alarm, saying that there was another group of Marashea
> attacking us. They came and surrounded the camp while others went
> from house to house searching for her. It was easy for them because

there were only a few men; most had gone to Randfontein for a stokvel. Those who remained resisted but they didn't stand a chance and some of them were killed. After about thirty minutes Moelo was found and taken to their taxis, which they had parked some way from the camp. . . . Houses were damaged and destroyed; I have never seen such an atrocity. ('Mè KW)

Clearly the danger involved and the losses suffered in initial raids and recovery expeditions outweighed the material value of any one woman. Despite the economic imperative to control women, the cycle of raid and counter-raid with high-profile women as the targets indicates that women possessed an emblematic value that transcended economics. For Marashea, capturing a high-profile woman from a rival group was in many ways analogous to capturing the enemy's colors in European conflicts.

Perceptions and experiences of kidnapping indicate the centrality of gender domination in the Marashea. There is an obvious contrast between the typical, matter-of-fact attitude of men — "When you loved a woman from Ha-Molapo you just kidnapped her without any negotiations. When you were attracted to a woman you just told your members and they would assist you to go and kidnap her" (HM) — and the experiences of women victimized by such actions. 'Mè LW was kidnapped in 1992 by a group of Marashea who spotted her at a shebeen in Soweto. They followed 'Mè LW to her employer's house, where she worked as a domestic servant, and the next day they broke into the house and assaulted and abducted her. She was taken by taxi to a neighboring township and endured terrible abuse. "My wound [from the initial assault] was so painful but nobody cared and they said they would beat me again. I was told to sleep with that very man who stared at me when we were at the shebeen. I think he is the one who suggested my kidnapping. I was told that if I tried to run away they would go and burn all my relatives' homes [in Lesotho] and kill my family. Hei! ntate, Marashea are not good people. We had sex right there, sleeping one couple right next to the other."

After about a year 'Mè LW's mother learned of her whereabouts and came from Lesotho to beg for her release, fabricating a story about a death in the family. The leader allowed her to go back to Lesotho for the funeral, and 'Mè LW never returned.

'Mè KW was abducted from her husband's house in Bekkersdal in 1991 during a visit from Lesotho. Her husband had a Russian friend who visited them and whose secret advances 'Mè KW refused. Her abductor waited to strike until her husband worked the night shift. After she had been settled in a Marashea camp she was required to brew and sell beer, handing over the

proceeds to the man who had engineered her kidnapping. She secreted away small amounts until she had enough for taxi fare to the Lesotho border. Eventually her captors relaxed their vigilance and 'Mè KW was allowed to go into town accompanied by other women. On the pretext of going to the toilet she managed to separate from the women watching her and quickly ran to the taxi rank, where she boarded a taxi to Lesotho. Just like 'Mè LW, her ordeal with the gang had been horrific.

> At night as I was sleeping alone I heard a noise at the door and then about ten men burst in. They woke me up harshly and covered my mouth with a scarf to prevent me from screaming. They threw me into a bakkie [pickup truck] and drove me to a place I didn't know. When we arrived, M raped me and then I was locked in a house. I was always guarded by women and was tied with a rope. M would come at any time to rape me and then leave. The worse part was that I was beaten like a dog on the way and was badly hurt, but no one cared and my wounds were not even treated. I was unable to wash myself or even eat, but no one helped me. Instead he just came and forced me to have sex by undressing me and doing what he wanted and then just leaving me undressed. I stayed with them for a year without a chance to escape.

The Marashea relied on intimidation and violence to terrorize kidnapped women into submission. When asked what prevented an abducted woman from attempting escape, KI responded, "She is told that she must not run away or she will be killed. But above all she is guarded by men and women who don't work. If she is wild we beat her so that she is unable to walk for several weeks. If she then looks calm we keep her tied with a rope for many days and then we untie her but still watch her closely." LG recounts the fate of a group of kidnapped women who managed an initial escape: "We found them at Merafe Station. One of them was thrown on the train tracks and her leg was cut off by the train. She was sent to the hospital and the others were severely beaten." Despite their violent entry kidnapped women were eventually integrated and participated fully in group life, including all the various support capacities.

The relationship between women, mineworkers, and Marashea that remains the lifeblood of the organization is explored in chapter 5 and their auxiliary roles will also be examined as part of the groups' survival strategies, so a brief outline here will suffice. Long-term female members guarded kidnapped women and, of course, women did all the domestic work. In addition, the women of Marashea often acted as messengers and couriers when men were

jailed and at trial. On such occasions they would deliver food and clothing that contained moriana to assist in winning the cases. Crowds of women also provided public support for men on trial by appearing at the courthouse dressed in blankets that were the insignia of their particular group.[62] Women encouraged the men as they prepared for battle, singing their praises and participating in rituals to bring the men good fortune. The famo dance was instrumental in this regard as Coplan has noted. "[It]was both a lusty good time and a preparation for battle, at which women did and said everything possible to fire up their men."[63] 'Mè TF remembers that when the men were "going to fight they put their melamu down and we as women take our clothes off to show our breasts and jump over the melamu."

Hiding men's weapons was an important responsibility. When groups of Marashea traveled on trains and taxis and were at risk of being stopped by the police, women carried the guns in their undergarments. "We hide their weapons, especially when we travel in taxis; the guns are hidden under our breasts. We even cross the Lesotho border like that because the police do not normally search women" ('Mè ID).[64] When police raided Marashea houses and settlements, women were also responsible for concealing weapons.

In the years before guns became commonplace, Marashea women sometimes took an active part in street battles. KP remembers the crucial role played by women in a victorious encounter: "We fought the Zulu and Mapondo together at Meadowlands. We defeated them because we were using bricks and our women helped us. They wanted to force us out of our houses, so we chased them, and when one of them would fall the women would throw bricks at him and many were badly injured." Both male and female informants reported that women fought only in defense of their homes. "When our men were fighting we would help them. We threw stones at their enemies but that only happened when our place was attacked." Debby Bonnin notes that women played a similar role in the recent fighting in KwaZulu-Natal. "While it may have been primarily men who were directly involved with the fighting, this did not necessarily mean that women were unconcerned with it, but they operated in a supportive capacity, which did not necessarily challenge or shift their traditional gender roles."[65]

There has been little change in the status of Marashea women over the years. Women in the rural Free State and far West Rand remain firmly under male control. Basotho women naturally gravitate to informal settlements populated by Basotho, where the language is familiar and there is a greater chance of linking up with relatives or friends from their home areas. Many of these camps are run by Marashea, and the women who settle there are usually allowed to keep some of their earnings but pay rent or protection fees or both,

contribute to burial and legal expenses, and are subject to group (that is to say, male) discipline. Their business and personal lives all take place within the confines of a Russian-controlled area. Marashea women on the Rand were probably not as constrained as the women in rural shack settlements, because they had greater occupational diversity and would not have been monitored as closely. They almost certainly had more opportunities to manage their finances and engage in personal relationships beyond group scrutiny.

Borashea was harsh for all members but more so for women, who had to contend with male violence as a fundamental condition of group life. A few relatively privileged women exercised a greater degree of agency than their less fortunate counterparts. However, even these women were forced to submit to the male concept of gender relations and abide by group regulations designed to ensure their subordination. In its most heinous form, gender oppression in the Marashea was no better than slavery. Women were abducted, beaten, and raped into submission and held as captives. Furthermore, the practice of fighting over women as a group display of masculinity has resulted in a great deal of bloodshed. This gendered violence has been a definitive feature of Borashea from its inception to the present and has, to a large extent, determined the history and activities of the society.

Like any other society, and especially one as diffuse as the Marashea, the Russians have changed over time. However, it remains a Basotho organization made up largely of migrants and retains many of the cultural trappings of former years. Funerals, dances, and feasts continue much as they always have. The basic organization and rules have changed very little. Gangs extract protection fees, as they have done since the society began. The Matsieng-Matsekha divide remains a source of tension, and the gangs continue to fight over women, albeit probably not to the same extent as in former years. The Marashea draws its livelihood from the mining industry, as it has done since the expansion period, and still survives largely through the patronage of mineworkers.

The longevity of the Marashea is testament to a remarkable story of adaptation. Its affiliation with the mines has provided a constant stream of recruits and a reliable source of income. The Marashea has retained its Sesotho identity, a development that has contributed to the integrity of the gangs. The economic contribution of female members is another unique aspect of Borashea. This combination of factors differentiates the Russians from other gangs and criminal organizations in South Africa and has ensured that the Marashea remains a power to be reckoned with in that country's gold-mining areas.

3 ↶ Making a Living

Survival in South Africa

> We called ourselves that name because we knew that Russians were those
> people who were fighting the world. That's why we called ourselves Rus-
> sians. We took the part of Russians — Marashea — because we said, "We
> are fighting the world."
>
> —SC

OVER THE COURSE OF its fifty-year history the Marashea has been faced
with a formidable array of obstacles to its survival. As black, foreign, often illegal migrants partially dependent on criminal activities, Marashea have carved
out an existence in hostile environments. They developed strategies to deal
with a state dedicated to the maintenance of white domination, a police force
tasked with subjugating the black population, a justice system stacked against
blacks, an economic climate inimical to black advancement, and the enmity
of various black South African groups. The resilience and autonomy of the
Marashea underscores the limitations of the apartheid regime to regulate
African lives. The nature of Marashea-police interactions, characterized by
shifting alliances, situational cooperation, and occasional episodes of conflict, highlights the inability of the resistance/collaboration model to capture
the complexities of the relationships between black South Africans and the
apartheid state. The Marashea has survived because of its ability to marshal
various resources to adapt to and exploit the structural opportunities provided
by the state-supported migrant labor system.

ECONOMICS

In the words of KI, "Marashea have to make money for living. Whatever comes
their way, they use it to gain money." The development of the compound system, which effectively confined male mineworkers to single-sex hostels, pro-

vided a market for the primary business of the Marashea—supplying miners with alcohol, commercial sex, and recreation in the form of dances and feasts. Basotho men had a long history of working on the mines by the 1940s, and the different Russian gangs actively cultivated this market. Each gang had close connections with particular mines, and their members working on the mines directed fellow mineworkers to Marashea settlements. The steady stream of new migrants also ensured that the Marashea had a large pool of Basotho men from which to recruit new members.

A key to the survival of the Marashea gangs throughout their history, but especially after the 1950s, when they became more reliant on mineworkers as a source of income, has been their ability to exploit women as an economic resource. As we saw in the previous chapter, the Marashea controlled large numbers of female migrants. These women were instrumental in attracting mineworkers to spend their wages in Marashea settlements. Additionally, new recruits, so important to maintaining and replenishing the strength of groups that lost members to death, imprisonment, desertion, and retirement, were attracted to the Marashea largely because membership provided access to women. Matsieng morena BM, who presides over a number of Marashea settlements in mining areas, acknowledges the importance of female members: "If there were no women here, these men from the mines would not come." The wealth derived from women's commercial activities generated a substantial share of group revenue; however, the Marashea did not rely on these proceeds alone.

Marashea men on the Rand before 1963 were usually engaged in waged work on the mines, in secondary industries or in the commercial sector. In fact, Guy and Thabane claim that "there was no income to be derived from one's activities with *Ma-Rashea*."[1] When their informant Rantoa was out of work he robbed as a member of a separate gang. Bonner's broader study led him to conclude that while most 1950s Russians on the Rand were employed, "from a relatively early stage a section of the Russians remained unemployed . . . and it may have been they who levered the Russians' general propensity for violence into more anti-social and personally remunerative directions."[2] The 1963 legislation, coupled with the exhaustion of the gold mines around Johannesburg, forced the "Russians on the Reef" to diversify their economic activities, as they could no longer rely on obtaining waged jobs. Non-mineworker Marashea in the Free State and West Rand were almost all mal-ofa—those without formal employment. These men functioned as squatter lords, collecting rent and protection fees and overseeing the women who supplied liquor and commercial sex to mineworkers. However, in the absence of

waged work outside the mines, many Marashea men were compelled to find alternate ways of generating income and some developed a degree of financial dependence on more visible criminal activities.

With the exception of marena and perhaps a few of their closest advisors, individuals did not make money simply by being Marashea—no salaries were paid. The income generated from protection fees, dances, stokvels, and mercenary endeavors went into the central treasury, as did fines and membership dues. These funds supported the marena and were allocated for group transport, legal, and burial expenses, for bribery, to purchase guns, and to pay traditional doctors. Marashea groups on the Rand in the 1940s and 1950s catered to the needs of mineworkers, but these activities, while important, tended to supplement wages from the formal economy. As the mining industry declined in importance on the Rand and the number of miners dropped throughout the 1960s and 1970s, the remaining urban gangs became increasingly reliant on financial contributions from criminal activities.

The basic economic unit of Marashea was the household, and each man and the woman or women he stayed with were responsible for their own upkeep. "An individual Lerashea together with his nyatsi has his own ways of making money, which he keeps. As for the group—stokvels, contributions, protection fees, and fines are for the group and the morena" (KI). When jobs were plentiful on the Rand most men were able to live on their wages, along with whatever their linyatsi brought in as domestic servants, brewers, and prostitutes. When jobs became more difficult to obtain, both around Johannesburg and in the rural mining areas, men had to become more entrepreneurial. This sometimes meant engaging in blatantly predatory practices such as robbery, but also branching out into the informal sector. The ways in which Marashea men raised funds can be divided into two basic categories: monies acquired through violence, which usually involved a collective effort as Marashea; and those accruing from entrepreneurial activities, including illegal practices, which were primarily individual initiatives.

A limited range of options existed for unemployed Marashea men. Women were expected to raise money but a man could not always depend on this. Obviously, "loafers" needed money to live and they were also under pressure to pay their membership dues. HL testifies that this provided the impetus for stock theft. "Every man must pay his contribution. Every Thursday he must pay. Those who were not working used to go and steal cattle and sheep so they could pay the contribution." One popular alternative was selling dagga. KI, who worked as a miner, supplemented his income in this way. "I used to sell dagga with the woman I was staying with. She would go to Lesotho to buy big bags of dagga and smuggle it into South Africa. My role was to take this dagga

into the mine hostel and sell it there. I had a friend who was a mine security guard and I would enter when he was on duty at the gate. I only gave him R50 to take in twenty liters of dagga that I packed into matchboxes and sold for R2 each. I made a lot of money that way."

Many malofa forged economic partnerships with mineworkers. Miners who stole gold entrusted Marashea on the outside to peddle it for them. "Those who have connections with those who work at the gold plant . . . would buy some raw stuff and refine it on their own and sell it. In Thabong most of the Marashea make their living selling gold. Some are rich; now they have bought taxis and most of them are owners of the Majakathata Taxi Association" (WL). DS's connection with diamond workers in South Africa allowed him to become an intermediary in a lucrative network: "I was involved in diamond dealing. The miners brought diamonds and I was an agent between the buyers who, were white people, and the suppliers, who were miners. I negotiated the prices."[3] Some Marashea also marketed diamonds smuggled out of Lesotho into South Africa. It appears, however, that such dealings are individual initiatives rather than organized group activities. The Russians are well placed to acquire and transport gold and diamonds because of their connections with the mines and their involvement in the taxi industry, but the extent to which different groups have participated in the illegal trade is difficult to ascertain. Although gold was the most common material obtained from mineworkers, GB spent two years in jail for selling copper he purchased from miners.

Miners were an important market for Marashea entrepreneurs. Men visited the mine compounds to hawk their wares and also relied on mineworkers, who frequented the settlements on weekends, to buy their products. "We sell clothes to the miners on the compound. . . . Some buy and sell things like saddles. I remember one old man who was Lerashea. He bought saddles from Johannesburg and sold them to miners who took them home. Marashea do whatever they can to get money. Some have small shops and others are singers and they make money from that music—from concerts and from selling tapes" (KI).[4] In addition, some Marashea groups ran money-lending operations in the compounds as well as in the townships.[5]

The darker side of Marashea economics indicates that the organization's reputation for violent crime is not without foundation, despite the claims by many veterans that Borashea opposed robbing and victimizing ordinary people. These contradictions may, to some extent, reflect the heterogeneity of the Marashea. Different groups had different policies and engaged in different activities. Some marena seem to have enforced strict injunctions against robbery while others made no such stipulations. Various Marashea groups have

reaped financial gains by engaging in robberies, assassinations, and hiring out as "muscle." Johannesburg newspapers are littered with dozens of references to robberies conducted by Marashea, and police reports paint a similar picture in the Free State.[6] Oral evidence confirms that many Marashea committed muggings and break-ins as a matter of course. As with Rantoa, it is likely that some men participated in criminal activities as individuals separate from the group; however, it is evident that members sometimes took advantage of their numbers and strength to rob and kill collectively as Marashea.

Marashea robberies have followed two general patterns. Looting rival Russian settlements has been a favorite activity. Successful attacks were concluded by wholesale plundering. LG reports that after one such raid, "We came back with women, televisions, and other household articles." Additionally, common people were robbed and mugged. Some malofa made a career of robbery. "Every Friday Marashea go for what they call *ho tsoara poho* [getting hold of the bull; a euphemism for violent robbery], where they go to a certain place to break in and rob—money, property, and especially clothes. These clothes were given to us women to wash, even if they were stained with blood" ('Mè LW). Marashea men tell stories of how they went out in groups searching for victims to rob. SM states that "because we were not working we would rob people on payday, taking their clothes and money. . . . we would see a person at the station and ask him where he was from, then we would ask him for money and if he didn't give it to us we would beat him." Marashea also augmented their wardrobes through robbery. "Our clothes came from other people, because if you were wearing beautiful clothes we would stop you and take them from you" (PK). And contrary to their image as ferocious fighters, KL states, "We went on the night trains to rob people of their luggage, especially women." In SM's case, one of the robberies backfired. "One day we took a box from a train that was going to Johannesburg. The train was slowly going up a hill and we climbed on it and pushed a big box off. We loaded it onto a lorry and took it to a house, locked the door, and opened the box. That was when we found that it contained a snake going to the zoo. We were afraid and shouting and there was no chance to open the door, and the people outside heard us trying to escape. The police came and we were all arrested." Occasionally, Marashea would hold up stores and restaurants, but this was not a routine practice.[7] The emergence of a massive African-controlled taxi industry in the 1980s supplied Marashea groups with new economic opportunities. Enterprising Marashea invested in the taxi business, while others hired out as mercenaries in the numerous conflicts between rival taxi associations.

Throughout the society's existence, Marashea have been hired to intimidate or kill people. The *World* characterized the 1950s gangs on the Rand as

"won't-work Basuto Russians who have made a profession of killing and fighting. For a small fee they will go and attack, kill and cause damage to an area."[8] Intimidation was obviously cheaper and less hazardous than assassination. SO describes how Marashea terrorized their appointed targets: "When we found that person we would take him to an isolated area and frighten him. We told him that we were going to kill him and we would ask him about the trouble with the person who hired us and we told him that that man was our brother. We would then beat him and put him in the boot of the car and drop him near his house. We warned him never to interfere with that man again or we would kill him."

PK states, "If you want us to kill someone, it depends on how hungry we are," but for the right price, some Marashea would do contract murders. "If you want to have someone killed, you hire Marashea to do that job for you and they will kill that person. . . . Because that is a tough job that can send someone to prison we ask R5,000 but sometimes we negotiate the price. We are usually hired by businesspeople to kill their rivals" (MM). People in Lesotho knew that Marashea provided this service. "Even in Lesotho, if someone wants to move you out of his way he can hire Marashea to come and kill you" (DG).

Finally, gambling was a very popular pastime that is almost invariably mentioned when Marashea are asked how malofa made money. It seems that many Marashea were habitual dice players (some also played cards and bet on horse races), but with the exception of a very few sufficiently lucky or skilled players it is difficult to envision people supporting themselves through gambling.

RELATIONS WITH THE POLICE

Given their participation in criminal activities and the day-to-day regulation and harassment to which all Africans were subjected, the Marashea came into frequent contact with the police. In fact, the police and different Marashea groups occasionally worked together against a common antagonist (typically one with ANC affiliations). The apartheid state did not consider the Marashea to be a subversive group that posed a threat to its authority. The police cracked down on the gangs periodically, but as common criminals not dissidents. This distinction was crucial, as the National Party government devoted tremendous resources to destroying black political groups that challenged its legitimacy. And, for all the violence in which the Marashea engaged, whites were very rarely victimized. The Marashea's value as vigilantes, especially in the 1980s and 1990s, when nationalist groups began to openly confront the

government, more than compensated for its criminal activities. As a result, while the Marashea was sometimes regarded as a nuisance, the state made no sustained attempt to eradicate the gangs.

Whenever possible, Marashea gangs purchased the assistance of the police through bribery and by acting as informants. To curry favor and make money, the Marashea sometimes assisted the police, occasionally even assassinating police targets. "They would hire Marashea to kill people they did not like at the location. They would pay Marashea for that" (OE). The most common method of gaining police assistance was outright bribery, and the different groups cultivated specific officers in this manner. Bonner's research revealed that of all the Russians' stratagems for dealing with the police, "The most favored was to gain the ear and support of a Basotho [Mosotho] sergeant in the charge office or police station with a view either to incriminating the opposing side or gaining advance notice of arrests."[9] Oral testimony confirms that this was a popular tactic employed by many Marashea groups. "Some police helped the Matsieng group and others helped Molapo depending on which area they lived in" (HM). Basotho police were even known to join internecine fighting,[10] and AT reports that police assisted in other ways: "When Lerashea has a friend who is a policeman he would tell his group and they would call that policeman to come and train them how to use guns so as to help them in their fights."

The Marashea enlisted police to assist them with specific situations — often fights with a rival group. "We might work with the police if we realized the other group was stronger. Then we would go to the police and pay a bribe with the money from contributions and tell them to arrest those people so they would be dispersed. If we wanted to defeat them we would go to the police and give them money and the police would use their guns so we could defeat them" (SO).[11] ML remembers that the police could be hired to get rid of a particularly feared or hated enemy: "In an incident in Thabong some time ago, Marashea bribed the police to go and help them kill morena of a rival group. . . . The police came and provided them with a searchlight. He was on the ground hiding and they shot him dead." The Marashea also sought police assistance for more routine procedures. "If we had cases we could go to them and give them money to destroy the information" (MM).

As Brewer has pointed out, the SAP had insufficient resources to adequately police black residential areas, was poorly trained, and lacked investigative skills.[12] It is hardly surprising that they relied so heavily on informants (and coerced confessions). Some Marashea worked closely with the police in this capacity, both as individuals and on behalf of their groups. PL, a Matsieng morena on the Rand in the late 1950s and 1960s, was approached by the police to be an informer.

They gave me a letter to show I was a police informer and I was not to be arrested by the police. If I showed them the letter, they left me alone. I helped them to arrest the most wanted tsotsis and robbers. I knew them because we played dice together. They were playing with us because we as Marashea depended on dice to have something to live on. There were many tsotsis in that group so I helped Frederick [police handler] catch those tsotsis. I didn't do that for nothing. When I helped them catch a tsotsi, the police gave me money. (Welkom, 21 May 1999)

This association had multiple benefits for PL and his group. Not only was it lucrative, PL's position also allowed him to finger rivals and enemies for arrest, a situation he was quick to take advantage of.

SAPS inspector K "managed" a group of Marashea in the Free State from the 1970s to the early 1990s to their mutual benefit. K's main contact was Mokhemele, a powerful Matsieng morena who also had ties to the infamous Bureau of State Security (BOSS) (see chapter 6).

Mokimbelele [Mokhemele] started things at first. He just called me one day. I was always working to get crime down, so we always caught a lot of people for trespassing and so on. We took in eighty to a hundred of them in a weekend just to get the crime down, because all the people were saying the MaRussians were doing murders. If there was something wrong they said it was the MaRussians. After I worked about a year like that catching them, Mokimbelele invited me to, you could say, his kraal. And we talked and we came to an agreement that if there was something wrong I could contact him and tell him what's wrong and he would hand the criminals to me.

QUESTION: So you reached an agreement that he would help you—what would you do for him?

No, from my side I didn't make any agreement, but as soon as he started helping me it wasn't necessary for me to arrest all those guys to get information. If crime is down it isn't necessary to do all that work.

In return for their cooperation Mokhemele's group was allowed to operate without interference.

MB's observation indicates the extent to which some Marashea were given carte blanche by the police: "The police gave me a gun to do away with the tsotsis and other gangs in the locations. The police realised that we were the strongest movement that could help them stop crime. They became our

friends and even came to our feasts, where they would celebrate with us." Current Marashea state that they enjoy congenial relations with the police. "We are friends these days, we do not fight. Let me tell you one thing. If the police want to arrest one of us here they just tell me—We want to arrest so-and-so in connection with a certain crime. I tell them to come and take him. Even if he has hidden somewhere I order him to come and surrender to the police. All in all we work together with the police" (BM).

Not all police were corrupt, nor did Marashea groups command the resources to purchase blanket immunity, so a degree of conflict was inevitable. If they were unable to neutralize the police through bribery or other means, Marashea usually tried to avoid confrontations. When threatened with arrest gang members typically fled and even when cornered would often submit. However, in desperate circumstances, or when they had the advantage, the gangs sometimes chose to fight. Oral testimony, police reports, and newspaper accounts are all replete with stories of clashes between Russians and the police. Fighting seems to have been more prevalent on the Rand than in the Free State, probably because the SAP had a higher profile in the urban townships than the informal settlements bordering the mines. Marashea-police hostilities in the Free State erupted when town police were called out by panicked white farmers or mine officials to stop rival groups of Marashea from fighting. For example, in Stilfontein in 1970, a police patrol investigating a stokvel on farm property clashed with Marashea. They were forced to retreat and call reinforcements. A larger police force returned to the scene and engaged in a heated battle with the Russians.[13] However, the mining groups were generally able to operate with much less interference from the police than their urban counterparts.

The urban Marashea were particularly aggressive with African police. In Springs on the East Rand, for instance, nine municipal police were attacked by about fifty Marashea when they entered a house and demanded permits from the occupants, who were staging a party. "The blackjacks ran for their lives, leaving their bicycles and caps. Three of them were seriously injured and suffered gaping head injuries."[14] Municipal police, or "blackjacks," bore the brunt of Marashea assaults because they were present in the townships in greater numbers and were not as well armed as white police (many black police were not issued firearms until the 1970s), and attacks on white officers generated a much more forceful response. That said, white police were not immune from Marashea violence.

Russian assaults were sufficiently common for the SAP to treat seriously a 1956 report that Marashea from Evaton had been hired to attack the municipal police at Kroonstad. Apparently the Evaton Russians had been paid £40 to

"attack the municipality native constables because they were catching too many natives in the Kroonstad location for possession of illegal kaffir beer." Railway police were put on alert and commanding officers in neighboring towns were called out to set up roadblocks and search vehicles going to Kroonstad. The Kroonstad police blocked all the roads leading into the location. Door-to-door searches were conducted and weapons confiscated following information that resident Africans might be in league with the visiting Russians. As it turned out, several vehicles from Evaton were stopped and turned back and no attack emerged.[15] Nonetheless, the magnitude of the reaction indicates that the police believed in the possibility of a Marashea attack.

The police treated Marashea with caution precisely because they had first-hand experience of Russian belligerence. Rantoa relished an incident in which Matsieng had attacked Molapo prisoners in Benoni's magistrates' courts, "forcing the magistrate and other officers of the court into unseemly headlong flight."[16] Thus it is not surprising that when a group of Russians showed up at court to lend support to one of their members being tried for murder, police armed with Sten guns and drawn revolvers surrounded and searched them, locking up those in possession of weapons or without passes.[17]

A few Marashea assaults on white police attracted widespread attention from the media and politicians. In February 1950 eleven police (seven whites armed with revolvers and four Africans) intervened in a conflict between Molapo and Matsieng groups . As they arrived on the scene they were surrounded and attacked by the Molapo contingent. The police retreated, firing as they gave way. Most of the group sustained injuries, including Detective Constable du Plessis, whose ear was split in two with a battle-ax. When they reached safety it became apparent that a Sergeant Notnagel was missing. Once reinforcements arrived the police returned to the scene and discovered his mutilated body.[18] Notnagel's death sparked an inquiry in the House of Assembly and shortly thereafter Sten guns were issued to the Benoni location police station.[19] Molapo leader Matsarapane was arrested and sentenced to hang for the murder of Notnagel. As he was transported from court, several Marashea boarded the train, overpowered the guards, and secured his release.[20] In 1958, Brakpan police reportedly "declared war" on the Marashea after two white policemen and one African constable were injured in a pitched brawl with Russians,[21] and in 1965 Matsieng morena Tseule Tsilo became the object of a massive manhunt when he shot three white police officers.[22]

Most confrontations occurred when police attempted to separate groups during fights or to arrest combatants once a fight was finished. Beer and pass raids also led to conflict. However, Marashea were selective about confronting

the police. If flight was not possible, they occasionally resisted arrest. Maliehe Khoeli, a veteran of dozens of conflicts on the Reef, provided examples of both situations. Following a battle with Zulu antagonists at a railway station, Khoeli and his men were stopped by police who demanded to search them. The police were outnumbered and the Russians were well armed, so rather than surrender they opened fire and forced the police to retreat.

On another occasion, Khoeli's group was trapped by the police after a train battle with Matsieng rivals. During the fight, Khoeli had held a gun to the head of the white engineer to make him stop the train. The police came in hot pursuit and when they caught up with the Marashea, Khoeli's men had already given their guns to women who had returned to their homes. Armed only with melamu, the Russians had no choice but to submit.[23]

Marashea women also suffered at the hands of the police. Women were arrested and deported or fined for liquor and pass offenses, but, more seriously, women were sometimes tortured by the police to reveal the whereabouts of Marashea men. For example, women bore the brunt of police retribution following the murder of a police officer in the mid-1980s by a Matsieng group in Phiri. "The police took N and me and beat us to get us to tell them where the men were. . . . They took us to Protea police station and they beat us until I shit myself" ('Mè XL). Several other women reported similar occurrences, including electric shocks, and on one occasion a woman was put into a sack and thrown into a reservoir by the police ('Mè LW, 'Mè MD, 'Mè TW).

MARASHEA AND THE LAW

Rantoa's practical approach, as described by Guy and Thabane, is applicable to the Marashea as a whole: "Rantoa's conception of the law is the antithesis of the liberal one. There is no search for justice here: the law used correctly is one feature in life's struggle."[24] The Marashea's manipulation of the justice system was critical to its survival. The gangs depended heavily on lawyers to keep them out of prison and paid them accordingly. Relatively few Russians were imprisoned because they routinely bribed the police, employed excellent legal counsel, and intimidated potential witnesses. Furthermore, the nature of their activities often rendered prosecution difficult. Achieving convictions against individuals involved in large-scale confrontations was problematic. An advocate who represented Marashea on a number of occasions from the 1950s through the 1970s explained that the gangsters typically issued blanket denials of involvement and provided false alibis. The lawyer's job was then to "dispute identification and we usually got them off without any diffi-

culties" (Michael Hodes, Johannesburg, 3 March 1998). Marashea also devised strategies to assist in their own defense. "If ten of us were arrested we would put the blame on one man and the lawyer would represent that one man instead of all ten. . . . If such a man is found guilty, he will go to jail for us all but we will collect money to pay his fine" (KF).

The different Marashea factions had their respective lawyers on retainer and the decision to employ representation was made on a case-by-case basis. "In Marashea if a member is arrested we meet as men of the council and decide whether or not to get him a lawyer" (KI). Funds were usually provided for offenders arrested while on group business. Sometimes there were judgment calls:

> There are many cases when we make use of lawyers, like that man you met at CNC [settlement at Vaal Reefs]. . . . he has just finished serving five years. It was because of a lawyer that he was given five years instead of twenty or thirty. I sent some of my men to go to a certain place to fetch a certain man to come to me or submit to my orders. Instead of bringing him alive, they decided to kill him. We decided to get them a lawyer because they were sent by the group, even though they broke the rules. They lost the case in court but because of the lawyer they were sentenced to only five years. (BM)

Almost every man interviewed told of how a lawyer had saved him from incarceration or at least reduced his jail time. DB's example is typical: "Once fifteen of us were arrested and the people of Ha-Masupha were also arrested because people were killed. We won that case because of our lawyers. The Molapo people had come from Meadowlands to attack us and the lawyers made it clear we were attacked. The magistrate only fined us because it was bad to kill people, and we were warned not to appear in court again." So routine was the use of counsel that another Matsekha commander claims his group phoned their lawyer before prearranged conflicts to alert him to meet those who had been arrested at the police station to post bail (ST).

Because of his ability to speak English, PG1 liaised with his group's lawyers and was responsible for handling the legal fund in the 1950s. He dealt with one lawyer in particular, Isaacs, "the best lawyer in my life," who regularly charged up to £500 for his services. Isaacs delivered value for money, especially in the case of a Masupha leader arraigned on murder charges: "[Matsabang] shot about three people dead in the night. We were working together in the general post office in Johannesburg. He was arrested and immediately I went to see Isaacs. He paid the bail for him. Really the case was very, very

difficult, but he was discharged on those murders." PG1's experience was not an isolated event, as Bonner's research demonstrates: "So extensively did the Russians use these professionals that my interview transcriptions at times read like a roll call of the Johannesburg bar: Loveday, Katz, Isaacson [possibly PG1's Isaacs], Laver—the list goes on and on."[25]

A large part of the Marashea's financial resources were spent defending its members in court, and each group had a communal fund for this purpose. A search of a Russian commander's room at Harmony Mine in 1956 uncovered a record of such funds. "During May 1956 Moketi's room was raided and notes of a meeting attended by 29 natives when he was elected leader of the group of Russians were confiscated. A list of names, a copy of which accompanies this, was also found in his possession. . . . Everyone on the list gave £1 towards legal advice."[26] Murder cases in particular required expert and expensive legal representation, and groups sometimes called on affiliated factions for financial assistance. This was the case in the 1980s when Matsieng members from Phiri were charged with killing a police officer, and two Matsieng groups in the Free State contributed several thousand rands for the defense (TS, 22 December 1998). When legal expenses were excessive, all people living in the area under a Marashea group's control were required to contribute to an emergency fund. Primarily because of good counsel and moriana (see below) those involved remember that they "used to win almost all the cases against our members" (MC)—an assessment substantially supported by archival and newspaper references.[27] Although some Marashea spent significant time in jail and a handful were hanged, capable legal representation spared many others from prison cells and the noose.

ETHNICITY AND NATIONAL IDENTITY

The fighting between ANC and Inkatha supporters in the 1980s and 1990s focused attention on Inkatha's attempts to appeal to, and manipulate, Zulu ethnic consciousness. However, ethnic mobilization in the context of urban violence predates the Inkatha campaigns. As a primarily Basotho association involved in countless conflicts with other ethnically defined gangs, the Marashea's role in heightening ethnic chauvinism illustrates the power and resonance of ethnic identities, especially in socially fragmented and dangerous urban settings. The gangs set aside internecine rivalries and invoked a national identity as Basotho when confronting outsiders. As both migrants and foreign nationals, these mostly unschooled and illiterate men drew on a common identity not so much constructed and informed by elite "culture bro-

kers"[28] as instilled by a linguistically and culturally homogenous society that had successfully staved off incorporation into South Africa. This martial history was emphasized during the initiation process that Marashea men underwent as youths. The Marashea reinforced this sense of ethnic exclusivity through its role as protectors of the Basotho, its cultural practices, and the violence it directed against non-Basotho. Rather than accepting ethnic conflict as the inevitable result of state and corporate policies, the practices of the Marashea illustrate how Africans interpreted and used ethnic identities in urban South Africa.

The Marashea has served two main purposes from its beginnings.[29] It operated as a defensive association for Basotho in the dangerous urban environs of the Reef. Moreover, the Marashea offered a haven of familiarity, a vehicle for survival, but also of cultural identification in the "ethnic and social chaos of the black townships."[30] Almost without exception male Marashea grew up in rural areas, herded their families' livestock as boys, and then went to initiation school before proceeding to the mines and factories of South Africa. Initiation reinforced a sense of nationalism, and migrants traveled to South Africa instilled with a distinct identity as Basotho.[31] Guy and Thabane reached this same conclusion based on their interviews with Basotho miners: "In the case of the Basotho workers whose evidence we have collected, the dominating feature of the testimonies was the existence of a sense of Basotho ethnicity. This ethnic culture was used to organize and to protect the workers in a largely rightless and dangerous environment."[32]

A Molapo veteran active in the 1940s and 1950s explains the sense of belonging and national solidarity that characterized Borashea:

> Borashea was like *mohobelo* [dance of male fellowship]—we danced mohobelo together, the men from different mines. I didn't want a Mosotho to fight with another Mosotho—it was a fight, but a kind of game that brought us together as one nation. People criticized us, asking what kind of men we are, and we told them that we are Marashea because we can fight. We kept our reputation as Basotho and also defended our places. When we said Molapo and Matsieng, we meant Basotho—we respected our country. We just wanted to see who knew melamu [here, the practice of fighting with sticks] better than others. We were fighting with our brothers. (PM)

In an extreme example of nationalist sentiment, a Marashea gang interrupted a soccer game in Johannesburg in which Lesotho was being defeated by a

South African team. The Russians invaded the pitch brandishing knives and guns to bring an end to the match once defeat seemed imminent.[33]

Despite factional rivalries, a common thread in the history of the Marashea has been the propensity to unite against outside antagonists. Indeed, many veterans insist that Borashea was born of a need to protect Basotho who were being victimized on the Rand. Rantoa describes these assaults as "one of the things that brought Basotho together, that united the Basotho in fighting."[34] Tsotsis are mentioned in these narratives but it is other ethnically organized gangs that posed the greatest threat. Tsotsis were viewed as cowards who preyed on lone travelers but were unwilling to risk battle with Marashea. Unlike tsotsis, Zulu and Mpondo adversaries organized themselves for combat and engaged Marashea in open confrontations that sometimes involved hundreds of combatants. In such circumstances, Marashea would temporarily shelve internal disputes and come together as Basotho to face the common enemy. "Our group had about one hundred members but there were many other groups in different places. When we had a problem with a fight we would send a man to collect Marashea from other places. They would hire taxis and come to help us" (NN, 13 May). Although Mpondo figure most prominently in stories of conflict and some truly epic battles were fought against Zulu *impis* (groups of warriors), Marashea gangs clashed with numerous ethnic groups. These battles took place in the townships, in mine compounds, and in the squatter camps surrounding the mines. Perhaps the best remembered and documented of these conflicts occurred between Basotho and Zulu, the first in Benoni in 1950 and the second in Meadowlands in 1957 (sometimes referred to as the Dube Hostel Riots). In both episodes Molapo and Matsieng joined together and the Basotho emerged victorious. MK supplies a vivid description of the Benoni conflict:

> We attacked from the fence side and pushed them toward the location. Some hid in houses and some were chased into the hospital and were killed there. The head constable of the police told us not to chase them into town because they would disturb and shock the white ladies and their children. We promised that we would not go after them if they ran in the direction of the white quarter, but during the fight this was forgotten. We drove them in any direction they took. . . . Many Zulus died in this fight and the police took a week to collect the bodies. Some were in the toilets, some were in the rubbish pits. They were all over. That is how it went.[35]

According to consistent Marashea testimony, the 1957 fight began after a member of a Matsieng group was killed and mutilated at a shebeen by Zulu hostel dwellers. A Matsekha veteran recalls, "Although we did not have a good

relationship with Matsieng people, a message was passed to us that a Mosotho had been castrated by the Zulus" (ST). PG1 left his Matsekha group in the mid-1950s yet claims he still took part in the fighting. "At that time I joined [the fight] because it was binding each and every one—it was a national thing. Matsieng and Molapo came together." The conflict had been simmering for some time and the murder of Malefane was the spark that ignited the conflagration. "We took Malefane's body from the mortuary to prepare for the funeral and the burial date was published all over. All the different mines and locations were told of the burial date. The Zulus informed their people and they collected others from Natal who came by lorry. We joined together with Molapo because of this. We came together because we learned there was a group of Zulus who wanted to destroy Marashea" (HM). The funeral procession of hundreds of armed Marashea passed by Dube Hostel, where the Zulu reportedly attacked. This was the start of several days of conflict that left more than forty people dead. In the end, the combined forces of the Marashea inflicted a severe defeat on their Zulu enemies.[36]

Newspapers and police reports note several clashes between Marashea and Zulu groups over the years, although these were usually isolated affairs that did not require or involve Marashea alliances. A typical example is provided by a 1959 account: "Nineteen passengers lay unconscious and injured on New Canada station after a train had come to a halt after a nightmare journey, from Naledi to town. A faction fight between Zulus and 'Russians' was raging in a rear coach. Men were being flung through the windows."[37] Even in these lesser conflicts, a sense of nationalism and pride in the collective strength of the Marashea sometimes emerges. "There were many [Marashea] from Phiri to Naledi. They would leave Naledi and visit here [Phiri] and we also visited. We went to Moletsane and Molapo. We occupied all the space in a train when we went to places like Germiston. People were afraid of us and Zulus would not ride the train if we were in it. They were afraid of us because as we walked through the carriages we beat them with melamu" (BT).

One informant claims that Marashea joined people from the townships in their conflicts with Zulu hostel dwellers during August and September 1976. Soweto students had called a stay-away and assaulted hostel dwellers who refused to comply. The Zulu migrants responded in kind and an all out battle soon ensued. According to Matsieng veteran TS, township residents called on the Marashea for help. His group responded largely because the Zulu had allegedly killed people from the Molapo faction.

> In 1976 I was involved in a fight against the Zulus at Mzimhlope.
> The Zulus were fighting with everybody. . . . There were Marashea
> from Ha-Molapo and they were near that place and were hated by

the Zulus. The people at the location thought that Marashea were the ones who could fight the Zulus. We waited at Dube Station to get them when they left their places to fight. Tsotsi was morena at that time. He was good in fights because he was brave and controlled the fight. . . . We fought the Zulus because we had a witness that they killed our people, they killed people from Ha-Molapo.

Mpondo migrants occupy a special place in the history of the Marashea. The fighting between Mpondo and Basotho migrants, which figured prominently in the formation of the Marashea, spread to the mining areas of the far West Rand and Free State. One example illustrates how Marashea reacted to assaults against Basotho by other ethnic gangs. In order to collect protection fees with a minimum of opposition, the Marashea had to demonstrate the ability to safeguard their clients. This financial imperative explains the forceful response to the rape of a Mosotho woman by a group of Mpondo.

It happened that the Mapondo raped a Mosotho woman who had just been married. They took her from her husband and raped her. . . . At that time we had no particular dispute with the Mapondo. But then we were told what they had done to that lady. . . . I told my men that I intended to attack as soon as we were told. . . . At sunrise I released thirty-eight men. I said to them, "Men, these Mapondo are said to be at that side of the valley, go and fight them!" We then waited outside and some men were playing dice. I heard women exclaiming, "Look at that!" Some men were running and I was confused. I didn't know whether they were my men or Mapondo because the Mapondo sometimes also wore red blankets. We went to meet them and on the way we met one man. I called to him and he said "Baba" and I saw he was Pondo. I told him to come to me and when he approached I hit him in the forehead with my sword and he died. I turned him over and chopped his head in two. Then we climbed the hill to the location where there were some squatter camps called Matjotjo. . . . My men came to me and reported, "We have killed six Mapondo; here are their swords." I asked where the rest were and they said they didn't know. I said, "Go and prevent them from going to that side, make them come this side so we can kill them all." We then killed seven more. (MK)

The Marashea's Sesotho identity did not prevent the organization from attacking fellow Basotho. The association embraced ethnic solidarity when it

served its purposes, but much of the mine violence addressed in chapter 5 pitted Basotho affiliated with the ANC and NUM against Russian groups. In the end organizational survival superseded national identity, and when Marashea felt threatened by Basotho, they did not hesitate to employ violence against their countrymen. Perhaps because of the importance of national identity to the Marashea, veterans typically referred to fights against NUM and ANC supporters as clashes with Xhosa. Basotho who supported the union were seen by the Marashea as the "dogs of the Xhosa."

In order to survive, Marashea groups could not be completely insular, they needed support from surrounding communities and on occasion from fellow groups, even fierce rivals. Their status as foreign migrants was not forgotten and when push came to shove Marashea would rally together against outside antagonists. This is a consistent theme throughout Marashea history. "We formed different alliances. If any of the groups had problems they called their members from other places. If we were attacked by other tribes, Matsieng and Matsekha would come together as one group, but after that we went back to our own fights" (NN, 20 May). Although infused with an ethnic identity as Basotho, gang members' first loyalties were to their groups and then to the association as a whole. Outside rivals were usually defined in ethnic terms, but this was not always the case and the gangs occasionally attacked fellow Basotho who posed a threat to the organization.

TRADITIONAL MEDICINE AND MAGICAL PROTECTION

Basotho society, like many societies worldwide, has a deep-seated belief in magic and the powers of magical practitioners. People seek the assistance of traditional healers in Lesotho for any number of situations: for ill health; to encourage success in business, politics, or at school; to thwart enemies and thieves; and to protect animals, crops, and homes. "The use of medicines does not stop at the curing of sickness," Hugh Ashton observes, "but extends far beyond, to almost every situation where a man [sic] requires help to control natural and social phenomena, or is faced with difficulty, danger, and uncertainty."[38] In their most sinister guise these beliefs are manifested in *liretlo* (ritual killings or medicine murders), in which body parts are used to make powerful potions. Most Basotho have lived a tenuous existence in an impoverished environment and the use of and belief in moriana is one way in which people have attempted to acquire a measure of security against misfortune and to improve their position in life. Moriana is especially critical in situations when people feel threatened and the Marashea's reliance on magic

was a natural development. When veterans were asked how the Marashea has managed to survive, the vast majority attributed the society's success to the potency of its magical protection. "We made use of lingaka; we could not do without them. . . . The Marashea has survived for so long because of moriana" (KL). In general, moriana was used to strengthen the Marashea, to ward off evil, and to bring good fortune. "Morena finds the ngaka for the group, who incises members with strong moriana to strengthen them. The ngaka also sprinkles some moriana all around the area where Marashea are living to protect them from witchcraft and sorcery. The other moriana is used when a stokvel is held. It is used to call customers from the mines to come and buy beer" (KI).

Moriana was a part of everyday life but it assumed added importance in two specific circumstances—during fights[39] and when facing criminal charges. It was inconceivable to enter into battle without being properly fortified with medicines, and each group had a doctor or doctors on retainer, much the same as lawyers. Medicines could take the form of powders inserted into incisions or concoctions that were smeared on the body. It was imperative not to impair this treatment by engaging in sexual relations. To do so was to invite disaster. "If one does not follow this rule and it happens that we fight, he will certainly die" (MB). Many of the male informants related stories of how traditional medicine served them well in a particular situation, usually a fight or court case. Traditional doctors also sometimes assisted the morena and council with battle plans. "We had ngaka who advised us about the fights. He would assess the fight and make a map of the fight before it began, and all our weapons were touched by him" (TG).

Moriana could be helpful in several different ways, including rendering the enemy's weapons harmless. MM's group fought against ANC comrades in Odendaalsrus and emerged victorious because of the protection proffered by their medicine. "They attacked us but their guns produced only water instead of bullets and we managed to shoot them. Six of them were killed and many wounded." KI describes the consequences of confronting an enemy who had engaged a more powerful doctor: "Moriana played an important part in that fight near Beisa Mine. Those people from Gauteng [a rival Marashea gang] had strong moriana; if not for that we would have killed many of them, but some of our guns shot only water and fruit instead of bullets."

Sometimes more elaborate preparations than the simple doctoring of weapons was called for. BH, a veteran of conflicts in the 1950s and 1960s, relied on a type of battle indicator supplied by a traditional doctor. "There was a man called Magubane who was staying at Natalspruit. He gave us a small bottle with moriana inside. You were supposed to shake it when you went to the fight. When the liquid turned white you knew you would win the fight,

but if it turned red that meant danger and you were supposed to avoid fighting because you would be killed." Rantoa's group preferred the string method: "Supposing we intend to fight people on the other side of the road. A string would be prepared with the appropriate moriana. When we approached those people, we'd pretend as if we were running away. They would follow us until they passed over the string. Then we know that they would be drugged and easy to fight" (Bonner transcript). If all else failed, one tactical option was to demoralize the enemy by targeting their doctor. PK remembers this was the key to victory in a bitter dispute with Zulu opponents. "We fought with Zulus in Gauteng at White City. The Zulus were beating people at the locations. They even killed some Basotho. There was only one thing that enabled us to defeat them. Lenkoane attacked their doctor and cut her head off. We took the head and went to the fight. When we arrived, we found that the Basotho were winning the fight. Lenkoane knew that their doctor was very strong." In a grisly aftermath: "The head of the Zulu doctor that Lenkoane cut off—we used it as moriana for our group."

It should be mentioned that the use of charms and magical protection by combatants is common in South Africa. In the recent fighting between Inkatha supporters and ANC comrades, combatants from both sides used such measures. Ari Sitas discovered that while comrades propagate an image of themselves as fearless warriors, "this fearlessness needs treatment against fear: there is a proliferation of *muti* and war medicine in their daily lives and battles."[40] Heribert Adam and Kogila Moodley note that magic rituals were important to both sides in the conflict and that combatants levied a tax on residents under their control to help offset the cost of war medicines. An informant's explanation of the purpose of these medicines echoes that of Marashea veterans: "Before we go to fighting, some people at the houses near the battlefield stand outside with buckets of water and muti. They dip a broom into the mixture and sprinkle it over us as we run past. . . . Comrades believe the muti will stop the bullets from hitting them and will give them courage."[41]

No matter how much faith Marashea placed in magical treatments, doctoring did not substitute for fighting skills and common sense. Guerrillas in Zimbabwe's liberation struggle used charms designed to protect them but did not dispense with more conventional methods. David Lan investigated the links between spirit mediums and guerrillas and concluded that "few if any of the guerrillas relied exclusively for their safety on magical precautions. . . . Ancestral protection and rigorous military discipline were both essential."[42] Thus the use of moriana was a method of maximizing protection in battle but not to the exclusion of careful preparation and sound tactics.

The situation was much the same when the battles shifted to legal terrain. The Marashea made a point of engaging expert legal counsel, but at the same

time the judicious use of moriana could only bolster one's chances of beating the charge. Women delivering provisions to Marashea in custody fetched powdered medicines from the doctor and mixed them with food or rubbed them into clothing, strengthening the prisoner and bringing him good fortune in his courtroom encounter. DG supplies a typical account:

> Tanki, our morena, was arrested and I went to a woman at Khutsong who was called Machakane. She told me to come with Tanki's clothes and not to wash them. When we arrived she slaughtered two chickens and soaked the clothes in the blood. She cooked the chickens and gave me back the clothes to take to Tanki and to exchange them for the clothes he was wearing. On the following day Tanki was with us and I believed that moriana really worked. He was discharged.

Sometimes, medicine could invoke the powers of nature: "Marashea are very strong with moriana. It can happen that while a case is proceeding a storm will come and take all the papers from the magistrate's desk and the accused will be discharged" (LG). The lizard method is a particularly impressive example of moriana at work:

> When our members were taken to court our ngaka would give us a lizard and it was put inside a bottle and taken to court by the women. When the case proceeded members of the jury were there in order to decide the case. The lizard was nodding its head inside the bottle and all the jurors became sleepy and did not follow what was said and our member would be discharged. One Lerashea named Moruti was falsely accused of killing a policeman and our women took a lizard to court and all the people fell asleep and Moruti was found not guilty. (MC)

Traditional doctors and magical powers could also play an important role in group relations, specifically between marena and their followers. Some marena pointed out that they were careful to keep essential secrets regarding moriana from their men lest this information be turned against them. PL reported: "I was morena and I would find ngaka for the group. My members should not know him because if they turned against me, they could then find moriana that could kill me" (Welkom, 21 May 1999). He had witnessed his morena, Lenkoane, killed by an ambitious subordinate and was not eager to suffer the same fate. BM is adamant that moriana allows him to rule:

You asked me about moriana. You cannot lead people without the use of moriana. The moriana is used to strengthen, unite, and make these men brave. But above all it is used to make the men listen and obey the leaders. The moriana that makes them strong must also make them submissive to their morena. That is my responsibility— to make them obey me. If I don't do that they will rebel against me. These men could defeat me in a fight; that is why I have to give them something to make them listen and accept me as their morena. You know how long I have been morena? Twenty-five years. You think I don't make mistakes, or that they love me? No, it is my moriana that makes them believe in me.

Marashea were discriminating when it came to their doctors. Some were given trial runs and if they proved unsatisfactory their services were dispensed with. It was essential to employ a reputable practitioner and to avoid charlatans. "We would learn from the first fight if the ngaka was good or not. We would pay him half and give him the balance after the fight" (NN, 20 May). BH observed, "Some lingaka were very good, but others were just cheating."

This attitude about the contingency of magical protection fits what I believe to be the wider utility of moriana to Marashea. A belief in magical protection allowed members to rationalize defeat, either on the battlefield or in the courts. Failure could be attributed to the group's doctor or alternately to the power of the enemy's medicine. Either way there was hope for the next confrontation because doctors could be changed or in extreme circumstances the opponent's doctor could be killed and his or her remains used to produce potent medicines. In all circumstances moriana was used to fortify Marashea in the harsh world they inhabited and to supplement other protective measures.

COMMUNITY RELATIONS

Much like their relationship with the police, Marashea relations with the communities in which they were situated were a study in cooperation and conflict. The most common intersection between Marashea and non-Marashea was the payment of protection fees. Without exception, Marashea informants, both male and female, report that residents in areas under Russian control were expected to pay for their protection. Rantoa, who resided in the Russian stronghold of Newclare in the 1950s, explains how this policy was developed: "We would say that every house would have to pay so much. Originally we

would collect from Basotho only. Later we realized we were also protecting people of different ethnic groups who were not contributing. Then the collection was extended to everyone who stayed in the same area, irrespective of ethnicity" (Bonner transcript). People had no choice regarding payment. GB lived in a succession of informal Marashea settlements in the Free State until he retired in the early 1990s. "We meet the people who are not Marashea when we collect protection fees and when Lerashea is dead we collect burial fees. We claim protection because everyone is under our protection. If you do not want to pay that money, you have to leave and find another place." The fees people were required to pay varied from group to group and according to the circumstances. Some groups levied a set amount, while others collected on a contingency basis. Morena PL operated on the latter system. "They paid whatever we paid. When we wanted R50 they had to pay it. For instance if the lawyer needs money in the middle of the month, they pay it" (Lesotho, 23–24 May 1998).

The "protection" to which Marashea refer was primarily protection from assault and robbery by tsotsis, but also from other ethnic gangs and Marashea rivals. Marashea veterans are quick to claim that they were more effective than the police in controlling the tsotsi menace, and people regularly turned to them for assistance. In this way, the Marashea functioned as an alternative justice system. "If the people who were not Marashea had problems with tsotsis we would go and find that tsotsi and order him to return what he took from that person, and we even gave him some strokes. . . . We chased tsotsis, so they admired us very much" (NN). Morena BM argues that safety is what attracts people to stay in camps under Marashea control: "These people prefer to live with us here because they are protected and they live a safe life here. In the locations and on the farms where there are no Marashea they are robbed of their property. With us they are safe. There is no one who can drink their beer without paying them, or do anything without the consent of the owner. They have to pay something because we provide protection."

In Soweto the Marashea's campaign against tsotsis gained further legitimacy in the 1970s, when some Russian groups joined hands with the *makhotla* (traditional courts) set up by local residents to combat crime. The makhotla were strongest in the townships designated as Sotho, including Naledi, Tladi, Moletsane, and Molapo. Suspected offenders were dragged to the court, tried, and then flogged or fined or both. Marashea would assist the makhotla when suspects resisted its authority. Glaser classified this arrangement as "an alliance of convenience. The Russians had a long history of antagonism towards tsotsis and they felt comfortable with the traditionalism of the Makgotla [makholta]. The Makgotla, for its part, needed the muscle of the Russians."[43]

Makhotla groups often operated with the approval of the police and sometimes even received official sanction. This arrangement undoubtedly suited the Russians, who consistently sought cooperative relations with the authorities. The Russians' link with the makhotla continued until the early 1980s, when these more conservative groups were eclipsed by youthful ANC supporters who set up street committees and informal courts. However, rampant crime ensured that vigilante groups continued to receive some support from beleaguered township residents.

This type of relationship could only exist in an insecure environment in which the state offered little protection or hope of justice to the African majority. Vigilantism has flourished in South Africa largely because black residential areas have been so poorly policed. The state abrogated its role as protector of this segment of the citizenry, and people often felt forced to pursue justice through informal channels. The Marashea was, and remain, a beneficiary of these circumstances.

South Africans living in townships and informal settlements, especially unattached females, have always been vulnerable to criminal violence. Consequently, some residents probably paid protection fees quite willingly. The Marashea did not limit their activities to controlling tsotsis. Retribution was exacted against those who victimized people under Russian protection, as with the Mpondo gang suspected of having raped a Mosotho woman. Assorted offenders were judged and punished, presumably with a measure of community support. "I remember when one man made a mistake; he was Motswana and he slept with his daughter and made her pregnant. So the rule of Marashea was that man was supposed to be killed. We blew the whistle and went to his house. We took him and pushed him to the lekhotla and we beat him until he died. The people were all under Marashea control. Like that man—he was not Lerashea but he was living in the same location as Marashea" (MS).

Many Marashea claim the group had a positive reputation that resonated beyond their immediate community. "When we were arrested there was a jailer at No. 4 prison who was called Two Boys. He would say that he liked Marashea because Marashea controlled tsotsis better than the police. When we were riding the train, people were safe because tsotsis would run away" (BT). This idea of Marashea as the arbiters of social order is a consistent theme in Russian testimony, and newspaper reports lend some credence to these claims. For example, the infamous Rope gang was put to flight by Marashea in Alexandra when they were terrorizing guests at a party. "One guest advised the host to send an SOS to the Russians. They came faster than was expected and in no time members of the Rope gang had disappeared."[44]

Some Marashea veterans report that they worked with the authorities to combat the tsotsi menace. "When tsotsis were robbing people of their properties we were called, especially during the Christmas period, when many people were in town and on the trains. The town council would call us to chase them away" (WL). GL maintains that their role was recognized and appreciated by railway employees.

> We patrolled all the train coaches, looking for tsotsis. When we arrived at the train station we paid for one ticket, even if we were twenty or more. The one who bought the ticket entered first and we followed him. We went to places like Springs and Germiston with a ticket for one person and we were not disturbed because we were government people who controlled the tsotsis on the trains, so we were not required to pay for the train. We stopped crime, so when the ticket examiner saw us he would not say anything.

He does not seem to consider the possibility that the ticket examiner was too intimidated to question twenty men belonging to a group with a reputation for violence.

The idea of Marashea as crime fighters, however ironic, is deeply ingrained in Marashea identity. This is especially true when Basotho are the perceived victims, as KI's story makes evident:

> There is a place near Thabong, just above the Mothusi railway station. It is a big shopping complex where most of the miners go for shopping. Miners from President Steyn, President Brand, and Saiplaas go there for shopping. There were tsotsis who used to rob Basotho of their property, especially at month's end. As Marashea we could not allow anything that hurt Basotho. These tsotsis made many Basotho afraid to go to that area for shopping, and that made us take a very serious step. . . . On a certain Saturday we went to that area in the morning around 9 o'clock. We surrounded the whole complex but we were all in disguise, hiding our weapons beneath our blankets and going in groups of two or three. There were Marashea in every corner of the area and there was no way to escape. . . . We had instructed some of our men to go and buy things in the shops and to expose their money in order to attract the tsotsis. After about thirty minutes someone raised the alarm. We had placed a man so he could see what was happening on every corner. A whistle blew right next to the place where I was positioned and immedi-

ately I saw three men in black suits running toward me. I waited until the first one was close to me and I pulled my assegai out and stabbed him in the chest and he was down on the ground bleeding to death. When I turned around I saw that the other two were also lying on the ground dead.

KI reports that he and several others waited for the police to arrest them. The case was dismissed because the police had no real interest in prosecuting. "They said they only arrested us because we committed a crime, but we were also preventing crime that even the police failed to prevent."

There is, of course, another side to the relationships between residents and Marashea. Many people have viewed Marashea as predatory criminals. Even in Lesotho people are split in their assessment. Some regard them as protectors of Basotho in South Africa, while others condemn them as hooligans whose activities bring all Basotho into disrepute. The small contingent of middle-class Basotho on the Rand—educators, clerks, ministers and the like—had no time for the blanketed gangsters. A few felt compelled to publicly distinguish between Marashea and the Basotho people as a whole. Simon Matolo addressed a letter to the editor of the *World* in response to a previous missive that had criticized the criminal behavior of "foreign" Africans from the protectorates, specifically Basutoland. He implored, "Admittedly a few of them—the 'Russians'—are well known criminals but is it fair to assume that the whole population of these territories are criminally inclined?"[45] Although African newspapers often spoke out against the Russians, the relevance of this is questionable as the literate classes were not the people the Marashea were attempting to win over. Their support, such as it was, came from fellow migrants—particularly, but not exclusively, Basotho. These were the people the Marashea gangs needed to cultivate in order to establish solid bases in their urban enclaves. That said, it is unclear to what extent the Marashea achieved popular, as opposed to coerced, support.

Newspaper and archival records indicate a level of resentment against Marashea activities, primarily robberies and extortion rackets, but also internecine Russian violence that threatened township residents. Rival groups favored trains and train stations as battlegrounds, and hapless commuters were often forced to flee when the fighting began. A 1970 cartoon in the *World* satirized the crime situation on the trains by observing that the chaos caused by Russian conflicts created opportunities for thieves to steal from distracted passengers.[46] People who objected to paying protection fees received firsthand experience of Marashea violence. In 1951 the director of native labor in Johannesburg noted in a report regarding Russian protection schemes,

"Refusals to pay are met by acts of extreme violence on the persons concerned."[47] In the same year, the *Sunday Express* proclaimed that the Marashea "fleece the poorest families, by demanding protection money every week, which they are forced to give as the only alternative to assault and possibly crippling injury."[48] Marashea were occasionally arrested for extortion,[49] and newspapers carried stories of protection rackets through the 1970s. In 1968, Russians were reportedly harassing residents of Daveyton on the East Rand, demanding R30 per household,[50] and in 1975 the more philanthropic gangs in Phiri required working households to pay R5 and business owners to pay extra.[51] In both cases residents were threatened with violence.

Newspapers also reported Russian robberies and assaults and recorded the victims' expressions of outrage. Under the headline, "End Russian Terror, Angry Women Plead" the *Post* (Johannesburg) announced that women from Mapetla (Soweto) marched to the Moroka police station "to ask for protection against the notorious blanketed Russian gangsters."[52] Such stories appear throughout the period of Russian activity on the Rand.

It was difficult for the Marashea to force resident populations into compliance on the Reef. In the urban setting, township dwellers could more readily organize resistance against Russian depredations or, alternately, move to areas free of Russian influence.[53] Spontaneous resistance also occurred. Passengers' objections to Russian harassment on a train traveling from Soweto to the East Rand in 1957 led to a full-scale brawl and the hospitalization of several participants.[54] In Chiawelo (Soweto) in 1965, Marashea were reportedly indiscriminately assaulting people in the streets "when all the men in the area came out armed with an assortment of weapons. The fight was sharp and short. One of the Russians was hacked to death. Several men on both sides were severely injured."[55] Exasperated urbanites also appealed to the police and local government officials, yet even in this more regulated environment, the Marashea were a formidable presence.

In the Free State and far West Rand mining areas, the Marashea established settlements over which they maintained complete control. People coming to settle in a Russian camp knew they were placing themselves under the dominion of the Marashea. There was no police presence in the settlements, no local officials to appeal to, and no media to take up people's appeals. In their squatter camps the Marashea were a law unto themselves.

Male Marashea are quick to admit that protection fees were demanded from residents and that those who refused to pay were forced out of their homes or dealt with in an equally violent fashion. Without exception they insist, however, that the Marashea enjoyed harmonious relations with their neighbors and fellow residents because of the protection they provided. A few

women tell a different story. 'Mè RW provides a balanced account: "Some liked them—the place we were living was nice because Tsotsi did not allow any disturbances; he gave people soft loans. But other people said that Marashea kill innocent people, and they hated them." Other women did not equivocate. 'Mè MG declared that people "were afraid of Marashea. They pretended to like them because they had no choice. People hated Basotho because of Marashea; even now it is still the same." No doubt, popular support for Marashea was highest among their Basotho compatriots, but it is difficult to gauge the degree of that support.

LESOTHO AS SANCTUARY

Marashea wanted by the police for serious offences often fled to Lesotho. South African police were not authorized to cross the border and were unfamiliar with the country. There was no extradition treaty between Lesotho and South Africa, so if Marashea fugitives gained the border they were safe. Since Marashea as an organization operated exclusively in South Africa, these fugitives usually returned once they were confident the police were no longer giving priority to their pursuit. The police were aware of this tendency and sometimes set up roadblocks to intercept Marashea fleeing the Rand for Lesotho. A police raid in Soweto in 1967 resulted in the arrest of fifteen Russians suspected of a number of offenses. The remainder of the targeted group were reportedly "heading for hide-outs in Lesotho."[56] In a 1975 case against fifty-eight Marashea, who participated in a station battle resulting in the deaths of three men, only thirty-two appeared at the hearing. "Some of the [absent] men are reported to have died during faction fights, some have been arrested for being in South Africa without necessary documents and have been deported to Lesotho and others are said to have skipped the country to Lesotho."[57]

A number of informants testified that they fled South Africa to avoid arrest. TS killed a man in front of witnesses and knew the police would come looking for him. "I went to report to the manager where I was working that I was needed at home, and I got a leave and my money and went to Lesotho to escape that case. I spent a year in Lesotho and then came back." The majority of Marashea had family connections in Lesotho and had little problem passing time until they judged it safe to return. After a fight in Khutsong in which several people were killed, Matsieng leader Tsotsi Raliemere feared the police would seek him out. He returned to Phiri, collected 'Mè TW, and fled the country, returning only after a long while ('Mè TW). Mashai, the current

leader of a Carletonville group, is said to have escaped to Lesotho after shooting four men in a taxi war (MT). RC and HS spent time in Lesotho to avoid murder charges. Both returned to South Africa when they deemed it safe and neither was arrested. In these particular circumstances the Marashea's status as foreign migrants has served them well.

MYTHOLOGY AND SURVIVAL

Tseule Tsilo, Matsieng morena in the Carletonville area in the 1960s and 1970s, is revered by men as an icon of Marashea. His story and the manner in which he is remembered indicate that male Marashea have constructed a hero representative of their society. The Marashea had no specific ideology beyond survival. They had no political program—their reason for existence was to carve out a niche for migrant Basotho in the forbidding environs of South Africa. Tsilo is remembered by male informants as the quintessential Lerashea who possessed all the qualities necessary for survival (and prosperity) in the harsh world inhabited by Marashea. Tsilo is celebrated by those who knew him and remembered by others who have been told of his exploits. Every man interviewed had heard of Tsilo and many related stories of his powers and prowess. The heroic figure of Tsilo represents the larger set of values embraced by male Marashea. His deeds, powers, and code of ethics are eulogized, and an examination of the legend of Tsilo reveals much about the masculine culture of the Marashea.

Known to the press as Big King, Tsilo was accorded the status of public enemy number one after wounding three white police officers in a November 1965 shootout outside Carletonville, a small mining town southwest of Johannesburg.[58] Already wanted for the murders of six members of an Mpondo gang,[59] and having previously escaped from custody while being held on a charge of culpable homicide, Tsilo became the subject of a nationwide search. Two hundred officers, dogs, and a helicopter participated in the initial hunt, but Tsilo escaped—shooting his way out of a trap at one point. He then disappeared for the next eighteen months, despite the posting of a R500 reward and police assurances that "the search for Big King continues on every square inch of this planet."[60] Tsilo was finally caught near Theunnissen, in the Free State, in June 1967 and stood trial on a variety of charges over the next two months. Unfortunately, the trial records no longer exist and we know little about the proceedings other than Tsilo was acquitted on all charges with the possible exception of a passbook offense. The newspapers report that African witnesses refused to testify against Tsilo because they feared the power

of his muti. The widow of Sergeant M, an officer Tsilo shot through the head, was shocked and embittered by the acquittal. Her husband was unable to testify, but she is adamant that the other two officers wounded in the incident positively identified Tsilo as the shooter and remains astounded by the judge's verdict that there was not sufficient evidence to merit a conviction (Carletonville, March 1998). After he was discharged, Tsilo remained in the area as the leader of Matsieng until he was stabbed to death in the late 1970s.

It seems that Tsilo, like so many other Marashea, began his migrant life with a "join" on the mines. One report claims he began work in 1957 at Blyvooruitzicht Mine and rose to "boss boy" at Western Deep Levels before leaving the mines to become full-time Lerashea.[61] Tsilo "was influenced to join Marashea when his brother was attacked by a group of Marashea near the mine compound. He joined in order to get revenge and he became morena of Marashea" (MR). Despite his desire for revenge, Tsilo is remembered for his attempts at fostering unity between the rival factions.

The Matsekha-Matsieng divide has caused much bloodshed over the years and many veterans lament the schism. BF, who joined Matsekha around 1950, reminisces somewhat wistfully, "Marashea began at Benoni; people from Lesotho were friends. There was brotherhood from Leribe to Matsieng but we ended up separating because of women." Informants acknowledge the destructiveness of these fights and stress how rival groups of Marashea united in the face of outside threats. Members report that some leaders worked to achieve peace between warring groups but that squabbles always resumed, in part because a warrior mentality was central to Marashea identity. The ideal of Basotho unity was recognized despite the internecine violence, and Tsilo is remembered as an advocate of Basotho solidarity. He arbitrated between warring Marashea factions and was quick to come to the aid of other groups embroiled in conflicts with non-Basotho antagonists. Tsilo "was respected by other marena. When a morena from another place had a problem, he would write a letter and then we would go to his rescue" (DS). One of Tsilo's subordinates recalls that "he did not like us to fight with other Basotho; he wanted cooperation to fight against MaPondo" (SO).

Tsilo is venerated as the Mpondo slayer who mercilessly pursued these enemies of the Basotho. A man who served under Tsilo remembers that "he fought tough fights, especially in the times of the Mapondo fights. He fought Mapondo and he finished them because of his bravery in those fights" (PK). Another Lerashea, who never laid eyes on Tsilo, relates that "he was famous for killing many Mapondo—that is all I know of him" (KK). The founding purpose of Marashea was to unite Basotho against outside threats, of which the Mpondo were judged particularly dangerous. Tsilo, then, represents the

ideal Marashea leader, who worked to overcome rivalries within the Basotho community while at the same time waging a relentless campaign against the Mpondo enemy.

Miners provided contributions; bought beer, dagga, and prostitutes; gambled with Marashea; and paid protection money for their women. It was essential to maintain a good working relationship with these customers, and Tsilo is remembered for protecting mineworkers to preserve a strong client base. "Tsilo loved miners," remembers ML—a judgment shared by one of Tsilo's subordinates:

> People from the mines would visit the locations and some Marashea attacked them. Tseule was against that. If he saw you as Lerashea robbing someone who was not Lerashea he would call all Marashea and summon you and ask why you took the money and how you thought Marashea would make money since you were robbing miners. . . . he told us that all the miners were not to be robbed or beaten because they brought money to Marashea and that they were allowed to propose to our women because they brought money to the location. (SO)

His keen business sense benefited his group and enabled him to amass significant personal wealth—"Tseule had three taxis, two vans, and one private car" (GK)—yet another measure of the successful Lerashea. Tsilo's interest in protecting miners and uniting Basotho against outside enemies came to the fore in the ethnic conflicts that occasionally broke out inside mine compounds. In one account he is credited with originating the practice of Marashea gangs from the locations and squatter camps coming to the aid of Basotho mineworkers in these clashes (GB).

Because deadly confrontations played such a prominent role in the lives of Marashea, the groups valued courage, perhaps second only to intelligence, in their marena. Tsilo was seen as both brave and cunning. "He was a hero. His leadership was remarkable. He not only sent his men to fight, he led them himself" (KB). Most marena were proficient fighters, and strategists were appointed as leaders. Tsilo, more than any other Lerashea, is famed for the strength of his medicine. Stories of his special abilities abound and account for his success in battle and against the forces of the law. When chased by the police, Tsilo outwitted them by shifting shapes into a dead dog, a sickly old ram, a hen with young chicks, a mother suckling an infant, or various other guises. "When the Boers came to arrest him he would vanish around a corner

and turn into a dead and rotten dog because of his moriana. As soon as the police went away disappointed, he would turn back into a man" (ML).[62] On other occasions, Tsilo simply vanished into thin air—"He was using strong moriana and when his enemies came to attack him he would feel it in his blood and run away. One time I was with him and the MaPondo came to attack us and he disappeared and we did not see him anymore. Tseule was strong in moriana" (PL).

According to legend, Tsilo's extraordinary powers enabled him to evade the massive search for so long and to eventually be acquitted on all charges. "He had very strong moriana, if he was on a hill or a peak that was surrounded by the police, he could escape, even from a helicopter" (MB). During his time as a fugitive, Tsilo's reputed powers were detailed by the *Post*: "He claims that his warnings of danger come from small straps which he wears around his upper arm. On the straps are rolls of muti. These give off sensations as soon as the police start a new search for him anywhere in the country, he claims. . . . He also believes that this muti will protect him when he is found by the police."[63] Thus, it came as no surprise to the Marashea when he was set free—"he was discharged because of his moriana" (TB).

It is difficult to account for Tsilo's acquittal. Oral testimony and a newspaper report claim that African witnesses were reluctant to come forward. "The reason why Tsuelo [*sic*] Tsilo (32), alias 'Big King' was set free was that all the witnesses had run away. They have disappeared and are nowhere to be found." The prosecutor told the court "there was no case if all the witnesses who were to give evidence against 'Big King' had gone."[64] These statements, however, refer to the charges of murder and culpable homicide stemming from the killing of the Mpondo gang members; the English-language papers carry no references to the trial concerning the shooting of the three white police officers.[65]

Tsilo is remembered for working with the police:

> We used the money from contributions to bribe the police if we
> could see that a fight would be tough, and that was the idea of
> Tseule and Raliemere. They took the contribution money and
> bribed senior officers of the police, telling them that we will be at-
> tacked and we need their help. When the people came to attack us
> the police fired at them with guns, and when they dispersed Tseule
> and his men would beat them. That was how he won many fights. If
> the police were without money they would go to the shantytowns
> and meet Tseule, who would give them money from our contribu-
> tions, and no one would say anything. (PG2)

Other men recall that Tsilo was given guns by the police and that he worked as a police informer (TB, KL). NN remarked on Tsilo's connections with the local police: "Because of his bravery, the police trusted him. They put him in charge of the shantytown in Carletonville" (20 May). At the same time, as we know, Tsilo shot three police officers. This seeming incongruence is typical of Marashea-police relations. For every story of police bribery there is a corresponding one of arrests by, or battles with, police. Tsilo sought to consolidate his position by working with the police, but when directly threatened he opened fire.

Given the paucity of evidence, it is impossible to do more than speculate about Tsilo's acquittal and the fact that after being accused of the shootings of three white officers, two of whom reportedly testified against him, he stayed in the area and continued as the head of an organization involved in illegal activities. One respondent reports that Tsilo had a magistrate on his payroll, along with several police officers, and if this is so, it is possible that Tsilo was acquitted in return for his silence (AT). His courtroom demeanor indicates a certain confidence. A reporter noted that he was "smiling happily and gazing at the number of spectators in the small courtroom,"[66] and Mrs. M observed that he was "very arrogant and very sure of himself." Certainly, in the South Africa of 1967, it is mystifying that a black gangster accused of shooting three white officers was permitted to return to business as usual following his acquittal. Tsilo's ability to escape conviction and police retribution, which fellow Marashea credited to the strength of his moriana and his ability to influence state officials, cemented his stature as a mythical figure.

There are as many stories of Tsilo's death as there are Marashea willing to discuss it. These stories vary widely but the perfidy of a woman is almost invariably the critical factor in his demise. Tsilo was too powerful to die in battle or at the hands of the police; only the wiles of a seductress could render him vulnerable. Here too is a consistent theme in Marashea ideology—the ambivalent role of women. Women were prized for their beauty and their income-generating ability but were also regarded as the primary cause of conflict between Marashea gangs.

The most common version of the murder of Tsilo is relatively simple. Tsilo was reputed to be a relentless womanizer and the gist of the story is that a beautiful woman who was aware of Tsilo's weakness for female companionship made herself available to him on an ongoing basis. After a while, Tsilo grew to trust her and would visit her place. Thus the trap was set—only when Tsilo was asleep and defenseless did a man emerge from hiding and stab him to death. A number of Matsieng veterans claim it was an Mpondo trap, while a Matsekha member insists his group lured Tsilo to his death:

He died in this way: He was sent a woman who made him trust her. Tsilo, who had a good appetite for women, fell for her—she was big and beautiful. . . . That woman informed the man she was with that Tsilo would come. The man hid but was on his guard. Tsilo came to spend the night with that woman. He was relaxed when that man came out and stabbed Tsilo. The man who killed Tsilo was in our group but Tsilo didn't know him because the man was working in the factories. We plotted against him in this way because we couldn't get him in a fair fight. (ML)

In another popular account, one of Tsilo's lovers had taken up with another man with whom she plotted Tsilo's murder. She hid Tsilo's arm belt, which contained all his medicines, at which point her partner emerged to attack the Marashea leader.[67] This version speaks both to the inherent duplicity of women and the critical importance of magical protection.

It seems the police collected Tsilo's body. Mrs. M claims that the police brought the body to her house to show her husband that the man who shot him was finally dead. For the Marashea, the actions of the police were further proof of the power of Tsilo. "After his death, the police came to make sure he was dead. They even smashed his head with bullets to make sure he was dead, because they were afraid of him" (LG).

The Marashea is an organization dominated by migrant men who have struggled to survive in South Africa. They have created a hero emblematic of that struggle, one who prospered due to the powers and strategies that have served the association as a whole over the past fifty years. Tsilo triumphed over ethnic rivals, neutralized the potentially deadly forces of the South African state, minimized conflict between the rival Marashea factions, accumulated a significant degree of personal wealth, and was renowned for his prolific sexuality. Such a man could not be destroyed in battle but succumbed to feminine treachery—only in this manner can his death be understood and accepted. The life and death of Tseule Tsilo—a man among men—and the making of his legend are instructive in laying bare the fundamental values and survival strategies of male Marashea.

The vast majority of Marashea, both men and women, were poorly educated migrants, many of whom were forced to eke out a living on the margins of the formal economy. Originally formed as a protective association for Basotho on the Rand, the Marashea assumed a more commercial function over the years. The prearranged battles with rival groups, which were an integral part of Borashea in the early years, gradually died out as firearms proliferated. However,

the Marashea continued to engage in collective violence with a host of antagonists. Russian gangs battled each other to achieve prestige and for economic gain. They attacked criminal youth to increase the security of their home areas and to win popular support. They fought with other ethnic gangs over territory and to consolidate Basotho unity. They engaged in hostilities with political movements and unions that threatened to undermine their authority and economic base. Different gangs struck alliances with and bribed the police, manipulated township officials, aligned themselves with political movements, retained legal practitioners, appealed to language and regional groups on an ethnic basis, controlled and exploited female associates, and established profitable economic networks. In other words, the gangs negotiated the hazardous terrain of apartheid sometimes by challenging, but more often by adapting to, the urban conditions imposed by the South African state. The strategies employed by gangs to protect their interests underscore the limitations of state power and the ability of African groups to identify and exploit the "weak joints and soft spots of the structures of urban control."[68] These strategies have enabled the gangs to survive as migrant criminal outfits from the 1940s to the present.

4 ꙥ Urban Battlegrounds

Whereas much attention has been deservedly devoted to the violence employed by the state as a means of subjugating, dividing, and controlling township residents, the different ways in which black urban groups struggled to assert control over their environments have received relatively little scrutiny. These processes cannot be regarded in isolation from the state's quest for control, but neither should they be subsumed by the larger focus on the struggle against white rule. Rather, a more informed understanding of the conditions and challenges faced by black urbanites requires an examination of the nature of localized power and violence within the townships. African groups pursued agendas that served their own interests and had a considerable impact on social relations and perceptions of authority both within the locations and in the broader context of national and racial politics.

The 1950s was an exceptional period for the Marashea because of the large-scale battles that attracted much attention from the media and township officials. These records have been preserved and the availability of such evidence, combined with oral testimony, demonstrates the practical application of several survival strategies, particularly the gangs' success in negotiating the political terrain and achieving tactical cooperation between widely dispersed groups. Although the publicity served the Marashea well for a time, in the end it contributed to the state's determination to dismantle the gangs. The Marashea had become a public embarrassment to a National Party that could not control its "natives." Never again would the Marashea operate so openly. A declining presence on the Rand, the increasing availability of firearms, and state repression combined to ensure that the urban battles of the 1950s were a unique phenomenon in Marashea history.

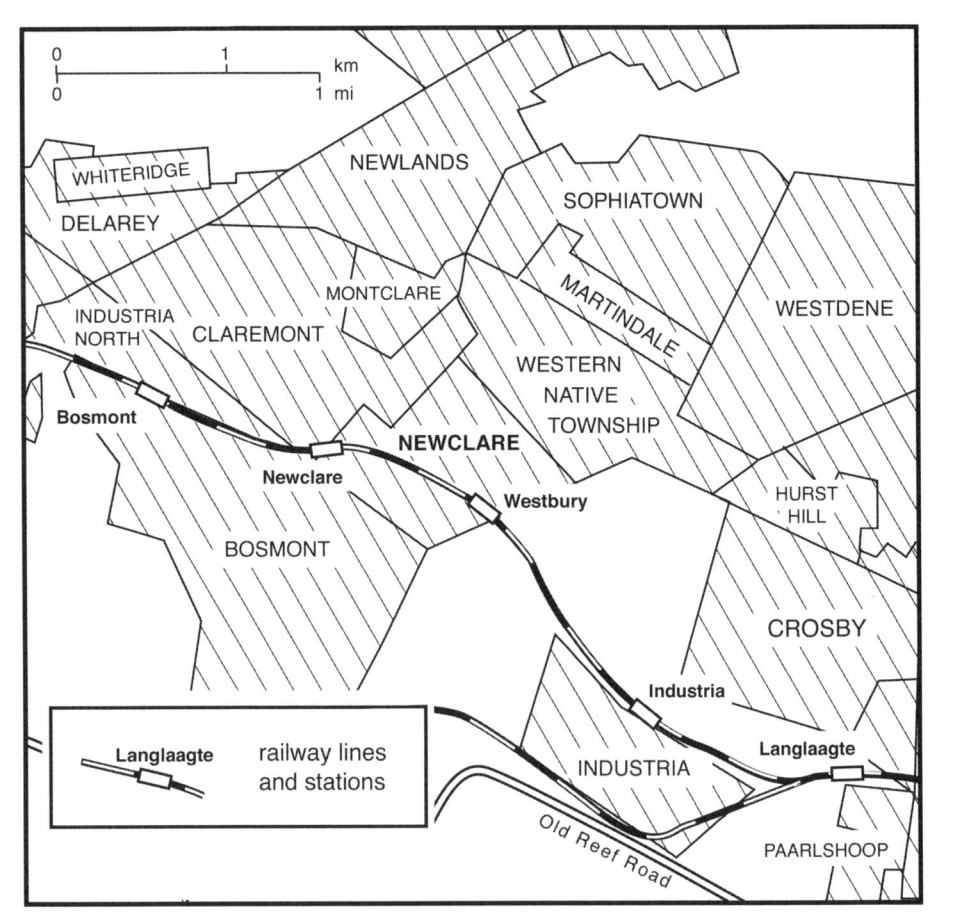

Western Areas of Johannesburg, 1950s

Among the many conflicts in the 1950s, two notorious and protracted cases stand out. The first was an eight-year period when the Marashea was the single most dominant force in the freehold area of Newclare (known by Basotho as Siteketekeng), a township on the western fringes of Johannesburg. With the collusion of the SAP, the Russian gangs emerged victorious from a series of battles with various opponents and effectively annexed the southern portion of Newclare. They maintained their dominance and functioned as an alternative form of government until Africans were expelled from the township as part of the Western Areas Removal Scheme at the end of the decade. The second conflict revolves around Marashea involvement in a bus boycott in Evaton Township, south of Johannesburg. These battles during the organiza-

tion's formative years illustrate the different living conditions and group priorities of the first generation of urban Marashea as compared to their successors in the mining areas of the Free State. Unlike Russian violence on the mines over transport routes, wages, and liquor distribution, the early fighting on the Rand was less about economics than controlling contested urban space. This was certainly the case in Newclare. For urban Marashea, the provision of housing in the overcrowded townships was an important concern. This was less of an issue for mining gangs, as there was little competition for space in the expansive farming areas of the Free State that bordered the mines.

SITEKETEKENG

The freehold township of Newclare was even more impoverished than the neighboring areas of Sophiatown, Martindale, and Western Native Township. Housing was of a poorer standard, overcrowding was more prevalent, and a larger proportion of the population supplemented their income (or supported themselves) through beer brewing. The southern portion of Newclare, divided from the north by a railway line, was regarded as an extremely rough neighborhood. Predominantly populated by Basotho migrant laborers and female beer brewers, Siteketekeng suffered from the highest reported incidence of crime in the Western Areas.[1] Free from city council control and sparsely policed (with the exception of beer and pass raids), Newclare, and especially the south, was known as a haven for criminals.[2] The Russians flourished in this environment and the Matsieng, which operated in various townships across the Reef, set up its Johannesburg headquarters here.[3]

Newclare occupies a prominent place in Marashea lore and history. It is remembered as a place where the gangs defeated their enemies to establish absolute control, and stories of the large-scale conflicts have been passed down over the years. A veteran, retired for many years, recalls, "My father was Lerashea. He was in Newclare, where he lost his left arm in the wars" (LT). Newclare acquired such a reputation in Lesotho that Monare, the protagonist in a popular 1950s novel detailing the vicissitudes of a migrant laborer's existence, implored his city-dwelling companion, "You should take me there one day. I might meet one of our women who lives there—Makalebe. I can remember her telling me of one big fight which took place at Seteketekeng between Molapos and Matsieng people. She said that men, women and children were running like animals, and the streets looked as though they had been painted with blood."[4]

The Russians of Newclare South began to appear in official correspondence and newspaper accounts in 1949 as a result of their conflicts with tsotsis and ethnically defined antagonists, as well as their demands for protection fees from Newclare residents.[5] Although tsotsi gangs rarely fought pitched battles with the Russians, their mutual animosity sometimes resulted in bloodshed. For example, following the funeral of a Russian believed to have been shot by tsotsis, the mourners charged through the streets of Newclare and "attacked every tsotsi, or whoever they deemed one, without warning."[6] A Matsieng veteran remembers that tsotsis "tried to fight us at Newclare but we beat them very much with melamu" (TT). Bhaca migrants and Marashea engaged in a series of clashes in early 1951. One fight, reportedly initiated by several Bhaca urinating against a Russian's door, resulted in the death of five Bhaca and the arrest of thirty-four Marashea.[7] The violent nature of Marashea activities did not escape police notice, and before the Civilian Guard–Russian conflicts of late 1951 and 1952, dozens of Russians were arrested in Newclare, mainly on charges of public violence.[8] The murder of an African detective who had arrested several Russians was widely rumored to be an act of revenge. In response to these activities, the Johannesburg city council, the native commissioner, and senior police officers convened a meeting in February 1951 to discuss strategies to break the power of the Russian gangs.[9] Up to this time it is clear an official consensus existed that the Russians represented a threat to security and order in Newclare. This was to change during the course of the conflicts with the Civilian Guards (also known as Civic Guards).

THE CIVILIAN GUARDS AND THE SQUATTERS

Communal policing initiatives had been in place in the Western Areas of Johannesburg since the early 1920s and were generally welcomed by residents frustrated by the high incidence of violent crime and the SAP's ineffectiveness. Military enlistment, which reduced the numbers of the Johannesburg police during the early years of the Second World War, resulted in the formation of the government-administered Civilian Protection Service (CPS). The CPS attracted over a thousand volunteers from across the black townships of Johannesburg, and while the neighboring areas of Western Native Township and Sophiatown contributed significant numbers of these volunteers, none came from crime-ridden Newclare. Following the demise of the CPS in 1947, disbanded by the authorities who regarded it as a wartime contingency, residents of the Western Areas persistently, albeit fruitlessly, petitioned for permission to form a replacement organization. Finally, in August 1951, in the

face of police opposition and despite the lack of official sanction, residents, acting through their advisory boards and ratepayer's associations, formed a Civilian Guard.[10] The self-proclaimed mandate of these Guards was to patrol the streets, to disarm people found with weapons, and to turn offenders over to the police. Just as in the past, this latest communal policing movement garnered little if any support in Newclare South, where the Russians had consolidated a power base.

Shortly after the northern-based Guards began their patrols in Siteketekeng in November 1951, fighting erupted. Given the mandate of the Guards—especially with regard to disarming residents—and the nature of the Russian gangs, conflict was inevitable. The following description of an early Guard patrol in Newclare South drives this point home: "In this 'Russian'-infested area, many armed with sticks and missiles were rounded up. Those who put up opposition against being searched were dealt with in the language they would best understand. A large collection of weapons was made in the thorough combing of the township at the weekend."[11] A number of Marashea veterans insisted that the Guards indiscriminately assaulted everyone they encountered south of the railway tracks. "Those people were whipping the people who were walking at night, and that became worse when they were beating innocent people. We came together as Marashea to fight them" (MC; also SC, 22 April, PP). A Matsieng member from Benoni reports, "The Civilian Guards were searching Basotho women at the railway station in Johannesburg. They would even search under their dresses. We did not like that and told them to stop, but they refused and . . . we traveled to Newclare to fight them" (MK). A former Matsekha commander, who was much praised by the police for his role in the Newclare battles, alleges that the larger conflict erupted when the Guards apprehended and assaulted suspected Russians: "The Civilian Guards arrested innocent people, saying that they were Marashea. They took them to an isolated place where there was a hall and they whipped them. That meant they were no longer interested in working with us. One person came running to my home to tell me people had been arrested by the Botswana Civilian Guards. I called a man named Maliehe, who is now dead, and I told him to blow the whistle. Marashea then came to my home. . . . We then went to the hall and . . . rescued those people. That was how the fight began" (ST).

The Russians retaliated with a vengeance and attacked patrolling Guards on Christmas Day, 1951. In the ensuing battle eight men were killed and twenty injured. Violence flared up again in March when thousands of Guards and Russians clashed. This time the death toll reached eleven, ninety-five were hospitalized, and "all available policemen were necessary to quell

the disturbance."[12] Russian reinforcements came from the mines and several townships, especially Benoni, while the Guards were supported by their colleagues in Sophiatown and Martindale.[13]

Several ingredients fed into the Newclare hostilities. The Guards were determined to police the Russian-dominated sections of Newclare and disarm the Marashea. The Russians relied on their weapons to protect themselves from tsotsis, rival Russian factions, ethnic gangs, and the police. It was inconceivable that they would surrender them to the Guards. Furthermore, the Russians felt that the Guards had been infiltrated by tsotsis, who took advantage of their new-found legitimacy to victimize their Basotho enemies. Finally, the Russians' status as migrants and foreign nationals was responsible for their antagonism to many of the ANC campaigns that were supported by the Guards. Most Marashea left their families at home in Lesotho and came to Johannesburg to find work. Thus, they were less likely than South Africans to participate in pass burning and other campaigns for which they might be deported. Bonner explains: "The ANC's main political campaigns, like the Defiance Campaign of 1952, the Bantu Education Campaign of 1955, and the various anti-pass campaigns of the 1950s seem to have little immediate pay-off or relevance to the Russians and were accordingly dismissed. To make matters worse such campaigns were often as not supported and enforced by the second-generation African urban population, which the Russians viewed with so much suspicion."[14] The Newclare Marashea fought to conserve the power and autonomy threatened by both the Guards' disarmament policy and the ANC's political agenda.

Following the March 1952 clash, the divide between northern and southern Newclare became increasingly rigid. The Guards controlled the north, where they continued their patrols, while the Russians maintained their hold south of the railway tracks. The conflict received much attention in the Johannesburg press, the vast majority of it unfavorable to the Russians, who were branded as thugs opposed to the crime-fighting agenda of the Guards.[15] By this time, however, the Marashea, under the leadership of Solomon Hlalele, had gained police support. Hlalele's stories of Guard aggression were sympathetically received by a police force that found it expedient to accept his portrayal of the Russians as staunch government supporters who abhorred communism. An examination of Hlalele and his followers' propaganda campaign demonstrates the Russians' understanding of the government's overriding concern with communism and political dissent, as well as their cynical appreciation of police hostility toward the Guards.

Both in his statements to the press and in various meetings with police and township officials, Hlalele claimed that he had initially supported the forma-

tion of a Civilian Guard because his people were also victimized by tsotsis. However,

> After watching the activities of the civilian guards we have come to the conclusion that: 1) We would not desire to associate ourselves nor encourage others to do so on the ground that they have little respect for the law and do not respect the police; 2) We would keep out of their movement because it has been refused recognition by the government of South Africa; 3) We would not have this movement in our sector because some of its members were desperate tsotsis who found it an opportunity to rob and assault people without reasonable cause. . . . All we desire is peace.[16]

Hlalele stated that tension between the Guards and his followers began when Guard supporters and ANC activists like J. B. Marks, Ben Kenosi, and Philip Vundla demanded that the Basotho join a pass-burning campaign initiated by the Communist Party of South Africa in 1950 and join in Freedom Day demonstrations that same year. The Marashea, "who as citizens of a British Protectorate were even more dependent than their fellow migrant labourers on possessing the right documentation,"[17] refused to comply, and as a result the Newclare Guards were comprised wholly of residents of Newclare North. Shortly thereafter, according to Hlalele, the Guards, which included a strong tsotsi contingent, began assaulting and robbing all Basotho they came across in their patrols. Naturally, Marashea mobilized to defend their people.[18]

Hlalele's campaign resonated with the police, who regarded ANC and communist activists as a political threat, but also because the Guards' very existence "was a powerful critique of their failure to tackle crime."[19] Reacting to township officials who praised the Civilian Guards and the generally favorable press coverage of Guard activities, the deputy commissioner of the Johannesburg SAP sent an eight-page indictment of the Guards to the police commissioner. Most of the report is devoted to listing the various Guard members accused of committing offenses (very few were convicted) while on duty. It claims that this list "provides constructive proof that the members of this body have in fact constituted a grave danger to their own people." For good measure, the report concludes that the Guards "are under the control of persons who are antagonistic towards the existing laws of this country for the control of natives and its present social structure."[20]

It seems that the convergence of police and Russian interests produced a marriage of convenience. Hlalele claimed he was in close communication with the Newlands police station and that when he wished to attack the

Guards, he would go there to complain that the Guards were molesting Basotho. He would then return to Newclare in the company of the police and on his prearranged signal his men would attack the Guards.[21] One of Hlalele's followers remembers: "We reported everything to the police and they would let us fight and only stop the fight when people were dying. We had a translator because our leader, Hlalele, did not know how to speak English. . . . He would tell the police what happened because those [Guards] provoked us and we did not allow them to do that" (MC).

There can be no doubt that the police endorsed the Marashea. Police correspondence and reports portray the Russians as trustworthy Bantu protecting their fellow Basotho in Newclare South from the blatant aggression and subversive influence of the communists. In a meeting of various officials to discuss the disturbances at Newclare, Major Talliard of the SAP informed the other participants that "after the establishment of the Civic Guard there were quite a number of murders and it was found that those murdered were Basutos. That is what put the Basutos against the Civic Guards."[22] One police report concluded, "The Civilian Guard was organised by known Communists, is still controlled by Communists and is directly responsible for the critical situation which exists at Newclare."[23] Such documents were forwarded to various government departments.

A new element was grafted on to the Russian-Guard conflict in May 1952, when the supporters of Mamalinyane Dhlamini, the leader of the non-Basotho people in Newclare South and a former ally of the Russians, were forced out of Siteketekeng. This group was often referred to as the "Hlubis" because Dhlamini and many of his followers came from the Matatiele area, on the southern border of Lesotho, home to a large Hlubi population. Dhlamini's people trekked across the railway line and squatted in Newclare North on land administered by the city council, a move that considerably expanded the number of parties interested in Russian activities. The Hlubi immediately sought the support of the Civilian Guards in their conflict with the Russians, and large-scale battles once again became a feature of life in Newclare. As political interest in the situation increased, the Marashea, aided by the police, stepped up their propaganda campaign. Dhlamini and the squatters were castigated as agitators indistinguishable from the communist Guards.

Documentary evidence indicates that the Russian-Hlubi dispute erupted over the misuse of funds collected by Hlalele and his supporters to provide for the legal defense of all residents of Newclare South engaged in the fight against the Civilian Guards. Although the Russians were at the forefront of the battles, non-Basotho residents, who also resented Guard activities, fought at their side. The fallout was explained by one of Dhlamini's supporters:

It was said by [Hlalele and his deputies] that the main objects and aims of the fund would be for the protection and defence of all tribes in Newclare should they find themselves involved in a court case. . . . At that time all other tribes living in Newclare South supported the Basutos in their struggle against the Civic Guards wholeheartedly. The disturbing factor came immediately after the members of the S.A. Police had effected the arrest of the persons suspected as ringleaders. Of the arrested persons were Basutos, Xosa, Zulu, Bacas, Shangaans and Hlubis and Betsvanas. This occasion offered a testing ground for the purpose of the tribal fund. The only people who got assistance from the fund were Basutos and the others were left to fight on their own.[24]

ST provides the Russian account:

One day while we were resting I was with Hlalele when Mathabane arrived to tell us that Mamalinyane was outside the location ready to attack. He was at the ground where I used to play football. I said that Mamalinyane was on our side so we organized ourselves and went to hear from Mamalinyane. He was with some Pondos and people were running all over the place because Mamalinyane was with many people outside the location. We went to them and asked what they were doing. They said we should fight, but Mamalinyane stopped them when we reminded him of our agreement. We asked him why he had turned from our agreement because we were given the authority to guard our location and we were friends. Some of Mamalinyane's people had even married Basotho women. They said that we misused the contribution because the money was supposed to pay for lawyers.

At this point Dhlamini, previously a close associate of Hlalele's, severed his ties with the Russians and, along with his adherents, refused to pay into the "protection fund."[25] While the disagreement over funds may well have sparked the conflict, the testimony of a number of Marashea supports the view of W. J. P. Carr, manager of Johannesburg's Non-European Affairs Department, that the fight was largely a struggle for supremacy between Dhlamini and Hlalele and their respective followers. MC remembers that the Hlubi were determined not to be dominated by Basotho: "We were staying together as one group and they separated themselves from the Basotho, saying they would not be ruled by Basotho and that was how the fight started." Another

veteran asserts, "We fought against Mamalinyane because he wanted to be the leader and we objected to that and told him to rule the people of Matatiele and then we beat him with melamu" (MC).[26]

Shortly thereafter, in mid-May 1952, open conflict broke out as the Russians reportedly insisted that "there can be no two bulls in one kraal."[27] Dhlamini and his supporters suffered considerable losses in a series of clashes and were forced to retreat to Newclare North, where between two and three hundred families took refuge by squatting on council-owned land.[28] Apparently the Marashea were given a free hand in this initial conflict with Dhlamini's people. "We asked the police for five minutes for fighting and we promised the police that by that time the Hlubi would be out of that place. They gave us time and many people died because the fight became uncontrollable" (MC). A second set of battles ensued as the Hlubi, now allied with the Guards, launched attacks on Newclare South in an attempt to drive out the Russians and regain their former homes. The Russians repulsed these invasions, retaliated with raids of their own, and maintained complete domination over Siteketekeng.[29] ST relishes the final humiliation suffered by the squatters: "We fought and beat Mamalinyane until they moved to the other side of the train tracks, and they were living in a shanty town during the winter. We stayed in Siteketekeng and ate all their chickens and cats."

During this time, the plight of the squatters, who were living in deplorable conditions, was featured in numerous press reports and caused considerable hand wringing among township officials, especially members of the city council. The Marashea had demonstrated their superiority on the battlefield. When the arena of conflict shifted into the realm of politics, public relations, and behind-the-scenes maneuvering, they proved every bit as proficient.

The local government departments' preferred solution to the crisis, which was garnering damaging publicity, was simply to repatriate the squatters to their former homes. This seemed the easiest and, most important, the least costly solution. The squatters, however, refused to return unless the Russians were removed from Newclare or, at the very least, the men identified as leaders of the gang were deported.[30] Various township officials urged the police to act accordingly.[31] However, neither the police nor the minister of native affairs were inclined to move against the Marashea. Once again the Russians' trump card proved to be the allegedly communist leanings of their opponents. The following excerpt from a police report further confirms SAP preferences: "A strong group of Hlubis, supported by Civilian Guards attacked the Basutos. . . . They entered a portion of the Southern Township occupied by the Basutos under Hlalele and commenced to loot the dwellings. They were met by about 50 Basutos under the leadership of Edward Mohale, a person who hates

Communism."[32] The account goes on to applaud the Russian victory. Every police report covering the conflict in Newclare identifies the Civilian Guards and Hlubi as the aggressors and emphasizes their communist connections. The Marashea, by contrast, are represented as a pro-government force standing up for order in the township: "The Basutos refused to co-operate with the Hlubis against the government . . . this is the reason for the hostilities between the two sections."[33]

Without the cooperation of the police, township officials were helpless to act against the Marashea and were forced to find another solution to the squatter crisis. In the end, no attempt was made to resettle the squatters in Newclare South. Instead, they were removed to an emergency camp in Moroka. Police condemnation convinced the government to ban all Civilian Guards in Johannesburg in mid-1952, and those who continued to patrol were arrested. Siteketekeng remained the exclusive domain of the Russians.

THE RUSSIAN VICTORY

It is useful at this point to examine the convergence of circumstances that resulted in the Marashea victory. The first stage of the conflict was won on the battlefield, where fighting prowess and the frequent superiority of Russian numbers allowed them to carry the day. Although one does not wish to make too much of this, Marashea were renowned for their bravery and fighting skills. They had learned the art of stick fighting as herd boys, and were extremely proficient in the use of melamu; battle axes and swords were also popular weapons. As one Newclare resident remembers, Russian ferocity was legendary: "We came to associate the name 'Russians' with violence. They would descend upon the township in great battalions, clad in brightly coloured blankets, pants belted high, white shoes and the inevitable stick which was a deadly weapon in the hands of a Mosotho. I had seen a man's jaw shattered at one fell swing of that stick. If you heard a whistle blow, you had to clear off the streets if you valued your life. They were insanely brave, those Russians. It seemed to them that violence was just a game."[34] A former Sophiatown tsotsi gang leader, Don Mattera, also remembers the Newclare Russians as impressive fighters. His gang avoided conflict with them if possible because "they were deadly guys. These guys never retreated; they came at you all the time" (Johannesburg, 19 February 1998).

Marashea did not rely solely on their proficiency with melamu. Throughout the 1950s guns became an increasingly important part of their arsenals. The gangs acquired firearms from several sources, including appropriation

from fallen enemies and through theft, but most were purchased from Chinese, Indians, or whites. "There was a white man who supplied us with guns. We met him at night and his car dimmed the lights. We would make appointments with him and we would contribute in order to buy those guns" (PP).

Just as important as fighting skill and battlefield tactics was the Russians' ability to call upon a wide network of affiliated gangs for reinforcements. These came from nearby mines and on numerous occasions fellow Matsieng were summoned from neighboring townships to lend assistance. A man who fought with Matsieng in the 1940s and 1950s explained: "Since Newclare was a place of many fights, we were always fighting there, and that was the place I used to fight with the group controlled by Hlalele."[35] Dhlamini also asserted that miners greatly augmented the Russian forces in Newclare South in the evenings and on weekends and it was these reinforcements that made the Basotho so formidable.[36] Hlalele's group had established strong links with the miners at nearby Rand Leases Gold Mine and it was observed that "the Induna and at least three of the Basuto Police-boys . . . are Hlalele's Underdogs."[37] The *Bantu World* also noted the movement of "foreign" Russians into Newclare: "The Basuto have been inviting comrades from all over the country and one lorry-load of men and taxis came from Benoni; from Kliptown men came by train; from St. Helena and Welkom in the Free State men came by lorries; three lorries came from Vereeniging—two of which were intercepted by the police and one escaped. These vehicles come to Newclare by night, and, after unloading, the men kept in the township in locked rooms."[38]

Police assistance was another valuable asset. On occasion, Basotho police actually fought alongside the Marashea, as was the case in 1954, when an off-duty Mosotho sergeant armed with his service revolver was arrested for participating in a large Matsieng-Masupha clash in Siteketekeng.[39] Throughout the conflict with the Guards and the Hlubi faction, Hlalele was in constant contact with the police and made public declarations time and again that "We of Siteke-Siteng regard the police as our friends."[40] Documentary evidence supports this claim. In the course of his investigation into the Newclare conflict Detective Sergeant Papendorp of the Special Branch reported, "Hlalele was neatly dressed, appeared friendly towards us and expressed himself prepared to assist the Police or authorities in any way possible in order to restore peace at Newclare. . . . I made a careful psycological [*sic*] study of this man. He openly replied to questions put to him and explained to me his desire to tell the authorities the cause of all the trouble." This favorable impression extended to the entire sector under Hlalele's control, where "people were friendly and keen to speak to us and assist in every possible way." Papendorp's assessment of Dhlamini was entirely negative. He emphasized Dhla-

mini's hostility toward the authorities and concluded, "The Hlubi leader, December Dhlamini, is trying to think out a story to suit his purpose, and I did not trust him."[41] Evidently, the police were able to persuade at least some local government departments to endorse their version of events. For example, in a letter to his superior, the undersecretary of native affairs advised, "The Police now have evidence (which we cannot refute) that the Civilian Guards alias Hlubis are the real aggressors and that they are communist inspired. The removal of the leaders of the 'Russians' who are said to support the Police and be in favour of law and order may therefore serve no good purpose. In fact, the Police fear that such a step would be regarded as a victory by the Hlubis who may then attempt to take further violent action against the remaining Russians."[42]

The Russians' confidence in the extent of police support is apparent in their request that a senior police official "who is fully conversant with the situation" be present when their lawyers met with the minister of native affairs, Hendrik Verwoerd, to discuss the situation in Newclare.[43] The Russians also gave numerous press interviews and often met with government officials to present their version of events. In an effort to elicit further sympathy, the Marashea petitioned Gideon Pott, agent for High Commission Territories, and convinced him that the Civilian Guards were dominated by a criminal element that preyed on all Basotho. Pott then recommended to the South African authorities that the Guards be disbanded. Through Pott, the Russians also corresponded with prominent chiefs in Lesotho, claiming they were the victims of the hostilities in Newclare.[44]

Dhlamini and some of the Civilian Guard leaders like Ben Kenosi also mounted public relations campaigns. However, Kenosi and his associates fought a losing battle in this regard as they were automatically stigmatized by police and government officials because of their political activities. For his part, Dhlamini's alliance with the Guards antagonized the police, and he alienated potential supporters among local authorities as a result of the illegal brewing and squatting activities he sanctioned among his followers. He especially angered township officials when it was discovered he had informed the squatters he was authorized by the Johannesburg city council to collect funds from them. The animosity toward Dhlamini reached such a level that Carr informed Dhlamini's lawyer that "this Department proposed separating the Newclare Squatters for settlement at Moroka with the obvious intention of breaking up the present groups and destroying the power of December Dhlamini."[45]

Because the conflict in Newclare South attracted significant publicity, the Russians retained the services of a law firm to represent their interests. Counsel met with the minister of native affairs to present their clients' version of

events and seemed to have found a sympathetic audience. Advocate Lakier's meeting with Verwoerd illustrates a number of Russian strategies. Lakier stressed to the minister that the English papers sympathized with the Russians' opponents; advised Verwoerd, "Communists are behind the agitation against the Russians"; and assured him that the Russians were in close touch with the police. Verwoerd replied that he was aware of the communist agenda of the Guards and the Hlubi.[46] His statements to the press indicate that Lakier's entreaties did not fall on deaf ears. Verwoerd told reporters that secret government sources had convinced him that "the so-called 'Russians' are at least as much, if not more, sinned against as sinning."[47]

Fortunately for the Marashea, the conflict in Newclare dovetailed with Verwoerd's political agenda to expedite the Western Areas Removal Scheme.

> After the passing of the Group Areas Act in 1950, which became the cornerstone of apartheid, Verwoerd was to become personally responsible for a whole string of legislation that not only aimed at manipulating urban space in order to create separate residential areas designated for occupation by specific racial groups, but also which gradually destroyed any existing rights which Africans might have had in urban areas. . . . The Newclare squatter movement therefore presented Verwoerd with a perfect chance to intervene actively in the Western Areas of Johannesburg in 1952, and thereby to make a preliminary attempt to implement his more grandiose apartheid schemes.[48]

Commenting on the problem that the conflict in general and the squatters in particular presented, Verwoerd made his intentions plain: "There is only one solution and that is that both South and North Newclare must disappear and their residents must be settled in better and properly municipal-controlled Native residential areas."[49] Verwoerd had no interest in resolving the conflict or repatriating the squatters, either of which would have meant taking action against Hlalele's Russians. A de facto alliance with the police, coupled with the complicity of the minister of native affairs, who turned a blind eye to their transgressions, enabled the Marashea to annex Newclare South.

The Russians benefited from a serendipitous set of circumstances—they were fighting a force that the police regarded as threatening, and the Newclare troubles suited Verwoerd's political ambitions. That said, Hlalele and his followers displayed keen political acumen. The violent tendencies of the Russians did not go unnoticed in either press or local government reports and, in order to support the Russians, their backers needed to demonize the Guards

and the Hlubi. This was achieved with the assistance of Hlalele and various other Russians, who assured white South Africa that the Basotho of Newclare supported the government and fought only in self-defense against communist agitators.

Once the Guards had been disbanded and the squatters removed to Moroka in 1953, the situation changed entirely. Neither the police nor any government department stood to benefit from the Russians' presence. Instead, a protracted war between Hlalele's Matsieng and a rival Masupha faction united the authorities in the view that the Marashea once again constituted an undesirable element in the township. Increasing numbers of Russians were arrested, imprisoned, and deported to Lesotho upon completion of their sentences. Indeed this was Hlalele's fate in 1953.[50] No longer useful allies, the Russians were subjected to intensive police pressure as the decade wore on. Having allowed the Marashea to become ascendant, the authorities battled for years to break the gangs' hold on Newclare and succeeded only with the advent of the Removal Scheme.

THE MATSIENG-MASUPHA FEUD, 1953–57

Masupha members living in Siteketekeng joined in the fight against the Guards and the Hlubi and coexisted peacefully with the Matsieng until a leadership dispute led to general conflict between the two factions in Newclare South in mid-1953. PG1 recalls that after the Russians vanquished the Guards and the squatters, "Hlalele wanted to rule all Basotho living in Newclare. Matsabang was the ruler of Masuphas and Molapos and he denied [Hlalele's claim], saying that no, he cannot be under Hlalele—that is where the division comes."[51] The old enemy of Matsieng, Mamalinyane Dhlamini, joined in the battle on the side of Masupha until his death in 1957.[52]

According to a Matsieng veteran, the Masupha-Matsieng feud in Newclare marked the beginning of the widespread use of firearms in Russian factional battles. "That fight was caused by Leshoailane from Ha-Masupha. They wanted to rule us and we fought with them and that was when the guns began. The people from Leribe were very strong because they were many and they used guns" (TT). Shortly after the fight began, the Masupha got the upper hand and many Matsieng people fled the area, while the victors "ran through the township, blowing whistles, brandishing battle axes, sticks and other weapons."[53] The Matsieng refused to accept defeat and the conflict continued even after Hlalele was jailed in 1953. Later that year, Hlalele's supporters informed the native commissioner in Johannesburg that they were

determined to return to their former homes, while the Masupha were equally adamant that they "were not prepared to have [the Matsieng] back in Newclare South under any circumstances."[54] The conflict intensified in mid-1954, when the Matsieng rallied their forces and reoccupied a section of Siteketekeng.[55]

Battles between the two factions raged for five years, often involving hundreds of participants. Many of the combatants were not Newclare residents. Since their initial defeat, the Matsieng constituted a minority in Newclare South and relied heavily on miners from nearby compounds to augment their forces. In one fight involving some eight hundred Marashea in 1956, the majority of the wounded were Matsieng supporters from Rand Leases.[56] "Every Saturday I knew I had to go to Newclare to fight," recalls a former Matsieng from Rand Leases (KP). Mineworkers also supported Masupha. A miner who worked in Springs remembers traveling to Newclare on three different occasions to fight Matsieng (SC). Marashea from throughout the Rand, and even from the Free State, joined in the fighting, with Matsieng from Benoni and Matsekha from Springs and Daveyton figuring particularly prominently.

At an open-air meeting in 1954, SAP Captain de Villiers pleaded with a large crowd to end the fighting and "strongly warned the Basutos that if they continued to fight they would be severely dealt with by the law. They would even be sent back to their homes in Basutoland."[57] However, it took little to spark renewed brawls and a few months later one of the biggest fights to date was reportedly initiated "when a Masupha woman went over to a Matsieng man."[58] In that same year the papers began referring to the fighting as the Newclare War, and in 1957 a police captain described Newclare South as "one of the hottest trouble spots. It is really a vicious place."[59] By the mid-1950s guns were causing the majority of serious casualties. In a 1957 battle involving one thousand Russians, some of whom were armed with revolvers and shotguns, an estimated 250 shots were fired.[60]

The Newclare Marashea's relationship with the police had significantly deteriorated by this time, not least because of casualties the police sustained when attempting to separate or arrest Russian combatants. Numerous police files refer to Russian attacks on patrolling officers in just such circumstances and former Russians confirm these clashes.[61] Animosity seems to have peaked in early 1957. The commander of the Newlands police station called the Masupha and Matsieng leaders into his office in an attempt to stop the feud. "I warned them that the continuation of the fighting would carry heavy penalties for the natives involved, and when I told them that in the end many of them would be shot by the police both groups said this would be the only solution." Shortly thereafter an officer was stabbed to death during a brawl between a

TABLE 1. Matsieng-Masupha Clashes in Newclare, 1953–57

Date	No. of Police	No. of Russians	Dead	Wounded	Arrested
25 Aug '53	50	200	1	1	13
4 May '54	36	150	—	9	11
19 May '54	62	100	—	9	24
30 May '54	39	100	—	—	8
13 Jun '54	17	40	—	6	8
4 Jul '54	61	200	1	11	26
22 Sep '54	90	400	—	4	—
6 Oct '54	42	500	2	14	—
20 Oct '54	24	200	—	3	—
21 Oct '54	69	500	—	1	8
25 Oct '54	47	700	—	5	—
30 Oct '54	22	200	1	5	—
5 Jun '55	53	400	1	14	31
12 Jun '55	30	1,000	—	5	30
18 Sep '55	26	200	—	—	62
27 Nov '55	.5	70	—	5	3
3 Dec '55	18	300	—	2	2
7 Dec '55	32	400	—	4	—
9 Dec '55	16	300	1	4	—
9 Sep '56	43	800	1	26	—
7 Dec '56	11	200	1	5	—
25 Dec '56	16	100	—	13	—
30 Dec '56	3	300	—	—	2
30 Dec '56	23	500	—	4	—
17 Jan '57	3	30	—	3	1
20 Jan '57	18	500	—	5	—
23 Jan '57	18	200	—	—	—
23 Jan '57	12	1,000	—	19	—
27 Jan '57	19	1,000	1	39	3
3 Feb '57	31	500	1	30	—
10 Feb '57	153	20[a]	1	87	26
Totals: no. of fights: 31	**1,089[b]**	**11,110[c]**	**12**	**333**	**258**

Source: CAD, NTS 7674 file 90/332, undated police chart. While these figures provide an idea of the scale and severity of Russian conflicts, they are merely a record of fights the police knew about and bothered to make official note of. They are not comprehensive even for internecine Russian disputes and do not include battles between Marashea and other ethnically organized gangs. On the other hand, police figures for the number of Russians involved can be only rough estimates and may well be exaggerated.

a It seems likely that this figure should be 200, given the number of arrested and wounded.

b Corrected from 1,079.

c If the number of Russians involved on 10 February 1957 was 200, then this figure becomes 11,290.

police patrol and a group of Masupha in Newclare South. The response was predictably ferocious: "The follow up actions of the police resulted in 70 natives including [Masupha leader] Ephraim ending up in the hospital with injuries."[62]

Exasperated police and township authorities were now making every effort to break up the gangs. The commander at Newlands, when invited to address a 1957 meeting of the Western Areas Resettlement Board, informed members about the conditions in Newclare South and asked that a start be made as soon as possible for the removal of residents to Meadowlands. Consequently, the Department of Native Affairs explored the possibility of changing existing legislation in order to expedite the deportation of those identified as Russians. In the words of the chief commissioner, "I don't see any reason why Basutos should have a right to stay in the city and make the lives of the officials, the police and other natives impossible." Later that same year, after summarizing the history of Russian violence in Newclare South, he recommended "that there should be machinery to push these aggressive Basotho out of the city."[63] The minister of native affairs also became an advocate of deportation. "In view of the continuous rioting at Newclare caused by Basuto factions and the difficulties experienced by the police in dealing with the culprits, I have drawn the attention of the Chief Native Commissioner, Witwatersrand, to these provisions and he in turn will discuss the matter with the police in order, if possible, to obtain the removal of the leaders of the two factions to Basutoland."[64] The police began identifying Russian leaders in Newclare South and concluded in their sworn statements that "it is in the interest of the State natives that he is sent back to Basutoland."[65] However, despite increased police pressure and numerous deportations, the authorities only won their battle with the Newclare Russians when the township was finally cleared of Africans in 1958.[66]

RUSSIAN RULE

What remains to be assessed is the legacy of eight years of Russian supremacy in Newclare South. Bonner claims that the Russians' activity on the Reef throughout the 1950s caused "a hardening of ethnic boundaries and a reworking of ethnic identities on all sides."[67] Perhaps nowhere was this more evident than in Newclare, where the Marashea succeeded in evicting many non-Basotho. Alongside the Matsieng-Masupha feud, the Newclare Russians continued to engage in large-scale conflict with other ethnic gangs. Both Matsieng and Matsekha members active in the 1950s remember occasions when

internecine disputes would be put aside and Basotho would unite to do battle with Zulu, Xhosa, or Mpondo adversaries.[68] These affairs may well have contributed to the strength of the Russian gangs, as they presented themselves as the defenders of the Basotho community. It is difficult to judge how Basotho residents on the Rand, and in Newclare in particular, responded to these ethnic appeals. However, according to the director of native labor, other ethnic groups made no distinction between the Marashea and Basotho as a whole: "The words 'Basutos' and 'Russians' in so far [sic] as their meaning is understood by the other tribes at Newclare are synonymous as is their opinion [that] all the Moshoeshoes (Basutos) living at Siteke-Tekeng are associated with the activities of the so-called Russians."[69]

Because the Marashea gangs were almost exclusively Basotho, the entire group was often castigated as Russians, or at least Russian supporters, and a degree of fear and resentment was directed at all Basotho. No doubt Hlalele's claims that Basotho were targeted by the Civilian Guards, the Hlubi, and other groups were to some extent accurate, although he never publicly acknowledged the reasons behind these assaults. During the clashes with the Guards and the Hlubi, a police officer stated that "anyone wearing a blanket at night was a 'dead duck' if found north of the railway line."[70] The plight of two men caught in this situation was reported by the *Bantu World*: "Two Basuto mineworkers had a narrow escape at Newclare North on Sunday morning when the police rescued them from a mob believed to be members of the Reno Square squatters camp. Neither man knew the Basuto side of the area and so when they alighted from the train, they entered the Northern side of Newclare. They were held up and thrashed by a mob suspecting them to be 'Russian' spies."[71]

This state of affairs forced some Basotho to make difficult choices. As one resident explained, "You see, at that time it did not matter whether you belonged to a group. As long as you were a Mosotho you would be a victim. For security and protection you had to join the group."[72] At the height of the battles with the Guards and the Hlubi, it was reported that Civilian Guard groups throughout the Western Areas were forcing Basotho to leave their homes, and while there may well have been an element of anti-Guard propaganda in this account, there is too much evidence of widespread animosity to dismiss it out of hand.[73] Basotho were attacked by urban residents who directed their fury with the Marashea against all Sesotho-speakers, while at the same time, the gangs demanded fealty from Basotho who lived in areas under Russian control and punished those who refused to support them.[74] It is likely that many residents of Newclare aligned themselves with the Marashea primarily out of a sense of self-preservation.

While the Russians invoked dread, in the absence of any formal political authority in Newclare South, they were also the foremost group dispensing patronage, protection, and justice. The gangs did not rely wholly on coercion to consolidate their support base, especially when it came to fellow Basotho. For example, both oral and documentary evidence indicates that housing in Newclare South was allocated by the Russians almost exclusively on an ethnic basis. TT remembers that this was a source of tension with Dhlamini's people and the Civilian Guards: "The Indians gave us accommodation in their quarters and we helped other Basotho so that when a vacancy became available we would invite only Basotho and not other tribes, and the fight started there." Once the Hlubi were forced out of Newclare South, their vacated houses were given to Basotho, including those from Benoni who had assisted in the conflict.[75]

Moreover, living under Russian rule would have appealed to many migrant Basotho. Newclare was a haven for such people, the majority of whom lacked any marketable skills and often the legal right to reside in South Africa. Relatively free from government scrutiny in Siteketekeng, these migrants were able to engage in income-generating activities that allowed them to scratch out a living. A 1950 survey of the Western Areas found that "in Newclare a considerable number of Basuto women were living either by themselves or with a group of unrelated men, and apart from brewing had no legal means of support."[76] Miners flocked to the locations on the weekends for Russian meetings and dances and were a key source of income for these women who sold beer and worked as prostitutes under Russian protection.

With marauding youth gangs victimizing many neighborhoods on the Rand, the benefits of Russian protection should not be underestimated. The rudimentary Russian code dictated that ordinary residents should not be robbed, old people were to be respected, and only tsotsis and members of rival ethnic groups or Russian factions were legitimate targets for assault. It is implausible that gang members uniformly obeyed these rules, but their very existence served to limit offenses against fellow residents. The Russians used a carrot-and-stick strategy to command the allegiance of the people of Newclare South—they offered a range of benefits to a significant section of the local populace and terrorized the remaining residents into submission. In this manner, the Basotho gangs turned Siteketekeng into the "Russian zone."

Newclare South was the headquarters of the Matsieng faction for a number of years, and the Masupha also established a strong presence in the area. Despite years of internecine conflict and police repression, Siteketekeng remained a Marashea stronghold throughout the 1950s. It is not difficult to conceive that the gangs' success in this regard helped to cement the Russians'

presence on the Reef and encouraged the expansion of affiliated gangs in areas like Benoni and Germiston as well as throughout the townships of what was to become Soweto. A Matsieng leader who joined in 1959 reports, "Our headquarters were at Booysens, which controlled other locations like Phiri, Naledi, and Molapo, but it began at Newclare" (PL, Lesotho, 23–24 May 1998). Many Newclare Basotho moved to the Sotho-designated zones of Soweto, and it seems more than coincidental that Russian assaults resulting in headlines such as "Sotho Site-and-Service Residents Live in Fear" began to appear at the same time, or that Marashea clashes became a feature of life in these areas.[77] Although the government succeeded in removing the Russians, along with all other Africans, from Newclare, the gangs established far-reaching networks during their decade-long reign. Thus, the removals in no way threatened the survival of the Russians. Instead, as the same Matsieng leader testifies, "We scattered all over Johannesburg and others escaped to the Orange Free State, where there are many Marashea now."

The Newclare conflicts reveal two contradictory elements of power politics in the apartheid-era townships. First, the importance for black groups of a well-placed patron, especially if a popular support base was lacking.[78] For the Russians' purpose, no entity was better placed to influence their activities than the SAP. Largely exempt from police persecution during their battles with the Guards and the Hlubi, indeed at times actively assisted by them, the Newclare Russians acted with impunity. Second, at least from the residents' perspective, the limits of the government's authority in day-to-day life in the township could not have been more apparent. The Russian gangs were the real powerbrokers in Newclare South. Access to housing, as well as the approval needed to operate informal and illegal business ventures, all required Russian sanction, granted only with the payment of "protection" fees. Nonpayment meant eviction from the area and quite possibly physical retribution. The Marashea also levied taxes for burial expenses and reportedly press-ganged recruits.[79] The SAP provided virtually no protection against these or any other Russian practices, and it was the Marashea, not the government, which wielded power in its most immediate sense in Newclare South. With no alternative, residents paid taxes to the gangs and depended on them to police and administer justice in the townships.

The Russian era in Newclare illustrates both the nature of state power and the ways that black South Africans were able to capitalize on its weaknesses. The gangs could not match the armed might of the state and were ousted from their stronghold. However, before the removals, government agencies did not exercise effective control over Newclare. The Russians, and various other African groups, took advantage of these openings to establish their authority.

The most powerful Russian faction residing in the Evaton area south of Johannesburg in the 1950s was a Matsekha group led by Ralekeke Rantuba. The Evaton People's Transport Council (EPTC) decided to boycott the buses of the Evaton Passenger Service (EPS) in July 1955 to protest fare increases, and when its supporters attempted to enforce the boycott, Ralekeke's group and the boycotters came into conflict. Sporadic fighting continued for almost a year, leading to numerous deaths, property destruction, and the internal displacement of thousands of people. The EPTC was led by ANC activists, and once again the Russians were painted as political reactionaries doing the dirty work of the state. An editorial in the *New Age* queried, "How is it that the 'Russians' always put in an appearance when the people are engaged in a political struggle?"[80] and the EPTC and its supporters complained bitterly that the police assisted Russian attempts to end the boycott.[81] However, unlike Newclare, there is no evidence that Ralekeke's followers opposed the boycott at the behest of the police, or that they received police support.

There are a number of possible reasons for Marashea opposition to the boycott. Tom Lodge suggests that the Basotho community's social and economic position in Evaton encouraged a rift once the boycott began. The EPTC was led by well-educated, relatively prosperous men active in nationalist politics. The Basotho were led by a man, widely perceived as a gangster, who had been convicted of killing a rival a few years previously. The Basotho resided in Small Farms, the poorest district of Evaton, and possibly were disinclined to support a boycott initiated by the more privileged. Finally, Lodge draws attention to the fact that Evaton residents resented the status of migrant Basotho, who were free to seek work in nearby Vereeniging, while those born in Evaton were prevented from doing so by the Native Consolidation Act.[82] According to this version a preexisting divide based on social, economic, and spatial distance between the Basotho and the rest of the Evaton population became further polarized once the boycott began.

Another possibility is that internecine Russian violence dictated Marashea participation in the conflict, at least to some extent. A Mosotho by the name of Khabutlane, described by the police as a self-appointed headman as well as a boycott supporter, was killed along with two of his "bodyguards" in December 1955. Police reports trace his death to a long-standing dispute with Ralekeke:

> During 1949 a number of Basutos from Leribe, Basutoland went to work in the factories at Vereeniging and settled in the southern section of Evaton Location. Ralekeke installed himself as chief of this

group and took a number of the unhappy residents and fighters and went to live in the northern section. Since then there was often friction between Ralekeke and Khabutlane and their followers. When the boycott began Khabutlane joined the boycott movement and Ralekeke refused to support any movement that Khabutlane was involved in. This worsened the friction between the two groups and caused aggression from the "Evaton People's Transport Council" towards Ralekeke.[83]

Smash Moweng, a leading member of the boycott movement, who was allegedly involved in much of the fighting, was reported to be "a member of the so called Russians under the leadership of the late Gabutlane [Khabutlane] who broke away from those under the leadership of Ralekeke."[84] Guy and Thabane's research also indicates that Marashea rivalries were behind much of the fighting in Evaton: "in the 1950s, the Matsieng faction travelled to Evaton in an attempt to oust Ralekeke's Ha Molapo from their position as recipients of the favours of the bus company, which was using them to break the Evaton bus boycott."[85] It seems that Russians fought on both sides of this conflict, which was considered another episode in the ongoing fight between Matsieng and Matsekha factions, albeit one that involved outside elements (SG, PM).

Ralekeke claimed that he was not consulted about the boycott and therefore did not support it. Basotho from Small Farms kept riding the buses and were assaulted by boycotters—only then did the fighting begin.[86] According to one veteran the Russians opposed the boycott because many of them were working in Johannesburg and relied on the buses to get to their jobs (SG). Ralekeke called on reinforcements from throughout the Reef and different Matsekha groups came to his assistance (BK, KM). At some point after hostilities commenced, the EPS hired Ralekeke's followers to escort the buses, protect the passengers, and attack the boycotters: "We helped the bus owner, he gave us a piece job to go up and down guarding those buses. They were ranking in groups. People put stones in front of the buses and burned them with people inside" (SG).[87] The violence on both sides was brutal. Maliehe Khoeli, a prominent Matsekha leader in Johannesburg, traveled with his men to Evaton to assist Ralekeke. He claimed that the strikers paid tsotsis to enforce the boycott and that "We hit all those who supported the boycott from children to grandparents. We crossed Small Farms to fight those tsotsis and one day we killed a certain priest" (Bonner transcript).

Police reports advocate the removal of members of both factions as a step toward ending the violence in Evaton and profess no sympathy for Ralekeke's

Russians.[88] In fact, Ralekeke was deported shortly after the boycott ended in 1956. Newclare veterans speak openly of how the police allowed them to attack the Guards and the Hlubi, but the oral testimony of Russians who fought in Evaton supports police claims of neutrality: "The police were stopping the fights, but the people who caused the strikes were many and the police could not control them" (SG). Although ANC activists were prominent in the boycott movement, there is no evidence that Ralekeke was doing the bidding of the police. Moreover, Matsieng Russians fought with the boycotters. Instead, in this instance it seems that factional rivalries played a key role in the conflict, as did the willingness of Ralekeke's group to work as mercenaries for the bus company.

Just as in Newclare, the fighting in Evaton underscores the difficulties the state experienced in controlling black residential areas. Without effective police intervention to prevent or even contain the violence, the fighting in Evaton dragged on for the better part of a year. Evaton was to be the last time the Russians figured prominently in media coverage, as the large street battles of the 1950s were not repeated in subsequent decades. The most spectacular episodes of violence in later years occurred on the mines in the era of unionization, but that fighting was far less public. However, while priorities and strategies evolved as the Russian presence expanded into the mining areas of the Free State and the far West Rand in the late 1950s and 1960s, many of the survival tactics employed by the founding generation of Marashea were also used by the various mining gangs.

5 ⇜ Marashea on the Mines

The Expansion Era

THE SMALL FRATERNITY OF SCHOLARS who have studied the Marashea consider the gangs to be an urban phenomenon that peaked on the Rand in the 1950s but then withered away as a result of increased police pressure and tightening influx controls. Bonner argues that "the more rigorous application of the pass laws began to take its toll on confidence and strength so that by the mid-1960s the Russians' heyday had come and gone." Coplan acknowledges that the Marashea has continued to the present day but maintains that "harsh enforcement of apartheid and influx control regulations in the mid-1960s reduced formal Russianism."[1] To be fair, Bonner's research focused solely on the Marashea on the Rand in the 1950s, and Coplan mentions the Russians only in passing. Nonetheless, these assumptions are erroneous. The 1950s and 1960s were a turning point in Marashea history but not one that marked a decline. Rather, this period was a watershed in the expansion and reorientation of the Marashea, which established a powerful presence in the Free State and far West Rand goldfields. The Russian gangs employed a range of strategies that facilitated their survival in South Africa, but the single most critical factor in the society's survival and expansion over the past fifty years has been its association with the mines.

EXPANSION

Following the 1963 passage of the Aliens Control Act, the number of Marashea employed in urban areas other than as mineworkers decreased accordingly.

Dunbar Moodie notes that, "the earlier pattern of proletarianized Sotho working one or two shifts on the mines and then moving into secondary industry was hampered if not stopped altogether by the 1963 legislation."[2] By contrast the number of Basotho working on the mines expanded dramatically, especially following the opening of the Free State mines in the 1950s. By the mid-1970s over one hundred thousand Basotho men worked on South African mines, and "Lesotho nationals became heavily concentrated on Free State mines because of their proximity to Lesotho."[3] In this same period, mineworkers experienced significant wage increases.[4] Basotho women and women from the various homelands migrated to the Free State to service mineworkers, and the Russians moved in to capitalize on these developments.

With urban employment more difficult to obtain, the divide between Russians who worked on the mines and their unemployed compatriots became increasingly evident. These distinctions were not absolute in that some mineworkers augmented their earnings through illegal weekend activities; also men drifted between these categories, working for a period and then "loafing," depending on family circumstances, personal preference, and the availability of employment. However, mineworkers' wages remained the one stable financial source available to the Marashea, and the gangs, which had always had members working on the mines, became more mine oriented after the 1950s. Marashea in the Free State and other mining areas established informal settlements on farm properties adjacent to mines. In so doing, Marashea gangs strategically placed themselves close to their target market. Many mineworkers frequented nearby Marashea settlements that supplied dances, concerts, liquor, dagga, and women rather than incur the expense and traveling time to get to urban townships. When mines were close to larger towns like Welkom, Marashea groups also established themselves in the neighboring townships.

The move to the mines began while the Johannesburg Russians were at the height of their power in the 1950s. Asked when Marashea began in the Free State, ST responded, "I don't know the year, but they started when the mines were established in the Free State. Many of the people working in Gauteng went to the Free State mines." Many Marashea joined the society in Johannesburg in the 1940s and 1950s and then moved with their groups to the Free State, or they migrated from the Rand independently and joined newly formed groups in the Free State. These movements were noted in the press. For example, a 1956 court case revealed that Scotch Sepula, "the alleged leader of a notorious gang of Basutos on the Free State goldfields known as the Russians," was sentenced to eight months' imprisonment on a charge of public violence stemming from a fight with a rival Russian gang.

Sepula had a 1952 conviction for a similar charge in Springs.[5] A long-serving mine employee from Virginia with intimate knowledge of the Marashea witnessed the beginnings of the society in the Free State: "You see when the Free State mines started you already had a lot of activity of Marashea in Gauteng. And then as you had new mines the so-called bosses of the Marashea established themselves on those mines as soon as a handful of Basotho were around. Because as early as the 1950s the Marashea were already active here when I was a young man" (NT).[6] Part of this movement was a response to state and police pressure on the Johannesburg gangs, along with the exhaustion of Johannesburg-area mines and the declining employment options for township Russians. However, the primary factor was almost certainly the opportunities created by the opening of the Free State mines, which employed tens of thousands of Basotho.

Russian gangs in the Free State began appearing in newspaper accounts and police reports in the mid-1950s. In the course of a 1975 inquiry into mine violence a white employee of Welkom Gold Mine from 1951 to 1958 offered, "During those years, the Basotho workers, in groups of 20 to 50, terrorised the nearby Bantu during the weekends and sometimes on evenings. These groups called themselves Ma russians."[7] The SAP district commander for Welkom observed in 1957 that "The gangs known as 'Russians' are kept under constant surveillance. There is no doubt that the so-called gang still exists not only in Virginia but throughout the mine fields."[8] Newspaper headlines such as "Welkom Is Plagued by Russian Menace" and "Russian Menace Spreads to Quiet Village in Free State" confirm that the Marashea were firmly established in the Free State in a period when the Johannesburg gangs were attracting much greater attention.[9] The Marashea have maintained a presence in the Free State ever since. In 1992 the Goldstone Commission's investigation into mine violence took note of the prevalence of the Marashea: "In Thabong township there flourished a criminal gang of Sotho known as Russians. This phenomenon in mining area townships with Sotho mineworkers is fairly widespread."[10] Visits to Marashea *mekhukhu* in the Free State and far West Rand in 1998 and 1999 confirmed that every mine that employs substantial numbers of Basotho has miners who belong to the society, along with a Russian presence in a nearby informal settlement, township, or both.

SYMBIOSIS

In the 1950s and early 1960s many of the Russians who lived in the townships and squatter camps were employed in waged positions outside the mines, but

since 1963 the vast majority have been unemployed except for piece jobs. The malofa and mineworker factions have had a symbiotic relationship: the unemployed relied on the miners for financial support while the miners depended on the "full-time" Russians for access to and control over women. Additionally, group membership provided a measure of security from attacks by tsotsis and other Marashea. When fights occurred, mineworkers and malofa united against their enemies. Both groups operated under the same rules and had one leader, who was invariably located on the outside. The current leader of Matsieng in the Free State, who quit working on the mines in 1976 after he became morena, explains why this is so: "Morena of Marashea cannot be from the mine, he must rather stay in the squatter camp or location because he has to be available at all times. If he is in the mine compound he will not be able to solve all the problems that come up everyday; he will not be able to get reports and visit all the places where Marashea stay. He must be unemployed to enable him to be available for consultation" (BM).

To the extent that there was an imbalance in the relationship, the aggressive recruiting of mineworkers indicates that unemployed Russians relied more heavily on mine employees than vice versa. A 1960s Matsieng commander outlines their recruiting tactics:

> A person can leave Lesotho not intending to join Marashea, but when he reaches the mine we used women to attract him and that would cause us to have many Marashea. If we wanted to attract new members we would tell the women to go to the mines and the miners would propose to them. The women would agree to their proposals and they would invite the men to the location, giving them good directions. They would then make good food and make the men feel at home, and after seeing that they are welcome they would see that the place is good and then the men would join and every weekend they would be there for the meetings. The women were under our control and we would tell them how to treat a man so he would not leave and he would pay the contribution to the group. We would send the women to the mines because we wanted our population to grow. That would help us to raise funds, because miners had money. The miners would come with money and buy at our stokvels, and if you as a member interfered with a new member from the mines, you would be punished for threatening a customer who brought money to the group. We were not working and our funds were only coming from stokvels and playing dice, and that was not enough. (PL, Lesotho, 23–24 May 1998)[11]

Marashea who worked on the mines recruited fellow mineworkers. TS, a mineworker at West Driefontein in the Carletonville area in the 1970s explains: "For instance, you are my friend and you are Lerashea and I am not. You encourage me to join, telling me that it's nice to join Marashea and women are available. There are dances and drinking of joala and moriana, which will help you to get promoted in the mine. So it was easy for people to join. We even used Marashea who had good positions on the mines as examples for the others" (22 December).

The report of a concerned official describes the relationship between mineworkers and outside members in Hlalele's Matsieng:

> It is certain that the Induna and at least three of the Basuto
> Police-boys at Rand Leases are Hlalele's "Underdogs" and are
> responsible for intimidating the Basuto mine natives of Rand
> Leases and forcing them into paying subscriptions to the organisa-
> tion. Members once accepted, are free to visit locations for the
> purpose of visiting women and going to liquor dens. In many cases
> where a mine native is known to have a wife or woman in the loca-
> tions he is immediately forced into paying "protection" money for
> the woman.[12]

An active member of a Free State group explains that the relationship is essentially the same almost fifty years later: "Mineworkers are the customers of Marashea—they buy beer from us. When their wives or linyatsi visit them from Lesotho, QwaQwa, the Transkei, Ciskei, and other places, they keep them at our squatter camps under our protection. They even rent rooms from us" (KK).

The experiences of a Matsekha veteran of the 1950s to 1970s in Welkom and Rustenburg illustrates the value that the Russians placed on their employed members:

> The rule was that when we were going to the mekhukhu from the
> mines bringing money to our wives we were supposed to be wel-
> comed and no other Marashea were supposed to insult us, and if
> anyone said anything bad he was punished. The Marashea from the
> mekhukhu were required to treat us well. The one who provoked
> you was supposed to pay R50 as a fine. The money was given to the
> morena, and if the Lerashea beat you he was required to lie down
> and you got revenge in front of the group by beating him, and you
> were given R20 when you left that place. (NN, 20 May)

Russian mineworkers paid membership dues on a regular basis and spent a portion of their wages in the settlements and locations, where they were required to attend meetings. Mineworkers not affiliated with the Marashea were also valued customers, although they were free to frequent the mekhukhu or not as they saw fit. The proximity of Marashea-dominated squatter camps to the mines, and the range of services provided by the Russians, ensured that a significant portion of some mineworkers' wages went into Russian pockets. WL, a Matsieng commander active during the 1960s through the 1980s in the Welkom area, summarizes this situation: "The miners are our market. We sell beer and dagga and they are the ones who buy these things. Some put their women under our protection and they pay protection fees. They also rent our houses for these women. Marashea get most of their money from the miners."

Prominent Matsieng morena Mokhemele was well known to the authorities. He presided over a settlement near the South Vaal Hostel, where it was observed that "he keeps a shebeen and is a known supplier of dagga, liquor and prostitutes."[13] A 1972 report on a series of fights at Vaal Reefs, in which Russians were said to have played a leading role, emphasizes the extent to which gangs had infiltrated the compounds and their reasons for doing so:

> It must be stressed that to have the support of hundreds of mine Bantu employees is very lucrative indeed when considering the increased earning power of Bantu mineworkers over the last five years, and it is therefore inevitable that rival leaders and their gangs, come into being. This then was the assumed situation at No. 3 compound where two rival bosses and their gangs operated, not so much from within the compound but from the outside, although each group had their respective followers, supporters and lieutenants within the compound.[14]

The Marashea depended on mineworkers for more than financial support. On many occasions the mines provided sustenance and sanctuary. Unemployed Russians were able to live on the mines under the protection of their fellows without being discovered by mine management. A former liaison division manager with the Employment Bureau of Africa (TEBA) explains how this occurred: "Some of these guys who just came in looked after the property of the Basotho, and some of the Basotho were head clerks; they were people in authority. It was really easy for them to manipulate the system for somebody to be fed and housed and allocated a bed in the hostels because the hostel manager, with ten or twenty thousand people, he would never know who the hell was in the hostel" (R. de Boiz, Johannesburg, 16 June 1998). This was common practice at many mines. Inspector K claims that in the 1970s and

1980s "most of them lived out of the compound; it wasn't as controlled as these days. They went into the hostels and ate there, came out, and that's how they made their living" (Potchefstroom, 7 June 1999). A 1980 investigation of Marashea gangs in and around Welkom concluded, "There is evidence going back several years that such groups can infiltrate mines and obtain accommodation and food illegally for sustained periods without the management of the mine being aware of the state of affairs."[15] Another dispatch claimed that Tseule Tsilo had lived for several months in the Western Deep Levels compound.[16] Marashea seeking to avoid the police and those who lost battles with ANC comrades in the townships during the 1980s also reportedly took refuge on the mines (ML).

RUSSIANS IN THE COMPOUNDS

Historically the Marashea has avoided conflict with mine management. Virtually all criminal pursuits and fighting took place outside the mining compounds when the mineworkers were off duty. Weekends in the townships and squatter camps provided the time and stage for most Russian activities. The mines were a haven and source of income and recruits, and the gangs tried to keep a low profile. A security officer employed at Harmony Mine since the 1980s did not consider the Marashea to be of any real concern because "they were not involved in criminal activity in the hostels. They didn't actually interfere with the mining operation" (29 October 1998). Matsieng and Matsekha operated on the same mine and fought each other outside the mine on weekends, yet there was almost never conflict between the Russian factions inside the compound. Numerous interviews confirm that KP's experience was typical of Marashea relations on the mines: "It was peaceful inside the mine, everything happened on the weekends. Some of the Molapo were even the cooks at our mine, but we were not afraid they would poison us because everything happened outside the mines. There was a man named Simon from Masupha who was in charge of the cooks and he served us very well — the problems came only on weekends."

Management was aware of the Russians but as a longtime mine employee explains, "Mine management knows they exist but there is nothing they can do about them; what happens off the mine premises is a municipality issue" (HF, Lesotho 23 April 1998).[17] A former Masupha member who worked on various mines in Gauteng and the Free State during the 1950s and 1960s confirms that there was little management could do to prevent Marashea activities outside the mines: "The compound in the mines can't stop anybody from

going outside the premises of the mine. . . . Anybody could go out and do tsot-sis' work, and we also went out like that. We also went out for fighting. No-body knew that we were going to fight" (SC, 22 April). Some mining officials made use of the Russians' talents. One former mineworker remembers that the hostel manager hired Russians to force men, reluctant to leave their beds on Monday mornings after a weekend of indulging, to get up and work their shifts (RA, Lesotho, 9 May 1998).[18]

Various mining authorities monitored the Russian gangs and periodically expressed concern over their potential for disrupting work. Reports of faction fights occasionally noted that the dispute originated outside the mine as a result of Marashea attacks on other workers,[19] but despite sporadic friction, neither archival records nor oral testimony reveal any sustained attempt by management to purge the mines of Russian gangs.[20] My research uncovered only two episodes in which the Marashea earned the widespread enmity of mining authorities.

Basotho miners' involvement in a volatile domestic political climate some-times spilled over into South Africa with violent consequences in the mining compounds. Without exception Marashea informants insist their groups had no interest or stake in South African politics. They might admire the ANC as individuals but the purpose of the group was to protect its members and to make money. This neutrality did not extend to political developments in their homeland. The irony of the Russians being labeled as conservative collabora-tors is illustrated by their involvement in the politics of Lesotho. When Prime Minister Leabua Jonathan of the Basotho National Party (BNP) annulled the 1970 elections he seemed certain to lose and declared a state of emergency, the opposition Basotho Congress Party (BCP) under Ntsu Mokhehle was forced into exile. Over the next several years BCP supporters attacked police stations and other symbols of government authority in Lesotho, and many were killed in government reprisals. The South African mines became a key point of organization and funding for the exiled BCP and its armed wing, the Lesotho Liberation Army (LLA). Mineworkers contributed heavily to BCP coffers, and although the ruling BNP had spies on the mines, the compounds were beyond the reach of the BNP's military. The majority of Basotho mi-grants living and working in South Africa seem to have supported the BCP, and Marashea were no exception. Some gangs took up the cause of liberation and many other Russians supported the BCP as individuals. Russian groups held fundraisers for the BCP and a number of Russians joined the LLA. MB remembers, "Marashea supported the BCP because many of them were ill treated by Leabua Jonathan's soldiers. . . . Marashea contributed money to the BCP, especially after 1970, when it was in exile. The purpose was to strengthen

the BCP so it could go back to Lesotho and win the elections. Some of us fled the country to join the LLA and we felt very glad when some of our members joined the LLA."

Mining and police records, as well as Russian testimony, all confirm that the BCP was solidly entrenched on the mines and that the Russians often were important supporters.[21] TEBA's liaison division believed the Russians were operating largely at the behest of the BCP: "Anti-Jonathan, pro Ntsu [Mokhehle] 'Russian' gangs have operated in the hills behind Western Deep Levels for the last 20 years. Their object is to sow confusion and cause trouble amongst the Basotho miners leading to the discharge of the Basotho and forcing them to return home where there is no employment. Presumably, the next step would be to foment rebellion against the Lesotho government."[22]

Political activity on the mines escalated when Basotho mineworkers protested against the imposition of deferred pay in 1975.[23] They reacted violently to the Lesotho government's decision that 60 percent of mineworkers' wages be deposited in the Bank of Lesotho and be accessible to the miners only on their return to Lesotho. Basotho on a number of mines rioted, attempted to enforce stay-aways, and fought with other workers, especially Xhosa. While many Marashea sympathized with the BCP's political goals, it should also be remembered that the Marashea gangs were acting to protect their economic interests as the imposition of deferred pay threatened to substantially reduce mineworkers' financial contributions. Also, as the majority of Basotho miners supported these protests, Marashea gangs probably backed their customers to maintain their client base.

On some mines the Russians played a central role in the deferred-pay disputes. At Vaal Reefs, the notorious Russian leader Mokhemele (referred to as Kimberley by whites) is reported to have instigated much of the fighting against Xhosa workers, who refused to strike. Indeed, he was described as the "Chief Whip" for the BCP in the area.[24] Mokhemele had a long and fruitful association with the South African security forces. He worked closely with Inspector K for many years and during the deferred-pay disputes he enjoyed the protection of BOSS in return for supplying it with information on the political feuds in Lesotho. In 1975, when the deferred-pay disputes took place, Prime Minister Jonathan had fallen out of favor with the South African government for his criticism of apartheid. BOSS apparently encouraged the BCP in its efforts to destabilize the Jonathan regime.[25] To this end, BOSS operative Mr. Steyn approached mine management at South Vaal and asked them to allow Mokhemele into the hostel to organize the BCP. Mine officials complained bitterly of Mokhemele's special status as they claimed he was responsible for fomenting violence among mine laborers. It was also common

knowledge that although Mokhemele ran a shebeen near the mine and sup-plied miners with liquor, dagga, and prostitutes, he was immune from arrest. "The SAP and the Security Branch maintain he is a police informer and thus under their protection. In the past they continually refused to bring him to justice and stop a major source of trouble for South Vaal."[26] Mokhemele was living the Russian ideal. By assisting Basotho miners in their dispute he was consolidating his support while at the same time enjoying the protection of the security services.

PG1 was Lerashea in Johannesburg in the early 1950s but returned to Leso-tho to enter politics. He then served as the liaison between the BCP and many Russian gangs, recruiting for the LLA and raising funds. When the BNP im-posed the deferred-pay scheme, the BCP immediately began to organize protests: "I had to go all around the mines informing them what Chief Leabua Jonathan was trying to do to them. We were against that because our financial strength was mainly on the mines, because those people were contributing a lot of money" (PG1). The Russians were remarkably consistent in that they supported their client base—Basotho miners—in whatever disputes occurred.

A 1979 strike on Elandsrand Gold Mine (Carletonville) witnessed the sec-ond, albeit more isolated, conflict between mine management and Marashea. In this instance, Basotho mineworkers dissatisfied with bonus payments and living conditions led a riot that resulted in damages estimated at more than a million rands. Management blamed Marashea for inciting the strike and bringing in members from as far away as Soweto to enforce it. When sus-pected Russians were arrested by mine security, they were handed over to BOSS. Once again it was speculated that their involvement was politically motivated.[27]

As might be expected, some miners resented and feared the Russians. Notwithstanding their financial dependence on mineworkers, relations be-tween the gangs and mineworkers were not always harmonious. Marashea ac-quired a reputation for robbing mineworkers and despite the instructions of some leaders to refrain from such practices, police reports and the testimony of mineworkers and Russians confirm that this reputation is, in some cases at least, deserved. A Matsieng veteran states quite simply, "There are many Mara-shea on the mines because miners have money and Marashea can rob them easily" (KL). Security officials at Harmony Mine in Virginia report that the Marashea was greatly feared by some mine employees during the 1980s before it was driven out of the mine and the surrounding areas during a conflict with NUM supporters (29 October 1998). Moreover, a Russian was recently buried in the Mafeteng district of Lesotho after he and a companion were killed by a group of mineworkers they tried to rob (conversation, PL).[28]

Marashea gangs occasionally became involved in conflicts with other groups on the mines that resented their activities. Investigations into various fights list the causes as Russians robbing and attacking mineworkers and animosity caused by the high prices Marashea charged for prostitutes.[29] In a 1988 survey of hundreds of mineworkers following a spate of violence on the mines near Evander (east of the Rand), the most common response to the question, "What do mineworkers say about these men/What have you heard about these men?" was to identify the Russians as professional killers.[30] Mineworkers stress that despite hatred of the Russian gangs—"They only victimize innocent people who are not armed; they rob and rape" (MW, Lesotho, 19 April 1998)[31]—there was nothing individuals could do to resist Russian activities.

Along with supplying liquor, dagga, and prostitutes, and providing protection for mineworkers' women, the Russians also acted as security guards: "Target workers[32] . . . bought tremendous amounts of goods that they stored in their rooms to take home. Now, if that is stolen or destroyed, six or seven months is wasted. The Russians were essentially protectors of property. These were the guys who made sure the premises were secure and that nobody interfered with the property of the Basotho" (R. de Boiz).

Perhaps the single most effective way for the Russians to secure the support of Basotho mineworkers was by assisting them during faction fights with different ethnic groups. In the event of such conflicts Marashea interviewed for this study stated without exception that internal feuding was put aside in the interests of Basotho solidarity. "If there was trouble with other tribes—sometimes the fights started at the mine kitchen when one tribe cheated another in the line for food—Molapo and Matsieng would come together to attack that tribe," explains TB, a Matsieng member who worked at Libanon Mine (Westonaria) in the 1960s. WL vividly describes one such fight:

> I remember there was a conflict between Basotho and Mapondo on the mine, Geduld no. 2 shaft [near Welkom]. Somebody came to us and told us that the Mapondo had surrounded Basotho in the hostel. We told those who worked on the mine to go and help their colleagues—we only supplied them with weapons. The whistle blower blew the whistle and we gathered together to be informed of the situation at the mine hostel. We told the members working on the mine that we could only help them if they could drive the Mapondo off the mine premises. Then they left for the mine. When they entered the mine gate, they found that the Mapondo were at the gate blocking everyone from entering the mine hostel. The police [mine security] were behind the Mapondo, and the Basotho were on the other

side, so the police were between the two groups inside the premises. Most of the Basotho outside left the gate and went to the other side of the mine, where they jumped over the fence so they could join their brothers. Meanwhile the Mapondo did not realize that the Marashea at the gate had left. They told the police that the Marashea at the gate were trying to enter so the police rushed to the gate. The Mapondo thought that the Basotho inside would not attack, as they were the ones who started the fight and [the Basotho] were not actually ready to fight. But the Marashea had joined the Basotho in their position. When the Basotho realized that the police had left and their brothers had joined them, they took courage and attacked the Mapondo. The Mapondo ran to the gate and passed by the police. They scattered all over and many of them ran in the direction of the squatter camp where we were staying. They thought that all the Marashea had left to go to the mine—but we were waiting for them. The mine police said they were not responsible for what happened outside the premises. The Basotho were chasing the Mapondo and we had a chance to meet them. We killed many but some got away and gathered at the police station in town. They refused to return to the mine and they were all transported home by bus from the police station. By that time the mine fence had been pushed down so we could go into the hostels. Those Mapondo had bought so many cattle which they were to transport by train to their homes. We slaughtered all of them and ate them. That mine remained without Mapondo for many years.

In this instance, the Russians, both mineworkers and malofa, acted on behalf of their fellow Basotho and all enjoyed the fruits of victory.

Marashea have long been renowned as deadly fighters and their battle experience in the locations and squatter camps made them a valuable asset during large-scale conflict on the mines. Various Russian gangs played a leading role in mine violence over the years, but the Goldstone Commission's investigation into the violence at President Steyn Mine near Welkom provides the best documentation of such an occurrence. In 1991 the Congress of South African Trade Unions (COSATU) called for a nationwide stay-away scheduled for 4–5 November to protest against the introduction of the Value Added Tax. The management at President Steyn informed the NUM that workers who participated in a stay-away would forfeit their wages and be subject to disciplinary action. Despite appeals by the NUM, management refused to waver from this decision. The NUM indicated to management that the stay-away

was a COSATU issue and it had no jurisdiction to negotiate alternatives. The NUM stance was that workers who wanted to work would be free to do so without intimidation. At mass meetings in which NUM officials met with unionized mineworkers, the majority were in favor of the stay-away. However, a large number of Basotho workers had previously terminated their membership with the NUM, citing increased membership fees and disagreement with certain of its political activities.

On 3 November, when a group of Basotho attempted to go underground, fighting broke out as other workers, predominantly Xhosa, stopped them from doing so. This led to a series of clashes involving thousands of armed mineworkers that lasted throughout the night and resulted in fifteen deaths and fifty-five injuries. Almost all the casualties were Xhosa or Basotho, with Xhosa in the majority. On 8 November violence broke out at no. 4 shaft hostel. Xhosa workers isolated a number of Basotho in B block, where "they [were] savagely killed, having been beaten, stabbed, their throats cut and their heads smashed to a pulp." Over the next three days, 263 workers were injured and 25 more were killed. Once again Basotho and Xhosa dominated the casualty list, although this time the majority were Basotho. Included in the dead was a former Steyn employee and alleged Marashea leader, Stephen Nkhopea. Further fighting at no. 2 shaft hostel on 10 November resulted in another 38 deaths and 59 injuries, with Xhosa winning casualty honors. All was then quiet until the night of 24 November, when two taxiloads of Russians were transported from Thabong Township to the outskirts of the mine near no. 4 shaft. According to the Goldstone Commission:

> This episode was clearly a planned assassination, and unlike in the previous fights the Xhosa and Sotho workers had not separated into groups. The Russians had entered the hostel by stealth and killed 8 Xhosa workers and injured 26 workers. . . . This incident was apparently organised as an act of revenge for the large number of Sotho killed during the period of 8 to 11 November 1991. . . . The evidence shows collaboration between the Sotho at No. 4 shaft hostel and the Russians to take revenge. . . . The killing of Nkhopea was probably an added reason for Russian involvement. The Russians, with the assistance of Sotho workers, infiltrated No. 4 shaft hostel . . . and ruthlessly attacked Xhosa workers, killing and injuring many.[33]

The leader of a Matsieng faction near Welkom recounts the part he and his comrades played in this incident: "There was a fight at Steyn . . . and Basotho were defeated by Xhosa. We invited four Marashea from the Leribe

group, four Matsieng Marashea from Klerksdorp, four Matsieng Marashea from Virginia, and four Marashea from Power [informal settlement], where I was morena, and we organized ourselves and entered the mine to help Basotho fight Xhosa" (RC).

The connection between full-time Marashea and their compatriots on the mines could not be more apparent. Not only did the Russians avenge the death of one of their own, they rallied to the cause of Basotho mineworkers involved in a deadly conflict on the mine. Numerous investigations into violence on the mines led a TEBA investigator to conclude that Marashea were often at the forefront of the fighting on behalf of Basotho:

> We had meetings after severe fights when a number of people were killed. We'd have Russian people in there also as part of the debriefing, and when they spoke you would actually find the others listening to them and they would never be pooh-poohed. They seemed to have the inside information about attacks—who did what, when, and how—so that invariably one would get the impression that during the fight, even before the fight, there was some sort of game plan being followed, especially if they were the aggressors. (R. de Boiz)

A veteran who joined Marashea as a mineworker in Johannesburg and then migrated to the Free State explained malofas' willingness to assist their mining compatriots: "In many instances we are unable to enter the mine compound because of the security, but if we are able to enter, we help Basotho, as they are our brothers and customers who buy our beer and dagga in the squatter camps where we stay" (MB). Inspector K confirms that the Marashea routinely assisted Basotho during such conflicts. Whatever the motivation, it seems as if Russian gangs capitalized on ethnic violence among mineworkers to solidify Basotho support. This strategy benefited the gangs but the Marashea's murderous reputation almost certainly contributed to resentment of Basotho workers on the mines and a hardening of ethnic boundaries within the compounds.

The Russians have generally avoided antagonizing mine management. The gangs received the most notice from mining officials because of their role in faction fights, but these were typically viewed as ethnic disputes in which the Russians got involved as Basotho, not as a separate criminal society. Violence directed against the NUM almost certainly did not invite the disapprobation of mining officials, and, since the NUM has consolidated its position on the mines, the gangs have avoided conflict with the union.

Mining gangs also became deeply involved in the migrant taxi trade. In his study of taxi associations operating from QwaQwa, Bank uncovered the cen-

tral role played by a Marashea group based in Welkom. In early 1983 sporadic violence broke out between rival taxi associations, Mohahlaula and Majakathata, which were competing for passengers on the QwaQwa-to-Welkom route. By the middle of the year, Mohahlaula hired Russians from Welkom to protect them and attack their competitor. Majakathata mobilized their own forces—mostly friends, relatives, and unemployed men from QwaQwa—and the violence escalated. Bank summarizes the outcome, which resembled the massive prearranged battles of the 1950s more than any other subsequent conflicts:

> In these tense months small-scale clashes broke out at loading sites, street intersections and garages. These were periodically supplemented by full-scale battles arranged between the associations at places such as Hennenman, Ficksburg and Virginia [Free State towns]. According to taxi owners these "battles" occurred at neutral venues rather than on the home turf of either protagonist. The vehicles of the competing sides would be lined up in formation on a large open field. The leaders of both sides would then distribute weapons—guns, pangas [machetes] and sticks—and as soon as everyone was prepared the signal would be given to attack. These "battles" always took a heavy toll, leaving dozens of taximen and gangsters either dead or seriously injured.[34]

In the beginning the Marashea were mere guns for hire but over time they extended their influence and came to dominate Majakathata.[35] In 1991, one of Bank's informants explained: "The *Ma-Rashea* now runs this association. They are not people who have been paid for a service. They now have their own taxis given to them by the association. That is how they are paid now. When they arrive in Welkom or QwaQwa, they simply take their vehicles to the front of the queue and load them straight away. No-one is brave enough to stop them. You dare not let the *Ma-Rashea* go hungry!"[36] Taxi wars continue unabated in many areas of South Africa and Marashea with a direct stake in the taxi business inevitably become embroiled in taxi disputes. Even those not directly involved can be hired as muscle (BM). For example, in a 1990 conflict between N1 Speedy Taxi Organisation and Muhahlwule Taxi Organisation in Kutlwanong Township (Odendaalsrus), a group of Marashea was reportedly hired to attack the members of Speedy. Several people were killed and the house of a prominent Speedy owner was burned down.[37] The Marashea became an important broker in an industry that tied migrant workers and unemployed gang members together, increased the mobility of the gangs, and

preserved and intensified links with Lesotho. Control of long-distance taxi associations and transport routes to Lesotho not only secured legitimate income but facilitated the business of dagga and diamond smuggling.

URBAN REMAINDERS

While the mining gangs proliferated after the 1960s, Marashea groups on the Rand went into a slow decline. The various legal and economic conditions that pushed Basotho migrants to the mining areas drained the strength of the urban Marashea. The core of the Johannesburg Russians was composed of older veterans with jobs and houses in urban neighborhoods, along with the marena who ruled these groups. New recruits and veterans who had lost their jobs had little hope of formal-sector employment and were forced to rely at least partially on earnings from criminal proceeds.

Despite these difficulties, the Russians remained active on the Rand. Accounts of Marashea violence, both internecine and with other ethnic gangs, appeared in the Johannesburg papers throughout the 1960s and 1970s. A survey of press reports indicates that Matsieng were based in the Soweto neighborhoods officially designated for Basotho, particularly Phiri and Naledi. GK remembers, "In Phiri where I was living the whole street was Marashea." On the East Rand, Germiston and Benoni remained favorite haunts for Molapo and Masupha groups. Although the massive street battles of the 1950s gave way to smaller conflicts, these old rivals continued to engage in hostilities. On numerous occasions commuters and railway employees were forced to flee as rival gangs engaged in shoot-outs on trains or at train stations.[38] So ubiquitous was the violence between these various factions that a Masupha leader convicted of shooting a police officer pleaded in mitigation "that he was not aware he was shooting at the cops. He thought that they were rivals, the Molapo 'Russians' gang."[39] Miners seem to have played less of a role in these conflicts as time went on, and mineworkers are noticeably absent from arrest reports listing the occupations of Marashea. Instead, detained Russians included government clerks, post office workers, factory laborers, and on one occasion a municipal police officer.[40] One newspaper report claimed that the Russians were primarily composed of older men who relied on crime because they were forbidden to work in Johannesburg.[41]

Some township residents in the 1960s and 1970s commented that the Russians on the Rand were a nuisance, but that they no longer posed as much of a threat as in past years. A 1967 feature on crime in Naledi remarked that the Russians who had once dominated this area still existed, but the gangs had

Major goldfields of South Africa, present day

"moderated their sinister deeds."[42] However, with access to miners' wages steadily diminishing, even a reduced Russian presence resulted in robberies, assaults, and extortion schemes that were recorded by the African newspapers.[43]

Like their compatriots in the mining areas, the Marashea on the Rand became central figures in the emerging taxi industry in the 1980s. The Free State–QwaQwa taxi conflict spread to Johannesburg, and Molapo from Germiston and Matsieng from Phiri, already fierce rivals, backed competing associations in a drawn-out and bloody conflict. In April 1984 four leading taxi owners defected from Majakathata to establish their own association operating out of Soweto. This defection "was in direct contravention of the Majakathata codes of conduct and as such was a punishable offence," and Majakathata responded by hiring a Molapo group based in Germiston to punish the dissidents.[44] The leader of the dissident taxi owners then turned to Tsotsi Raliemere's Matsieng for help. The Marashea first became involved as mercenaries but were quick to seize the opportunity to infiltrate and assume control over taxi associations. With so much at stake, the conflict quickly escalated. Bank describes the outcome: "The warfare that broke out on the Johannesburg line was the most violent encountered in QwaQwa in the mid-1980s. . . . Running gun battles between the gangs were continuous throughout the latter half of 1984, and case studies reflect that dozens of gangsters and taximen were killed during these clashes. Many taximen claimed that their vehicles had been plugged with bullets and that they had witnessed the death of their colleagues on the streets in broad daylight."[45] It was difficult for the taxi owners to control Marashea once they became involved. Some owners felt that the Russians were simply using them for their vehicles and weapons to settle their own disputes and had no interest in the fortunes of the taxi associations. One owner explained, "I think that many of our people are getting tired of working with the *Ma-Rashea* because they are starting to exploit us. Every month they demand something else. Last month it was money to take the bodies of their members to Lesotho for burial. Next month they will be asking for more weapons. . . . I have no quarrel with the *Ma-Rashea*, but this fighting must stop!"[46]

This taxi conflict had particular consequences for the Matsieng Marashea operating out of Phiri. In the mid-1980s this was probably the strongest group on the Rand and it had managed to retain close links with a number of Matsieng groups in mining areas. Informants credit this success to the leadership of Tsotsi Raliemere, a famous and highly respected morena who died during the taxi war. According to both Molapo and Matsieng informants, Tsotsi's group was winning the fight against Germiston Molapo and had killed a number of Molapo members. Desperation and the desire for revenge led the Mo-

lapo to plan Tsotsi's assassination. Tsotsi was a frequent visitor to Turffontein racetrack and his affinity for the races was known to the Molapo group that paid local police to arrest Tsotsi on a trumped-up charge. Rather than resist arrest, Tsotsi simply told his companions to contact his lawyer as he was taken into custody. However, once they left the racetrack, the police drove Tsotsi to a designated location where they turned him over to his Molapo rivals. The Molapo men tortured Tsotsi before dumping his body. TS recounts Tsotsi's death and the resulting revenge attacks.

> Tsotsi died in 1985. He died because of Marashea. He killed many Molapo Marashea during the Majakathata taxi fights that involved people from Germiston, Soweto, QwaQwa, and Welkom. The taxi people were fighting among themselves and those from Germiston used Marashea and those who were attacked also used Marashea and they talked to Tsotsi and gave him money. We fought at QwaQwa, Fouriesburg, Maseru, and Van Rooyen, fighting against those who did not want other taxis to take passengers. After we defeated those people a man called Mokoena hired Marashea to kill Tsotsi. . . . He was captured at the racecourse—he liked the races very much and refused to miss them. When we learned that Tsotsi was arrested we went to different police stations but did not find him, then we went to the hospitals, but that was also in vain. . . . We received a message that Tsotsi's body had been found. His hands had been cut to pieces and he had been thrown in Katlehong cemetery. He had been kidnapped on Saturday—we searched for him on Sunday and Monday but with no success. Tuesday at 11 o'clock we got the message that he was dead. We found his car at the racecourse and it was not damaged. We drove it back and after that we wanted to fight. They tortured him from Saturday to Monday and then killed him. Sanki [a high-ranking member] had not allowed us to act immediately because he thought that Tsotsi had been arrested by the police. . . . But we learned that Molapo was involved, as after discovering about Tsotsi's death we captured one of them called Philate from QwaQwa—he was staying in Orlando. We came back to Phiri with him and he told us where Tsotsi had been captured and killed. Marashea do not go to the police, they kill to avenge their friends. So we avenged Tsotsi's death by killing Focatha, who had been involved in Tsotsi's death. We put him in the car boot and killed him. We went to Germiston, shooting and killing people. We killed Focatha, Lefu, and Lesole. Tsotsi's death hurt us. A woman

escaped from Germiston and told us that there were some old men called Motsoane, Letsekhe, and Nyefolo who had enforced Tsotsi's death. Some had argued for his release but those ones said if they let him go he would come back and kill them. So we chased them and killed them. We buried him, his funeral was very big, as you can see from the photos. There were taxis from Gauteng, Alberton, QwaQwa, Maseru, and Van Rooyen. (18 June)

Without a natural supply of recruits and source of income from the mines, urban Marashea were even more reliant on strong leadership to attract members and hold groups together. Tsotsi's death marked the beginning of the end for the Marashea in Phiri. Although Tsotsi was succeeded by his brother Teboho, the group never recovered from his loss and dwindled to an inconsequential level in the 1990s. KM, like many others, left the group following Tsotsi's death. "I decided to leave because there was no one who could rule Marashea the way he did. He was a good man, everyone in Phiri can tell you about him. After his death everything was stopped and Phiri's Marashea became inactive."

By the late 1980s the Russians on the Reef were struggling. A further factor to consider in their decline is the rise of the militant comrades of the ANC. The ANC established strongholds in many urban townships and conflict between the comrades and different Marashea gangs on the Rand reportedly weakened a number of Russian groups. Respondents stated that when Marashea came under intense pressure from a stronger group of comrades, many members would defect and move to the mining areas where the Marashea was more powerful. It was primarily younger men who left. Older veterans who did not retire to Lesotho generally stayed on the Rand, where they had homes and families. As the Marashea deteriorated these veterans cut their ties to the urban groups, many of which died out. There are still Marashea groups on the Rand, but they lack the power and influence of the mining gangs.

The Russians' long-term presence in mining areas casts light on the complex nature of relationships between outside communities and compound residents. Russian mineworkers and their compatriots in the locations and squatter camps "are one thing; they fall under the same leader" (MR). The relationships between the two sections of each Russian gang have intensified links between compounds, locations and informal settlements. Mineworkers have found their recreation in Marashea settlements on the weekends and have participated in township battles, while unemployed Russians have depended on mineworkers for financial support and often assisted their fellow members

during periods of conflict on the mines. Illegal activities such as smuggling and taxi wars have further strengthened these connections. The Marashea gangs have bound segments of the outside and compound communities together in a network of social, economic, and criminal interactions. The mining industry, with its single-sex hostel system of accommodation, has sustained an association of migrant gangs with a penchant for violence over the past fifty years, a development that has contributed to ethnic chauvinism and the interconnectedness of compound and township communities. The importance of the mines to the Marashea is apparent from the contrasting trajectories of the urban and mining gangs. The decline in the Russian presence on the Rand is directly attributable to the exhaustion of the Reef gold mines, while the emergence of the Free State and far West Rand gold mines was accompanied by a massive influx of Basotho and the establishment of a powerful Marashea presence that endures to this day. Perhaps the greatest challenge to both urban and mining gangs in the 1980s and 1990s was the difficulties associated with the political violence that erupted throughout so much of South Africa. The less powerful urban Marashea were not an important factor in the fighting, but the Russians, the NUM, and the ANC engaged in a protracted struggle for influence in the gold-mining areas. This violence takes the story of the Marashea to the end of the apartheid era.

6 ⤳ Vigilantism, "Political" Violence, and the End of Apartheid

The history of urban violence in South Africa lays bare the fault lines of township societies and demonstrates how the violence both reflected and exacerbated these fissures. Urban African communities were intensely heterogeneous and riven by divisions and tensions. To a large degree, urban violence mirrored the divisions in township communities—youth versus elders, "townsmen" versus "tribesmen," ethnic groups versus outsiders, the desperately poor versus the relatively well-off—all while males preyed on females. Episodes of violence encouraged these antagonisms and further entrenched social cleavages.

Identifiable groups within township communities also interacted with the police and vigilantes according to their position in township society. Employed adults and parents were more likely to support the police and participate in community policing initiatives like Civilian Guards. Indeed, generational tension, even hostility, is a consistent theme in urban violence. Older residents mobilized a variety of vigilante-style organizations to protect their businesses, pay packets, and families, first from the depredations of the youthful tsotsis and later from comtsotsis and overzealous comrades. Much of the fighting that took place during the civil conflicts of the 1980s and 1990s pitted adult males against youths.

That said, none of the divisions discussed above were definitive; township populations were not neatly segregated into compartments defined by ethnicity, generation, class, gender, or any other classification, nor were the interests of different groups always in conflict. Imbricating identities and agendas were as much a feature of township life as were confrontations. While still

highlighting the main lines of conflict, a focus on violence also illustrates the fluid and contingent nature of urban identities.

Any study of the political violence of the 1980s and 1990s must deal with the issue of collaboration. The South African struggle has been cast in stark terms, with ANC supporters in the role of liberation heroes and all black South Africans who came into conflict with them—Inkatha members, various vigilante movements, black local government bodies, criminal gangs, black police and soldiers, and homeland authorities—being classified as sell-outs and collaborators. A more nuanced understanding of the complexities of South African societies during the struggle for liberation requires a reassessment of the roles and motivations of these groups.

THE MARASHEA AND POLITICAL CONFLICT

The Marashea gangs have a long history of being painted as collaborators. As Bonner observed of the 1950s, "For those most active in the ANC and kindred organisations [Marashea] were not only viewed as socially disruptive but also as a politically reactionary force that operated largely at the behest of the police."[1] The police were comfortable with the Russians' political outlook. The gangsters were seen as conservative, "tribal," uneducated Africans untainted by communist propaganda and revolutionary ideals. Most important, the Marashea never campaigned against the government. Police investigations repeatedly judged that the gangs posed no political threat:

> I have the honour to inform you that the gangs known as Japanese and Russians *are not political groups.* (1950)

> There is no reason to believe that [the Marashea] have any grievances against whites or are undermining the state. (1956)

> The alleged "Russians" are in fact law abiding Basutos who strongly opposed the "Stay At Home Campaign." (1960)[2]

Marashea were a logical choice as police clients when the young lions of the ANC took to the streets to protest against the government in the 1980s, and the Russians' image as sellouts was reinforced during the last years of apartheid. The alliances that different gangs struck with the police served them well during episodes of conflict with ANC supporters. They were allowed to pursue criminal activities, were often paid for information, and sometimes were assisted in their battles with comrades. Inspector K's efforts to destabilize the

ANC in the Free State during the 1980s were made much easier by his affiliation with a particular faction of the Marashea. "They knew everything about the ANC. I knew things before they happened." The inspector reported that his association with the Russians ended in 1992 when he was placed under house arrest for his alleged collusion with Marashea in the murders of eight ANC activists (he was not convicted). With such examples it is not difficult to understand why the Marashea has been considered a reactionary force collaborating with the apartheid regime. Discussing recent Marashea involvement in violence with ANC and NUM supporters, Guy and Thabane go so far as to claim that "the Russians have been unable to discriminate effectively between their friends and their enemies."[3]

This assertion reveals a fundamental misunderstanding of the Marashea's quest for survival in South Africa. The Marashea was not a revolutionary movement. Its purpose was not to challenge or overthrow the existing political order but to survive and advance its members' economic interests. To achieve this, the gangs strove to neutralize the police and protect their own spheres of influence from encroachment. The Marashea did not, for the most part, oppose the political objectives of the ANC or the NUM, rather they objected to the methods used to achieve these goals. Many Russian veterans interviewed during the course of this study spoke admiringly of the ANC and its role in ending apartheid, but at the same time they stressed the apolitical nature of the Marashea. "Marashea were not involved in political matters. Comrades were fighting for liberation from oppression and we were concerned with business matters in South Africa" (KI). Marashea-ANC disputes were not ideological. Conflicts occurred when ANC actions threatened specific Russian gangs and possibly when Marashea were hired to disrupt ANC-backed campaigns. For example, it was alleged that Russians were paid to break the rent boycott in Soweto during the late 1980s. The Soweto Council reportedly "discussed a plan to enlist Sotho-blanketed 'Russians' and other vigilantes to help smash the street committees, whom they believe are sustaining the rent crisis."[4]

The Marashea began as a defensive association for migrant Basotho and members depended on the integrity of the group for survival. When ANC supporters threatened that integrity, the Russian gangs often responded with violence. Hostilities tended to be rooted in local, immediate concerns, and resistance to ANC initiatives at the local level should not be conflated with either a rejection of the ideals of the ANC or support for the apartheid state. The ANC did not have the organizational or administrative capacity to effectively control its supporters or those claiming to be acting on its behalf. The actions of some self-styled comrades were brutal and caused much dissension within the townships. Furthermore, the endemic violence and collapse of law-

and-order structures that characterized life in many townships and informal settlements in the 1980s and 1990s encouraged the proliferation of groups that justified blatantly predatory behavior in the name of the struggle: "The youth organisations vary from politically disciplined community defence and security organisations to outright criminal gangs; from comrades to ex-comrades turned criminals and hence called *comtsotsis*. . . . Irrespective of the ideological aspirations which gave birth to them, since the youth and civic structures face similar obstacles in meeting their communities' needs, they remain vulnerable for conversion into warlordism, corruption, criminality and extortion."[5]

It is not my intention to portray Marashea as victims. They were pragmatists and opportunists. They did not allow other African groups to dictate to them and jealously guarded their interests. The Marashea has a long history of mercenary activity and it is entirely possible that some groups were hired to undermine ANC initiatives and assassinate activists. Marashea veterans insist they did not oppose the ANC per se but fought with tsotsis, who called themselves comrades. Russian groups have a long history of antagonism with tsotsis and prided themselves on chasing them from the locations—this was to change in the 1980s. LG, who was Lerashea in the Johannesburg area from 1963 to 1997, noted this change: "Tsotsis were under our control; we beat them but they became stronger after the beginning of politics in South Africa. They were afraid of us because we killed them, but now Marashea are afraid of tsotsis; they are called the comrades and they fight as a group." Some Russian gangs fought with ANC supporters, but on occasion Russians also supported NUM and ANC actions.

The Marashea gangs did not publicly challenge the authority and legitimacy of the state; their resistance was more contingent. They fought with the police to avoid arrest and subverted the law for financial gain. Members of the Marashea had no love for the government, the police, or the whites, for whom they labored in the mines and factories. Tseule Tsilo is a hero partially because he shot three white police officers. SC observed, "White people were happy when we were fighting, as they did not take the deaths of black people seriously." Veterans relish memories of how they outfoxed "the Boers," but these triumphs were tempered by realism. Tsilo shot police as a last resort. He preferred to bribe officials, for this allowed his gang to operate with a minimum of interference. As we have seen, Tsilo's feats are representative of the grand strategies of the Marashea. It would have been counterproductive for the gangs to openly challenge the state. One of the keys to their survival was avoiding antagonizing mine management and the apartheid regime.

Dismissing the Marashea as government puppets obscures rather than illuminates their role in transition-era violence. A close examination of the

protracted fighting between some Russian groups and ANC and NUM supporters in the 1980s and 1990s reveals a more complex reality.

VIGILANTISM

"The term vigilante is itself a source of confusion. In South Africa, the term connotes violent, organised, and conservative groupings operating within black communities. Although these groups receive no official recognition, they are politically directed in the sense that they act to neutralise individuals and groupings that are opposed to the apartheid state and its institutions."[6] Nicholas Haysom also stresses that vigilantes enjoyed varying degrees of police support. Wherever possible the police sponsored and assisted the most powerful groups—political parties, criminal gangs, and business associations—whose interests clashed with ANC supporters. The collusion between state authorities and IFP members has been extensively documented. Another prime example of apartheid era vigilantism is the alliance between state security forces and a group that came to be known as *witdoeke* in the Crossroads area of the Cape Peninsula in the mid-1980s. In this case, an entrenched local elite, threatened by the increasing influence of new organizations aligned with the United Democratic Front (UDF), worked with the state to crush their mutual opponent. In 1986 "an estimated 70,000 squatters . . . became refugees in their own land as hundreds of 'witdoeke' with the uncontested support of members of the security forces declared war on these communities."[7] Such conflicts occurred throughout South Africa in the 1980s and 1990s as the state exploited tensions between ANC affiliates and various groups who opposed the comrades. The state's reliance on powerful local actors helps to explain why the Marashea had a higher profile in politicized violence in mining as opposed to urban areas.

BATTLES ON THE MINES

In the mid-1980s, Marashea groups were faced with the introduction of a powerful new movement on the mines as the NUM struggled to establish a strong presence and force mine management to grant recognition. To my knowledge the Marashea were the single most powerful African organization operating within the mines and mining communities of the Free State and far West Rand. As such they were a natural choice for mine management and police to turn to in the search for local allies. Different groups of Russians engaged in a series of bloody clashes with NUM supporters throughout the second half

of the decade and into the early 1990s. The causes of these conflicts were complex and varied but it is possible to determine some basic patterns. On one level a resident force with an established patron-client network felt threatened by the encroachment of militant unionism. Inspector K rationalizes NUM-Marashea conflict along these lines: "The MaRussians were feeling that [the NUM] wanted to cut them out and then they made a stand—fighting them. And the MaRussians also weren't for any strikes—they didn't stand for that because as soon as the people strike there's no money, and the women they protect wouldn't get any money from the men on the mines. . . . So, most of the time, they didn't agree with strikes on the mines."

The trouble that plagued Harmony Mine in 1990 is a good example of this phenomenon. Mine officials report that the Russians had strong links with the Basotho indunas[8] appointed by mine management. Through their influence with the indunas, the Russians had access to the hostels, where they directed money-lending businesses, recruited members, and intimidated men who defaulted on debts acquired in the shebeens run by Marashea women. The Russians were well-represented among long-term mine employees who had acquired positions of responsibility, particularly team leaders, who invested in Russian shebeens.[9] Many of these men were not in favor of unionism and resisted calls for the strikes and boycotts the NUM depended on to gain recognition. When team leaders and other mine employees refused to align themselves with the union and disregarded NUM-initiated strikes and boycotts, the situation quickly polarized and mineworkers divided into two antagonistic camps. The Marashea were no strangers to collective violence and the NUM was also quick to employ intimidation. The spark igniting a larger conflict was provided by the NUM's call for mine employees to boycott a Russian-owned concession store as well as Russian shebeens, where they claimed a number of their supporters had been assaulted. The story is picked up here by a mine employee who witnessed the events:

> The hostel people, via their union, decided to boycott that [concession store]. Now boycotting that place meant that the women with their little shebeens were not getting income, and if they don't get income, the Marashea bosses don't get income. So one day when the conflict started—because it was already simmering—you had two groups, one resisting the takeover by the union, which was entering their domain of influence. So it was on a Saturday when the announcement was made that nobody should go to the [concession store]. Then this group when they came up from work that afternoon went to that place with sticks ready for fighting because there

had been talk in the hostel that shit would break loose if anybody tried to stop them. So they went there and when they came back, the people who were left in the hostel, largely your comrades, blocked the entrance. . . . the group that was blocked off from the hostel were largely Marashea, reinforced by other Marashea who were not employed on the mine. . . . For the purposes of identification, the comrades on that particular day all took off their shirts, they were bare-chested, they had little doekies [head scarves], and then the other guys had blankets and kerries [knobkerries]. You had quite a bit of confusion inside the hostel, as there were some Marashea left inside who started fighting while the other chaps were outside. Because this was happening on the mine, management called in security, because it was chaos. Here are people who cannot go into the hostel, and there are people who are blocking others. Not understanding what the problem was at the time, because some people were already fighting inside the hostel, the Casspir [mine security vehicle] bulldozed the gate. This group went in . . . and it was fighting all over the show; [both groups] had illegal guns so it was a big battle during the night and several people died. (NT)[10]

The conflict spread to other shafts and some twenty people from both sides were killed in the next few days, some of them executed in front of large crowds of spectators. The fighting spilled over into Meloding Township and surrounding informal settlements and raged until the Marashea were forced out of the area. Marashea members on the mine, and those who had become identified with Marashea during the conflict, were taken to the TEBA depot in Welkom and bused back to Lesotho. A few were relocated on other mines.[11]

At the time, the NUM alleged that mine management hired the Russian gangs to break the union, and mine officials acknowledge that this was a widespread perception of NUM supporters but insist that the union was never able to substantiate this charge.[12] Marashea involved in the fight vehemently deny that they were hired by anyone to participate in the conflict. A member who left Virginia because of the fighting supplies his group's version of the conflict:

The comrades wanted to have control over everybody. Marashea did not start fighting them, they started fighting Marashea. . . . They left the mine compounds to chase Marashea from the squatter camps, where they lived in the farm area. The Marashea resisted this and the fight began. . . . [The comrades] said that Marashea were a thorn in the way of freedom but I did not understand what they meant by

this. . . . They killed everybody who was Marashea who worked on the mines with them. Some were killed underground. (KK)

The leader of a Marashea group that moved into Virginia a couple of years after the previous group had been expelled from the area states, "The ANC comrades were not on good terms with the Marashea because before I came to Virginia some of the Marashea were hired by mine management to fight NUM comrades." He claims, however, to have negotiated a peace treaty with the NUM.[13] Yet another cause of friction between the Marashea group in Virginia and the NUM is provided by a long-term veteran based in Welkom who heard that the morena "allowed his people to rob miners, which caused confusion, and the NUM and the ANC people attacked him and many people were killed" (SO). If there is any truth in this account, the conflict may have been exacerbated by mineworkers who nursed grudges against the Marashea and capitalized on the Russian-NUM rift to gain revenge for previous victimization.

It seems that some Marashea-NUM clashes occurred when Basotho workers resisted NUM intimidation. Moodie deals with this phenomenon in the context of Mpondo mineworkers. Groups of Mpondo were instrumental in breaking the NUM-initiated boycott of liquor outlets at Vaal Reefs no. 1 in 1985, and "for several days thereafter the strikebreakers roamed the compound and skomplas [family housing provided for administrative employees], allegedly in full view of management and accompanied by compound police, attacking shaft stewards."[14] Moodie notes that without exception, the mineworkers he spoke with, even those implicated in attacks on NUM personnel, applauded the merits of a representative democratic presence on the mines that championed workers' interests. Problems erupted when NUM supporters assaulted and intimidated mineworkers who did not observe UDF boycotts outside the mines or who refused to join the union. The violent actions of militant NUM marshals who openly supported the ANC posed a problem for the NUM just as some out-of-control comrades did for the ANC: "the militancy of the comrade element on the compound presented the local union organization with a dilemma. On the one hand, the amaqabane [comrades] disrupted compound life and gave the union a bad name, not only with management but with its more moderate members. On the other hand, they were useful as enforcers of decisions made at union meetings."[15]

The Goldstone Commission's report on the fighting at President Steyn in 1991 concluded that the violence was sparked by "a militant element consisting of certain NUM members [that] was determined to ensure as complete a stay-away as possible and took matters into its own hands."[16] After Basotho who

attempted to go to work were assaulted by this element, the violence escalated and Russians from the compounds and the township became involved. This may also have been the case at Vaal Reefs in 1986. Four Basotho team leaders on no. 5 shaft were killed and a NUM shaft steward was arrested in connection with the murders. The NUM called a three-day stay-away to protest his arrest. Seven Mojakisane, a known Russian who worked as a gang supervisor, refused to comply. He gathered some armed followers and went underground. The strike collapsed shortly thereafter.[17] The Marashea, whose support base on the mine was located among Basotho, many of whom occupied senior positions, could hardly have been expected to comply with an enforced stay-away in support of a man implicated in the murders of Basotho team leaders. Fights at the Bafokeng North Mine (Rustenburg) during 1992, which also drew in the Russians, seem to have started in a similar manner when NUM- and ANC-affiliated marshals attacked Basotho who did not support the union. A number of Basotho were set alight and general fighting followed.[18]

Russians engaged in a series of bloody clashes with NUM members in January 1995 at Vaal Reefs Mine during the Vaal Maseru Bus Company dispute. In support of the Transport and General Workers Union call to strike against Vaal Maseru, NUM members boycotted the bus service from September 1994. Many Basotho mineworkers depended on Vaal Maseru to commute to and from Lesotho and continued to ride the buses. After numerous instances of intimidation from both sides, fighting broke out in late January 1995, resulting in the death of eleven hostel residents and injuries to hundreds of others. Alleged Russian leader Tsepo Anetsi was at the forefront of the conflict on the side of the Basotho.[19]

There is no evidence that all Marashea groups were categorically opposed to the union; some members who worked on the mines belonged to the NUM.[20] Rather, resident gangs reacted when they perceived the NUM as a threat, or they supported Basotho mineworkers who were in conflict with the NUM, or both. On some occasions Russians fought alongside the union. For example, most Basotho working on Leslie Mine, near Evander, were NUM supporters. When fighting broke out between NUM members and Mpondo and Xhosa indunas' followers opposed to the NUM in 1987, local Marashea assisted their fellow Basotho.[21]

It has long been alleged by the NUM that mine management and police hired Russian gangs to attack union supporters and to cause faction fights with the aim of fracturing worker unity. James Motlatsi, president of the NUM, authored a 1995 report on the history of mine violence that laid the blame squarely on management's shoulders: "As we saw in 1986, the main source of violence was the determination of mine managers to crush the

union. Faction fighting became a form of union bashing and we [NUM leadership] produced much evidence to show how mine security forces allied themselves with non-unionists, scabs and those who broke union-initiated boycotts. Sometimes they provided arms for those who opposed the union and, on occasion, paid the 'Russians' to come into the compounds under the protection of security guards to do their dirty work."[22]

Personal testimony is provided by a Mosotho NUM organizer who was instrumental in establishing the union in the mid-1980s. He reports that management, in collusion with the police, approached Russian leaders and negotiated with them to pay individual Russians R500 to attack union officials and instigate faction fights:

> In 1984 during the first strike of the NUM at Vaal Reefs we happened to get three people. There were many running out of the hostel, but three were caught and the shaft stewards took them to my home and we interrogated them. They were told specifically to attack NUM leaders, shaft stewards, and organizers. . . . many were killed.
>
> I still remember one incident whereby one guy was right from my village and he said, "I know you; I have been told to come and kill you—but I didn't know it was you—we were just told to come and kill the leaders of the union." They killed people brutally but nothing ever happened. In the presence of fully armed police you could see Marashea killing people in the hostels.
>
> Some were even killed here in Lesotho. I remember in 1985, a leader of Vaal Reefs was killed in Mohale's Hoek, in his home, by Marashea. And in that gang of Marashea there were even the indunas from Vaal Reefs. (Puseletso Salae, Maseru, 5 June 1998)

A former TEBA official has no doubt that some hostel managers hired thugs to disrupt the union: "Some of these guys were out and out AWB [Afrikaner Resistance Movement], National Party types who believed the black man had to be kept in his place. Obviously they followed an agenda that was possibly different from what the mining house was propounding." However, he states that although these union bashers were typically referred to as Russians, they often had no connection to the Marashea (R. de Boiz). Active Russians interviewed for this study, who were involved in conflicts with the NUM, denied their groups were hired to attack union supporters. Even retired veterans, who spoke openly on such topics as collusion with the police and assassinations and described NUM-Marashea conflicts in detail, denied

they were paid to fight with NUM supporters. Some acknowledged that the police attempted to hire Russian gangs for this purpose, but to no avail: "Black police came to us saying that the Boers wanted us to attack the people who made strikes at the mines, but we would not agree to that" (MM). Other informants said that it was possible that some groups were hired, but none admitted their own participation.

Evidence of collusion between Marashea and mine security was provided to the Goldstone Commission by a taxi driver who transported a group of Marashea from Thabong to President Steyn Mine. Two taxi drivers reported that their kombis were boarded in Thabong by Russians who ordered that they be taken along back roads to Steyn no. 4 shaft. One of the drivers testified that as they passed a Steyn security vehicle a white man next to the vehicle waved them on toward the mine. However, his evidence was contradicted by the other taxi driver, and as a result Goldstone judged that mine security involvement was unsubstantiated.[23] The most damning account comes from Inspector K, who states that at some mines management "hired them to fight the people who were striking, and that's how [Marashea] would get involved."

Moodie's exhaustive study of the violence at Vaal Reefs in 1986 uncovered no end of accusations that mining authorities recruited Russians under the leadership of Mokhemele (Kimberley) to attack union supporters. Although unable to definitively prove these charges, Moodie gives his opinion that "Marashea were definitely hired to stir up trouble for the union at Vaal Reefs." He speculates that "it is possible that Marashea were hired by the Basotho establishment . . . independent of white management . . . but I doubt that hostel managers were unaware of it."[24]

Despite some compelling evidence, there is, to my knowledge, no documented proof that Marashea gangs were hired to attack union supporters. However, it requires no great stretch of imagination to envision members of management and security approving of such conflict and assisting the Russians in various ways—especially when they were acting as strikebreakers. As OB observed, "Marashea did not want their money to be deducted [for union dues], and Marashea helped the mine management to fight NUM." On mines where management was particularly antagonistic to the NUM, it is difficult to believe that at least some mining officials did not instigate and encourage violence against the union.[25] This does not necessarily mean that money changed hands, although, as long as most Basotho on the mine were opposed to the NUM, Marashea would probably have happily accepted payment to attack union supporters.

It is also important to acknowledge that the violent reputation of the Marashea made them convenient scapegoats for NUM officials eager to disavow

any responsibility for mine conflicts. This was the conclusion reached by an inquiry into fighting at Vaal Reefs in 1986. Russian elements were involved in breaking a NUM-initiated strike after some Basotho were killed, but the report found that these men acted on their own accord, not at the behest of management. As for NUM allegations that the Marashea were mercenaries, the report disagreed with Moodie's conclusions: "There was no evidence of this. If anything, on the evidence tendered at the enquiry, these were rumours emanating from and spread by the shaft stewards."[26] The NUM also blamed the violence at Bafokeng North Mine on tension between Tswana dagga sellers and Russians who undercut the Tswana by offering their product at a reduced price. The NUM presented this explanation despite the evidence of a number of witnesses who claimed the fighting began as a result of union marshals intimidating and assaulting those (specifically Basotho) who refused to support the NUM.[27]

One cannot overestimate the value of Basotho mineworkers to the Russian gangs. Had the majority of Basotho been in favor of the NUM, it is unlikely that the Russians would have opposed the union. Indeed, they sometimes fought in support of the NUM under these circumstances. Kent McNamara has pointed out that in the first phase of unionization (1982–85), Basotho were the chief source of union membership. "The Lesotho citizens appeared to be particularly keen to join the union to safeguard their future job security, being well aware of the shift in labour recruitment to South African workers after the 1974 clashes and the 1975 deferred pay dispute."[28] Conditions changed in 1986 when the new government in Lesotho, following South African instructions, urged its citizens to desist from active participation in the NUM. At the same time, the South African government announced its intention to repatriate foreign workers and the gold mines experienced a record wave of strikes.[29] Discouraged by their government and worried they would be retrenched for engaging in strike action, many Basotho withdrew their support from the NUM and clashed with NUM supporters.

Whatever their relationship in the past, now that the union is solidly established, NUM-Russian relations have greatly improved. KK, who left Virginia in the wake of the conflicts with the NUM and is currently a member of a group situated near Klerksdorp, testified, "We are now good friends with NUM members. The NUM protects workers who are our customers. When we have a problem with the workers we report them to the NUM officials at the mine. They also report to us if some of us have wronged their members." In true Russian fashion, the Marashea have also managed to stay in the good graces of mine management. KK paints a rosy picture of current management-Russian relations: "These days we have a good relationship. If we want to hire

a mine hall to stage our dances, they allow us. We have a musical band that holds concerts in the mine hall. We also hold other activities in the mine hall—the mine management has no problem with us." There are, however, still opportunities for Russian gangs to engage in violence on the mines. In 1999 a number of Russians accused of attacking subcontracted employees at Buffelsfontein Mine were acquitted for lack of evidence.[30] In this particular case, the violence was perpetrated against a group that is widely resented by NUM members. Union employees complain that subcontracted miners, who routinely accept dangerous conditions and poorer wages and benefits, undermine the NUM's bargaining position.[31]

THE MARASHEA AND THE COMRADES

I can find no record of Russian conflict with ANC-aligned forces from the beginning of the 1960s until the 1980s, when different Marashea groups clashed with ANC supporters on the Rand and throughout the gold-mining areas. This peaceful interlude can probably be explained by the quiescence of the ANC after it was banned in 1960. Only in the 1980s did its allies and affiliates reassert the presence of the ANC within South Africa through the auspices of the UDF and the NUM.

In mining areas, the line between the NUM and the ANC was difficult to distinguish for many Russians who categorized both as comrades: "NUM was organized by the ANC and we regarded them as the ANC, so we sometimes fought with them—they were our enemies" (GB). There was a great deal of fighting in some of the squatter camps and townships adjacent to the mines. Marashea testimony indicates that the clashes occurred as the ANC attempted to displace the Russians as the foremost authority in the camps:

> I took part in one event that was a fight between us and the ANC youth comrades. They claimed that the area where we had our squatter camp belonged to them. Two Marashea were killed in that fight. . . . There were great conflicts between the Marashea and the ANC. In the 1990s there is no group that is fighting Marashea except the ANC comrades. . . . They fight with Marashea over territory and in many instances they think the rules of Marashea are very oppressive to the people under them. (KB)

Inspector K confirmed that the disputes were essentially a struggle between an established force and a new group seeking to assert its presence:

There was tension. The ANC didn't recognize any other groups. . . .
They undermined the authority of the MaRussians and that led to
fights.

QUESTION: How did they undermine the Russians?

By talking to the youth, saying that the MaRussians haven't got the
right to take money. For instance, they collected money for burials.
The ANC went to the people and said, "You can't give your money
to them, they're not an authority."

Comtsotsis may well have exacerbated tension between Marashea groups
and ANC supporters. GB's description of the following conflict is consistent
with the Marashea's campaigns to eliminate tsotsis: "In 1989 I left Welkom
and went to Westonaria [far West Rand], and when I arrived there was a fight
between Marashea and the ANC youth. The cause of that trouble was that we
[the Marashea] stopped them from robbing Marashea and other people.
They robbed miners and we were not happy with that, and the fight lasted
about two months. We would not allow them to disturb miners because miners were our customers at our stokvels and dances."

Violence on the Rand between Russians and ANC supporters paled in
comparison to the fighting that took place between Inkatha members and the
comrades. And in contrast to the mining areas, there is no evidence that the
Marashea on the Rand received any significant police support in the 1980s
and 1990s. The lack of a Marashea-police alliance may reflect the decline in
power of the urban Russians since the 1950s. Inkatha had a much more formidable presence on the Rand at this time, and the preexisting Inkatha-ANC
dispute carried over from KwaZulu-Natal made Inkatha the logical choice for
security-force sponsorship. Despite a mutual enemy, the Russian gangs that
fought with the comrades did not forge a common front with Inkatha supporters. Such cooperation failed to materialize because of the ethnic exclusivity of both groups, the history of fighting between different Marashea and
Zulu gangs on the Rand, and the geographical separation between Inkatha
hostel dwellers and Marashea township residents. In fact, some respondents
reported that they fought with their communities against Inkatha. "We stood
with the ANC when they were attacked by the Zulus. We would throw them
out the windows of the trains" (PK).

In the urban townships of Soweto there seems to have been a definite generational character to the fighting between Russians and comrades. Russian
informants consistently stated that they objected to the behavior of the young
"tsotsis," who claimed to represent the ANC. Certainly this dynamic appears

to have been present in much of the "political" violence that occurred on the Rand and in the rest of the country. According to Campbell's research in Natal, "Part of the comrades' self definition has been to distinguish themselves sharply from what they regard as the backward older generation. 'The older generation only know about ancient times and ancient things,' Colin N (23 years) argued. 'The youth must correct all the mistakes they have made.'" Campbell suggests that Inkatha supporters were not exclusively anti-ANC, "but also [were determined] to put down the cheeky upstart youth who dared to think they could challenge the power of older men."[32] Elders held respected positions within Russian groups as advisors, and while membership encompassed all ages, from youth just out of initiation school to pensioners, positions of responsibility tended to be in the hands of seasoned veterans. Russians in the urban townships had a long history of animosity with the youthful tsotsi gangs and often took it upon themselves to discipline wayward youths in the locations. Such men were not likely to accept being dictated to by the street committees and people's courts set up by ANC youth in the 1980s. These structures were formed to arbitrate disputes and dispense justice to township residents, actions that effectively undermined the authority of the Marashea. In many instances this resulted in older people being beaten by the comrades.

TS, a Matsieng commander in Phiri in the 1980s, explained how the Russians became involved in fights with the comrades:

> Marashea did not fight with the ANC, but what I can explain is that the young comrades were silly. It would happen that when I quarrel with my wife and beat her she would go to the street committee, who would call the children, who would beat me. [Marashea and comrades] quarreled about that. . . . [Marashea] told them they must stop involving politics in family matters. . . .
>
> In 1986 a man whipped his wife and the wife ran away and reported to the street committee. Instead of settling the problems of that family [the comrades] beat the man. We disagreed and we fought with them. They burnt the house we used for dances and Lerashea called Malefetsane was inside and he was crippled. For that we killed many of the street committee. . . . The parents and elders came to sit down and settle the problem. We told them we are not against the ANC comrades but we hate a child who runs his father's family.

TS is at pains to establish that the Russians had no argument with the ANC as an organization but refused to accept the authority of its youthful members, especially in what they considered the private sphere. Just as with the NUM,

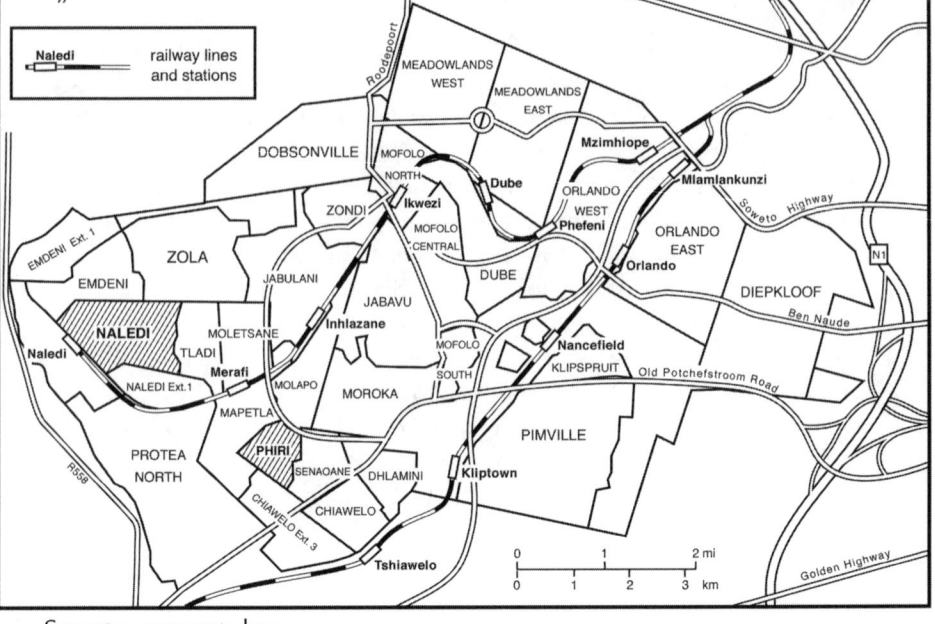

Soweto, present day

some Russians belonged to the ANC and proudly displayed their membership cards.

Another episode that received attention was Marashea resistance to the comrades' Christmas against Emergency campaign. ANC-supporting youth in many areas of Soweto attempted to enforce a blackout as a sign of solidarity with political detainees during the holiday period in 1986. In Phiri, the Johannesburg headquarters of the Matsieng faction, trouble began when residents refused the calls to turn off their lights. Youths allegedly attacked a house, setting it alight, and the Russians responded with a vengeance: "The skirmishes carried on until the early hours of the morning. Sources said that after the assault the 'Russians' went on a revenge mission, attacking and assaulting youths in the area. They said the 'Russians' launched house-to-house raids, flogging and assaulting youths who were found in homes."[33] A reported ten people were killed before the Soweto Civic Association brokered a truce.[34] Russian veterans did not view this as an ideological dispute but as an attempt to encroach on their territory. Phiri was one of the few areas left on the Rand that was controlled by the Russians and they were determined not to relinquish their authority to the comrades without a fight.

This snapshot of the Russians' interactions with the police, mining authorities, the ANC and the NUM will hopefully contribute to a body of literature

that is beginning to reveal the labyrinthine nature of transition era violence. The liberation struggle provided the backdrop against which an almost infinite number of more localized and intimate conflicts played out. The Russians' involvement in this violence illustrates the situational nature of both "collaboration" and "resistance" and therefore the limited value of these labels. Operating within this framework, how does one characterize the conflicts within the ANC, such as the bloody feuds that took place in Sharpeville and elsewhere between the self-defense units, composed mainly of ANC Youth League members, and the Umkhonto we Sizwe veterans who returned from exile in the early 1990s?[35] The Marashea's decisions to fight or assist the police and support, oppose, or ignore the ANC and its affiliates were based on each group's best interest in terms of survival and economic gain. Without an examination of specific local incidents of conflict, our understanding of this violent decade and its aftermath will remain woefully inadequate.

Epilogue ⤚ The Future of the Marashea

THE MARASHEA'S HISTORY DEPICTS the struggles of a criminally inclined migrant society to survive during the apartheid era. The gangs have been flexible and pragmatic and have adapted well to changing conditions in South Africa. Formed as a defensive association for migrant Basotho, the gangs developed into a fighting society that became notorious for its factional battles as well as conflicts with other adversaries across the length and breadth of the Rand. The expansion into the Free State and other mining areas, in response to South African legislation, police persecution, and economic opportunities, saw the Marashea assume a more commercial nature. The contemporary Marashea are markedly different from their predecessors of the 1940s and 1950s. The ritualistic battles involving hundreds of blanket-clad combatants wielding fighting sticks have given way to hit-and-run taxi raids by smaller groups of gun-toting Marashea. The fights of the formative years were principally about control of urban space and prestige, while modern disputes are often rooted in economic rivalries. The majority of first-generation Marashea were mine or factory workers who saw Borashea as a protective association for Basotho and an escape from the tedium of urban labor. These members expected no economic return but looked to the Marashea for access to women, a sense of social belonging, and recreation in the form of dances and fights with rival groups. Their successors have taken a more materialist attitude, and unemployed members rely on group activities for financial gain.

The early Marashea employed fighting skills learned in their youth and established an urban network of affiliated groups that replicated regional alliances in Lesotho. The distinctive blankets, which served as uniforms, along

with a common language, dances, songs, and other social customs, reflected the gangs' Sesotho heritage. At the same time, members developed specific practices that distinguished them from other migrant Basotho. Marashea relied heavily on traditional doctors and medicines to fortify them for battle and courtroom encounters. Such "traditional" practices and beliefs were married with new tactics—using firearms,[1] enforcing large-scale protection rackets, establishing control over migrant women, cultivating a market among mineworkers, manipulating the judicial system, managing relations with the police and mining authorities, and exploiting the political climate. This syncretic approach has served the society well over the years.

The lived experiences of successive generations of Marashea demonstrate some of the ways African groups adapted to the structural restrictions of apartheid policies and, to a certain degree, operated independently of white control. Marashea members were resigned to the reality of white rule and did not regard their society as a vehicle for political change in South Africa. Russian gangs' relations with the state and African nationalist movements were predicated on the protection of group interests, not on larger ideological or political concerns. Resistance and collaboration are important elements of modern South African social history; however, a focus on the myriad ways in which black South Africans managed their lives transcends the constrictive boundaries of struggle history and illuminates the complex range of strategies and relationships that emerged under apartheid.

In the townships and informal settlements of the gold-mining areas of South Africa and the villages of Lesotho, the Marashea are associated with violence. Ethnic solidarity and animus, gender dominance, generational disputes, political rivalries, competition over material resources and territory, and sheer acquisitive criminality all played a role in Russian violence. The Marashea's involvement in various types of violence over the past fifty years underscores the historical roots of the crisis in contemporary South Africa. Any attempts to address the current situation would do well to take account of the history of violence, crime, and policing.

The Marashea faces a precarious future. Clashes with NUM and ANC supporters have ended, but the gangs still engage in activities that bring them into conflict with the police and criminal rivals. And, while bribery remains an effective way of dealing with the police, the Marashea can no longer rely on political hostilities to gain the support of government security forces. When asked about the Russians' future, WL replied, "Marashea will survive as long as there are mines in South Africa, as long as there are women on the farms surrounding the mines." However, the South African mining industry is

in the midst of a long-standing economic crisis. The most immediate threats to the gangs are the massive retrenchment of Basotho mineworkers combined with reduced opportunities for novices.[2] The contraction of the mining industry seems to be having a differential impact on the Marashea. Some groups have been reduced: "There is no more money . . . so Marashea are becoming less now. . . . The source of money is blocked because of retrenchments" (RC). Other gangs report that their ranks are swelling as retrenched miners join rather than face almost certain unemployment in Lesotho (MK, WL).[3] Moreover, until the late 1980s, young Basotho men fresh from initiation school, with little or no formal education, typically began their working lives on South African mines. Now that option has been largely closed off and as a result "many of them come straight here to join us. Especially after initiation they flock to Marashea because there are no jobs in Lesotho or on the mines, where people used to get jobs so easily without educational requirements" (BM).

These conditions have created a number of problems for the Marashea. Some gangs may simply disband as their membership decreases. However, current members have few alternatives if they leave the Marashea. Employment prospects in Lesotho are abysmal. Most Marashea not employed on the mines are in South Africa illegally and the few who have obtained residence permits lack marketable skills. The primary options available to Basotho migrants are piecework and seasonal agricultural labor. Neither offers any security and both pay extremely poorly. And, despite low wages, difficult working conditions, and insecurity, there is a great deal of competition for these jobs. Additionally, the South African government is threatening to close the agricultural sector to citizens of Lesotho.[4]

The groups that are growing have to deal with a dwindling resource base at the same time as they are absorbing an unprecedented influx of new recruits. The ongoing process of retrenchment is eroding the financial foundation of the Marashea. Not only do miners purchase liquor and commercial sex in Marashea settlements, they are the primary customers for the entire range of products offered by Russian hawkers. The long-distance taxi associations and gold- and diamond-smuggling operations run by the Marashea are also largely dependent on mineworkers. The mining industry still employs approximately sixty thousand Basotho, but if this core of Marashea support continues to shrink, many gangs will have to make further adjustments. Three immediate possibilities come to mind. Some groups may increase their involvement in blatantly criminal activities such as extortion schemes, robbery, assassinations, taxi violence, and drug peddling. This reorientation would probably involve an expansion in urban centers and result in conflict with resident criminal organizations. Second, competition between Russian factions struggling to

control the remaining markets may cause a resurgence in internecine fighting. A third possibility is that township gangs in particular will expand their "protection" services and assume more of a vigilante or hired security function (or both). In response to rising crime rates and police ineffectiveness, vigilante movements have proliferated in recent years. Different Russian gangs have sought popular support by persecuting tsotsis in the past, and in desperate economic circumstances they may try to make such activities more remunerative, perhaps by offering their services to businesses. With their solid base and fearsome reputation in a number of townships, this seems like a natural niche for the Marashea to explore. All three scenarios raise the prospect of heightened levels of violence.

The final critical factor is the HIV/AIDS pandemic. The Marashea's primary source of income is derived from mineworkers who are attracted to Russian settlements by resident women, many of whom engage in sex work and are at particularly high risk of contracting HIV.[5] Many mineworkers refuse to use condoms and insist on the need for "flesh-to-flesh" contact.[6] Given the dependence on miners' patronage and the masculine identity that infuses Marashea, this situation is unlikely to change. Interviews conducted in 1998 with sex workers in an informal settlement located on the boundary of a Carletonville area gold mine revealed that while knowledge of HIV transmission was high, "no one used condoms. In conditions of poverty, and in the context of male-dominated social structures, women felt powerless to insist that reluctant male clients used condoms." Fierce competition for clients also reduced the likelihood that sex workers would insist on condom use, as clients would simply take their business to a more compliant woman.[7] Anecdotal evidence from Lesotho suggests that many Marashea women are coming home to die after contracting AIDS in South Africa. As the epidemic increases, the possibility exists that the commercial sex industry servicing the mines will decline, a development that could cause significant difficulties for the Russian gangs. Not only would this affect their economic base but recruiting could also suffer as fewer miners visited the camps. How the ravages of AIDS will affect the Marashea remains to be seen.

The Marashea has survived since its formation in 1947 in large part because of its ability to adapt to changing conditions during the apartheid era. Since the end of apartheid, the Russian gangs have been forced to deal with a new assortment of challenges, including the loss of state patronage, the contraction of the gold-mining industry so critical to the gangs' financial welfare, and the emergence of the AIDS epidemic, which threatens the lucrative commercial sex industry. The manner in which the gangs confront this latest set of obstacles will determine the Marashea's future.

Appendix

Marashea Interview List

Key

Initials: date and place of birth; duration and location(s) of term(s) as Lerashea; faction affiliation(s); occupation(s); highest rank within the group (location and date of interview[s]).

Male Informants

AT: 1940s, Lesotho; 1977–88, Kloof, then Kinross; Matsieng at Kloof, Molapo in Kinross; miner; regular member (Lesotho, 15 May 1998).

BF: unknown, Lesotho; 1950s, Brakpan; Molapo; miner; regular member (Lesotho, 8 August 1998).

BH: 1920s, Lesotho; 1951–69, Benoni and Springs; Matsieng, then Molapo; worked in bicycle factory in Springs; morena's assistant (Kwa Thema, 9 February 1999).

BK: 1920, Lesotho; 1947–49, Primrose; miner, factory worker; whistle blower (Naledi, 27 January 1999).

BM: 1947, Lesotho; 1968–present, Buffelsfontein and Virginia; when Matsieng and Molapo split, he went with Matsieng; miner, but left to become full-time Lerashea, became morena in 1976 (Virginia, 24 October 1998).

BS: 1954, Lesotho; 1981–96; Welkom, Matsekha; miner at President Steyn; morena's assistant (Lesotho, 8 August 1998).

BT: 1930s, Lesotho; 1950s–70s, Newclare and Phiri; Matsieng; miner, factory worker; regular member (Phiri, 16 December 1998).

CM: 1936, Lesotho; 1955–1970s, Welkom; Matsieng; miner at President Steyn Mine, then full-time Lerashea; whistle blower (Lesotho, 20 September 1998).

CN: 1943, Lesotho; 1973–present, Virginia and Klerksdorp; Matsieng; winch driver at Harmony, left mine in 1976 to become full-time Lerashea; whistle blower, then assistant to BM (Vaal Reefs, 23 October 1998).

DB: unknown, Lesotho; 1950s–60s, Newclare and Phiri; Matsieng; miner; regular member (Phiri, 16 December 1998).

DG: unknown, Lesotho; 1970–1990s, Buffelsfontein; Matsieng; miner; whistle blower, morena's assistant (Lesotho, 26 November 1998).

DS: unknown, Lesotho; 1968–92, Gauteng, then Welkom; Matsieng; miner at St. Helena; regular member (Lesotho, 25 November 1998).

GB: 1958, Lesotho; 1978–92, Welkom; Matsieng; miner at Geduld, then Rustenburg; whistle blower (Lesotho, 26 November 1998).

GK: 1947, Lesotho; 1977–79, Phiri; Matsieng; miner at East Driefontein; regular member (Lesotho, June 1998).

GL: 1944, Lesotho; 1964–86, Kliptown; Matsekha; miner at Western Deep Levels until 1981, then worked construction; whistle blower (Eldorado Park, 24 January 1999).

HG: unknown, Lesotho; 1961–70, Kloof and Robertson, near Crown Mines, jailed 1970–88; Matsieng; regular member (Phiri, 18 June 1998).

HL: 1934, Lesotho; 1950s–60s, Germiston and Carletonville; Matsieng; miner; regular member (Naledi, 18 December 1998).

HM: 1933, Lesotho; 1950s–early 1960s, Booysens; Matsieng; miner, then railway worker; regular member (Lesotho, 22 August 1998).

HS: 1922, Matatiele (KwaZulu-Natal, on Lesotho's southern border); 1940s–50s, Primrose; Matsieng; construction worker; regular member (Eldorado Park, January 1999).

KB: 1955, Lesotho; 1993–94, Klerksdorp; Matsekha; miner at Buffelsfontein; regular member (Lesotho, June 1998).

KF: 1955, Lesotho; 1976–89, Thabong; Matsekha; full-time Lerashea; accordion player (Lesotho, 25 November 1998).

KI: 1954, Lesotho; 1975–85, Thabong; Molapo; miner at President Brand Mine; literate, so acted as secretary (Lesotho, 16 December 1998).

KK: unknown, Lesotho; early 1960s–present, Virginia and Klerksdorp; Matsieng; miner for a few years, then full-time Lerashea; second in command to BM (Lesotho, 8 August 1998).

KL: unknown, Lesotho; 1950s–1961, Benoni and Newclare; Matsekha; factory worker; regular member (Lesotho, July 1998).

KM: 1918, Lesotho; 1940s–80s, Benoni and Alexandra; Matsieng; miner, factory worker; advisor to Tsotsi Raliemere (Naledi, 27 January 1999).

KP: 1933, Lesotho; 1950s, Newclare; Matsieng; miner at Rand Leases; whistle blower (Lesotho, 9 August 1998).

LG: 1933, Lesotho; 1963–97, Phiri; Matsieng; full-time Lerashea; whistle blower (Eldorado Park, 7 February 1999).

LT: 1939, Lesotho; 1959–84, Vereeniging; Matsekha; miner, then full-time Lerashea; regular member (Lesotho, July 1998).

MB: unknown, Johannesburg, but grew up in Lesotho; 1969–93, Crown Mines, then Odendaalsrus and Virginia; Matsekha; morena (Lesotho, July 1998).

MC: unknown, Lesotho; 1949–54, Newclare and Boksburg; Matsieng; regular member (Lesotho, 30 May 1998).

MK: 1933, Lesotho; 1948–1960s, Benoni, Klerksdorp, and Carletonville; Matsieng; miner, factory worker, then full-time Lerashea, morena (Lesotho, 8 August 1998).

ML: unknown, Lesotho; 1976–present, Orlando; Matsekha; miner and piece-work; whistle blower (Lesotho, 19 May 1998).

MM: unknown, Lesotho; 1970s–present, Theunissen and Virginia; Matsieng; miner, diamond dealer; regular member (Lesotho, 20 June 1998).

MR: 1928, Lesotho; 1953–56, Jabavu; Matsieng; piecework; regular member (Lesotho, 6 July 1998).

MS: 1918, Lesotho; 1950s, Benoni and Newclare; Matsekha; factory worker; regular member (Lesotho, August 1998).

MT: unknown, Lesotho; 1960s–1990, Vaal Reefs; Matsieng; miner, then full-time Lerashea; morena (Eldorado Park, 24 January 1999).

NN: 1933, Lesotho; 1952–73, Klerksdorp, Welkom, and Rustenburg; Matsekha; miner; whistle blower (Lesotho, 13 and 20 May 1998).

NT: 1928, Brandis, Free State; 1951–1960s, Pimville and Phiri; Molapo, then Matsieng; worked at Cleveland Engineering in Roodeport; regular member (Naledi, 14 December 1998).

OB: 1933, Lesotho; 1950–95, Vaal Reefs; Matsieng; miner; regular member (Lesotho, 4 February 1999).

OE: 1957, Lesotho; 1982–88, Virginia; Matsieng; miner at Harmony Mine; regular member (Lesotho, 13 September 1998).

OF: 1932, Lesotho; 1950s, Welkom; Matsieng; miner; regular member (Lesotho, 12 September 1998).

OU: unknown, Lesotho; 1940s–50s, Newclare; Matsieng; miner; regular member (Phiri, 16 December 1998).

PG1: 1929, Lesotho; 1950–53, Toronga; Molapo; worked at Johannesburg general post office; liaison with lawyers (Naledi, 20 December 1998, in English).

PG2: 1940, Lesotho; 1955–91, Daveyton and Vereeniging; Matsieng; coal miner; morena (Lesotho, 12 September 1998).

PL: 1934, Lesotho; late 1950s–60s, Booysens; Matsieng; morena (Lesotho, 23–24 May 1998; Welkom, 21 May 1999).

PM: 1916, Lesotho; 1940s–70s, Soweto; Molapo; miner at Crown Mines, then factory worker; regular member (Phiri, 11 December 1998).

PP: unknown, Lesotho; late 1940s–1950s, Jabavu; Matsieng; piecework; regular member (Lesotho, 24 May 1998).

RC: unknown, Lesotho; 1975–98, Virginia and Welkom; Molapo and Matsieng; full-time Lerashea; morena (Welkom, 20 May 1999).

RR: unknown, Lesotho; 1958–70, Springs, then Bloemfontein; Matsieng; miner, railway worker; regular member (Lesotho, 30 August 1998).

SC: 1934, Lesotho; 1953–59, Springs; Matsieng, then defected to Molapo; miner; whistle blower (Lesotho, 22 April 1998, in English; Lesotho, 7 June 1998).

SF: 1922, Lesotho; 1950–55, Newclare; Matsieng; worked at Crown Mines; regular member (Lesotho, 30 August 1998).

SG: 1928, Lesotho; 1950s, Newclare; Molapo; miner; regular member (Orange Farm, 15 January 1999).

SI: 1939, Lesotho; 1959–80, Evaton and Soweto; Molapo; started in mines, then piecework; regular member (Lesotho, 20 September 1998).

SM: 1920, Lesotho; late 1940s–1950s, Springs; Matsieng; miner; regular member (Lesotho, 29 August 1998).

SO: 1953, Lesotho; 1972–90, Roodeport; Matsieng, then Matsekha; miner; regular member (Lesotho, 13 September 1998).

ST: 1918, Lesotho; 1950s–60s, Newclare and Orlando; Matsieng; miner, factory worker; regular member (Lesotho, 23 August 1998).

TB: 1939, Lesotho; 1960–65, Carletonville; Matsieng; miner at Libanon mine; assistant to Tsuele Tsilo (Lesotho, 6 September 1998).

TC: unknown, Lesotho; 1970–present, Buffelsfontein and Vaal Reefs; Matsieng; miner, then full-time Lerashea; assistant to BM (Vaal Reefs, 30 January 1999).

TG: unknown, Lesotho; 1955–61, Newclare and Phiri; railway worker; regular member (Lesotho, 6 September 1998).

TS: 1954, Bloemfontein, but grew up in Lesotho; 1973–1980s, Carletonville and Phiri; Matsieng; miner; morena's assistant (Phiri, Soweto, 18 June 1998, 22 December 1998).

TT: 1914, Lesotho; late 1940s–1953, Benoni and Newclare; Matsieng; tailor; regular member (Naledi, Soweto, 18 June 1998).

WH: unknown, Lesotho; 1950s–60s, Phiri; Matsieng; miner at Rand Leases; left mine to become PL's assistant (Mapetla, 10 February 1999).

WL: 1930s, Lesotho; 1960s–mid-1980s, Phiri, then Virginia and Odendaalsrus; Matsieng; factory worker, then miner; morena (Lesotho, 8 August 1998).

Female Informants

In notes and text, female informants are identified with the title 'Mè (e.g., 'Mè KW).

EW: 1952, Orlando; 1979–90, Phiri; Matsieng; worked in factories as hawker, sold joala (Mapetla, 20 December 1998).

FD: 1939, Lesotho; 1972–present, Buffelsfontein and Vaal Reefs; Matsieng; sells joala (Vaal Reefs, 30 January 1999).

FH: 1943, Jabavu, but brought up and schooled in Lesotho; 1968–mid-1990s, Phiri; Matsieng; domestic worker (Phiri, 21 December 1998)

ID: 1959, Lesotho; 1985–93, Khutsong, Kloof, and Bekkersdal; Matsieng; sold joala (Lesotho, 29 December 1998).

KW: 1970, Lesotho; kidnapped by Matsieng in Carletonville in 1991, escaped in 1992; sold joala (Lesotho, 18 December 1998).

LW: 1969, Lesotho; kidnapped by Matsieng in Phiri in 1992, returned to Lesotho in 1993 (Lesotho, 15 January 1999).

MD: 1960, Mapetla; 1979–88, Phiri; Matsieng; factory worker (Pimville, 22 December 1998).

MG: 1925, Lesotho; 1951–73, Orlando; Matsieng; sold joala (Phiri, 21 December 1998).

OW: 1918, Lesotho; 1940s–50s, Springs; Matsieng; sold joala (Lesotho, 7 January 1999).

RB: unknown, Lesotho; 1980s, Thabong; Matsekha; sold joala (Lesotho, 25 November 1998).

RW: 1958, Mapetla (Soweto), but schooled in Lesotho; 1977–86, Phiri; Matsieng; domestic worker (Mapetla, 18 December 1998).

SL: 1959, Phiri, Xhosa, but grew up in Lesotho; 1970s–1986, Phiri; Matsieng (Phiri, 20 December 1998).

SP: 1956, Moroka; 1970s–1990, Phiri; Matsieng; worked in factories, domestic worker (Phiri, 21 December 1998).

TF: 1952, Lesotho; 1970s–1992, Welkom and Odendaalsrus; Molapo, Matsieng; sold joala (Lesotho, 20 September 1998).

TW: 1960, Phiri, but grew up in Lesotho; 1975–1980s, Phiri; Matsieng; (Phiri, 18 December 1998).

XL: 1952, Phiri, Xhosa, but married to a Mosotho; 1971–85; Phiri; Matsieng; factory worker (Phiri, 19 December 1998).

Notes

PREFACE

1. Marashea is the term for the group, Lerashea is a single member, and Borashea refers to the phenomenon of Marashea and might best be interpreted as Russianism. A number of the founding members of Marashea served with the British military in the Second World War and had heard that the Russians were formidable fighters.

2. The Rand (from Witwatersrand) or the Reef refers to the belt of urban settlement that runs some one hundred kilometers from east to west and has Johannesburg at its center. It has long been South Africa's mining and industrial heartland.

3. Basotho are natives of Lesotho, a small country completely surrounded by South Africa. Mosotho is the term for an individual of that country, and Sesotho is the language and culture.

4. See the appendix for interview dates and locations, as well as some biographical data. Informants are identified in text by their initials only.

5. Guttenplan, "Holocaust on Trial," 62.

6. Thomson, "Anzac Memories," 300–301.

7. Bonner, "Russians," 188.

8. Portelli, "What Makes Oral History Different," 67.

9. Blee, "Evidence, Empathy and Ethics," 335.

10. Mineworkers, mining officials, and numerous retired Marashea reported that BM's group battled with union supporters.

CHAPTER 1

1. For example, more than twenty thousand murders were recorded in South Africa in 2000. Nearly sixteen hundred police officers were murdered between 1994 and 2000, and reports indicate that South Africa trails only Russia and Colombia when it comes to the prevalence of organized crime. South African Police Services Official Website, http://www.saps.org.za; *Servamus*, October 2000; *Mail and Guardian*, 13 February 1998.

2. Many of the township residents interviewed for this study, as well as the media, make this linkage. For academic analyses see Taylor, "Justice Denied"; Wilson, *The Politics of Truth and Reconciliation in South Africa*; Segal, Pelo, and Rampa, "Into the Heart of Darkness"; Simpson, "Shock Troops and Bandits."

3. Van Onselen, *New Nineveh.*

4. Van Onselen, *New Babylon.*

5. For migrant and mining gangs see Van Onselen, *New Nineveh*; Breckenridge, "Migrancy, Crime and Faction Fighting"; Bonner, "Russians"; Guy and Thabane, "The Ma-Rashea"; Kynoch, "Marashea on the Mines."

6. Van Onselen, *New Nineveh*, 195.

7. La Hausse, "The Cows of Nongoloza," 108.

8. Breckenridge, "Migrancy," 63.

9. *Bantu World*, 22 June 1953.

10. Glaser, "The Mark of Zorro," 47.

11. Pinnock, "Stone's Boys and the Making of a Cape Flats Mafia," 427.

12. For a discussion of the different tsotsi gangs, see Glaser, *Bo-Tsotsi.*

13. A chilling glimpse into the world of the latest generation of young urban criminals is provided by Segal, Pelo, and Rampa, "Heart of Darkness." For a historical overview of South African gangs, see Kynoch, "Ninevites."

14. Van Onselen, *New Nineveh*, 55.

15. Brewer, *Black and Blue*, 200.

16. Glaser, "Zorro," 59.

17. See Kynoch, "Friend or Foe?"

18. Bonner and Segal, *Soweto*, 138.

19. See, for example, Adam and Moodley, "Political Violence, 'Tribalism,' and Inkatha"; Ellis, "The Historical Significance of South Africa's Third Force"; Jeffrey, *The Natal Story*; Marks, *Young Warriors*; Minaar, ed., *Patterns of Violence*; Morris and Hindson, "South Africa"; Segal, "The Human Face of Violence"; Sitas, "The New Tribalism."

20. Two notable exceptions include Pinnock, *The Brotherhoods*; and Glaser, *Bo-Tsotsi.*

21. A survey of the literature on colonial cities raises the specter of South African exceptionalism. The urban centers of South Africa seem to have experienced a greater degree of violence between the colonized than colonial cities elsewhere in Africa. For example, the gang wars so prominent in the South African setting do not appear to have troubled colonial cities north of the Limpopo. Youth gangs were a feature of urban life in cities such as Dar es Salaam, but they limited their activities to petty theft and the occasional mugging. See Burton, "Urchins, Loafers and the Cult of the Cowboy." Archival evidence, newspapers, popular publications like *Drum* magazine, biographical accounts, and academic works all portray South African townships as dangerous places where criminals terrorized law-abiding folk. Whether these differences are attributable to deficiencies in the

literature or accurately reflect social realities is impossible to establish without further research. It is apparent, however, that South African cities have bred criminal societies that have played a central role in urban violence.

22. Nuttal and Wright, "Exploring History with a Capital 'H,'" 38.

23. Bonner, Delius, and Posel, "The Shaping of Apartheid," 2.

24. Cooper, "Conflict and Connection," 1532, 1533.

25. Rose Hunt, introduction to *Gender and History*, 326.

26. Barnes, *"We Women Worked So Hard,"* xx–xxi.

27. Lodge, for example, in his discussion of Sophiatown gangsters, writes, "The gangs were popularly characterised as marauders in the white city, as heroes. . . . it was popularly believed that 'gangs seldom harm ordinary folk.'" Lodge, *Black Politics in South Africa since 1945*, 102. In an autobiographical account, a former tsotsi leader insists that some of the gangsters in Sophiatown functioned as "young Robin Hoods, fighting the strong in defence of the weak." Mattera, *Gone with the Twilight*, 102. A study of gangsters in 1980s Cape Town concluded that the gangs "are constantly on the threshold of resistance. They share with all Cape workers a long and terrible history of poverty and relocation. . . . It is this that has underpinned an understanding . . . of gang behaviour among ordinary people." Pinnock, *Brotherhoods*, 433. Austen argues that criminal gangs in South Africa "are one of the models for wider forms of youth gangs which . . . offer a degree of nonpolitical resistance to the repressive state." Austen, "Social Bandits and Other Heroic Criminals," 96.

28. Other analysts, keen to refute the social bandit ideal, have drawn attention to the destructive aspects of gang activity. Goodhew warns that "historians have tended to romanticise the gruesome impact of township crime," while Bonner emphasizes "the role of ethnic gangs in providing the nucleus and thrust for the growth of destructive ethnic chauvinism" in the townships. Goodhew, "The People's Police Force," 469; Bonner, "Russians," 186.

29. In any case it would be futile to attempt such a placement, as many gangs both acted in concert with state forces and joined antigovernment campaigns as it suited their needs. For example, in the 1950s tsotsi groups on the Rand frequently fought with ANC supporters, but on some occasions they rallied to ANC-led initiatives. In the 1980s and 1990s comtsotsis were generally classified as comrades-gone-bad or as gangsters who appropriated the "comrades" label in an attempt to legitimize their activities, but the distinction between comrades and comtsotsis was not always readily discernible, a state of affairs that further complicated the already murky definition of political violence.

30. Nicol, *A Good Looking Corpse*, 59.

31. Sampson, *Drum*, 107; Mokwena, "Jackrollers," 14.

32. *Business Day*, 11 February 1999.

33. Bonner, "Russians"; Guy and Thabane, "Ma-Rashea"; Kynoch, "Man among Men," "Marashea on the Mines," "Politics and Violence."

34. The Russians appear in English and Sesotho novels, including Chobokoane, *Ke lesheshele leo a iphehletseng lona*; Majara, *Liakhela*; Mopeli-Paulus and Lanham, *Blanket Boy's Moon*. They are also referred to in Huddlestone, *Naught for Your Comfort*; and Melamu, *Children of the Twilight*. A few academic works mention the Russian gangs in their treatment of related subjects: Bank, "The Making of the QwaQwa 'Mafia'?"; Coplan, *In the Time of Cannibals*; Goodhew, "Police Force"; Lodge, *Black Politics*; Van Tonder, "Gangs, Councillors, and the Apartheid State."

35. Bonner, "Russians," 175.

36. Ibid., 185.

CHAPTER 2

1. Bonner, "Russians," 169.

2. Between 1946 and 1948 the number of Basotho mineworkers on the Rand dropped considerably (from 55,136 to 26,672) while the numbers of Basotho working in secondary industry had increased significantly by 1946 (to 23,578) and continued to escalate thereafter. Bonner, "Russians," 176, 173.

3. Most respondents who were active on the Rand during the 1950s estimate that the majority of their members were employed as mineworkers. Arrest reports that list the addresses and occupations of Russians, as well as observations made by various police officers and township officials, indicate the same. See CAD, WRAD 352/1, Natives arrested in connection with faction fight in Phiri on afternoon of 18th May, 1958; CAD, NTS 7921, file 520/400 (12), Native Commissioner, Johannesburg, to Director of Native Labour, Lawlessness amongst Natives in Urban Areas and Urban Native Townships, 20 February 1951; CAD, NTS 7722, file 145/333, Director of Native Labour, Johannesburg, to Agent for the High Commission Territories, Johannesburg, Lawlessness and Unrest in the Pimville Location, 5 June 1950; CAD, SAP 367, file 15/660/44, vol. 2, Deputy Commissioner, SAP, Witwatersrand, to Commissioner, SAP, Pretoria, 9 September 1956; CAD, NTS 7674, file 90/332, Native Commissioner, Johannesburg, to Director of Native Labour, Johannesburg, 13 June 1952. See also *World*, 25 October 1958; *Golden City Post*, 5 October 1960.

4. *World*, 18 January 1965.

5. *Golden City Post*, 2 October 1960. See also *World*, 18 August 1956, 25 October 1958, 18 January 1965.

6. CAD, NTS 7722, file 145/333, Director of Native Labour to Agent for the High Commission Territories, 5 June 1950.

7. TEBA, NRC files, A. 9, pad 1, Director of Native Labour, Witwatersrand, to General Manager, Native Recruiting Corporation, Ltd., 14 June 1952.

8. Guy and Thabane, "Ma-Rashea," 437.

9. A police report contends that the society arose in 1947 as a result of fighting between Basotho who worked on the mines and visited the women in Benoni's lo-

cation and Basotho residing in the location who mobilised to defend their women against these interlopers. CAD, SAP 386, file 15/2/46, C. J. Lemmer, Chief Inspector, SAP, Boksburg District, to Deputy Commissioner, SAP, Johannesburg, 26 September 1949.

10. Bonner suggests, "As news of Hiroshima and Nagasaki began to filter through, the name *Japanese* was quietly dropped in favour of the common title of *Russians*." Bonner, "African Urbanisation on the Rand between the 1930s and 1960s," 127. For more on the Russian-Japanese split, see CAD, NTS 6490, file 125/313S, vol. 2, Deputy Commissioner SAP to Office of the District Commandant, 26 September 1949.

11. Bonner, "Russians," 175. Arrest reports support this statement. For example, the ages of sixteen Marashea men arrested for public violence following a fight at George Goch station outside Johannesburg, ranged from twenty-one to fifty-nine. *World*, 22 May 1970.

12. Litabe, "Marashea," 18.

13. Bonner, "Russians," 172.

14. Multiple interviews. CAD, SAP 386, file15/2/46, Division Detective, Pretoria, to Deputy-Commissioner, Johannesburg, 12 December 1950.

15. Marashea groups also operated on the platinum mines around Rustenberg and in the Eastern Transvaal gold-mining areas near Evander.

16. GB adds, "It was not common for brothers to join because there were many fights and it would hurt very badly if all the family members died in one incident."

17. See Pinnock, "Stone's Boys."

18. Older veterans made up the majority of my informants. It is possible that younger men, who joined in the more recent past, may have listed economic reasons as their primary motivation for joining.

19. TL is a former miner but not Lerashea.

20. Tshidiso Maloka, *"Khoma Lia Oela"*; Bonner, "Desirable or Undesirable Basotho Women"; Gay, "Wage Employment of Rural Basotho Women."

21. In a case study conducted in the late 1980s, 42 percent of prostitutes interviewed in a large mining town were illegal migrants from Lesotho. Steinberg, *Gold Mining's Labour Markets*, 33.

22. Unless they had documentary proof of continuous employment for a period of ten years.

23. Bonner, "Basotho Women," 228.

24. This happened to 'Mè FD personally. Other women reported that her experience was not exceptional.

25. *Post*, 20 August 1967.

26. *World*, 25 May 1967.

27. Coplan, *Cannibals*, 187.

28. Numerous other interviews confirm that Marashea began as one entity and then split into rival factions.

29. Bonner, "Russians," 164.

30. *World*, 8 March 1965; *Rand Daily Mail*, 4 May 1949; *World*, 10 September 1974. White newspapers occasionally mentioned the Russians, following attacks on white police officers or particularly spectacular battles, but Johannesburg-based African newspapers from the 1950s to the 1970s contain hundreds of stories of Russian activities.

31. FSA, PNV 1/2 and 1/3 contain numerous reports of Marashea conflicts in the Free State.

32. CAD, NTS 6490, file 125/313S, vol. 2, Deputy Commissioner SAP to Office of the District Commandant, 26 September 1949.

33. *Golden City Post*, 2 October 1960.

34. Guy and Thabane, "Ma-Rashea," 447.

35. For funeral fights see CAD, SAP 367, file 15/60/44, vol. 2, Riots at Pimville Location, 19 February 1958; CAD, SAP 397, file 15/21/4/, Unrest: Benoni Location, 10 May 1959; *World*, 16 May 1959, 22 March 1965, 29 August 1966; *Golden City Post*, 17 May 1959.

36. I am grateful to David Ambrose for bringing this incident to my attention as reported in *Lentsoe la Basotho*, 22 February 1997. Some of the details were later supplied during interviews.

37. CAD, NTS 4179, file 33/313, Native Commissioner, Vereeniging, to Director of Native Labour, Johannesburg, 6 December 1946.

38. *World*, 5 January 1957.

39. FSA, PNV, FS1302/vol. 1/21, Major, District Command, Welkom, to Deputy Commissioner, Bloemfontein, 3 June 1960.

40. These examples were described in detail by numerous informants.

41. Coplan, *Cannibals*, 188.

42. Catherine Campbell, "Learning to Kill? Masculinity, the Family and Violence in Natal," 625.

43. Glaser, "Zorro," 62.

44. Ibid.

45. Beinart, "The Origins of the *Indlavini*"; Mokwena, "Jackrollers."

46. For example, the Isitshozi gangs that operated from mining compounds on the Rand in the 1920s-1940s. Breckenridge, "Migrancy." For a discussion of the homosexual practices of the Ninevite gangsters based in prisons on the Rand, see also Van Onselen, *New Nineveh*, ch. 4.

47. Glaser, "Zorro," 51.

48. Guy and Thabane, "Ma-Rashea," 440.

49. Coplan, *Cannibals*, 191.

50. Coplan's informants also referred to Borashea as a *koma*. Coplan, *Cannibals*, 190.

51. *World*, 22 June 1964.

52. Morrell, "Of Boys and Men: Masculinity and Gender in Southern African Studies," 608.

53. Ibid., 619–22.

54. Bank, "A Culture of Violence," 135.

55. Campbell, "Learning to Kill?" 627.

56. Maloka, *"Khoma Lia Oela,"* 103. See also Bonner, "Russians," 170.

57. Both male and female informants stated that women sometimes assisted in their own "abduction" when they had been having an affair with a man from another group.

58. Bonner, "Basotho Women," 249.

59. *World* (Johannesburg), 2 July 1958.

60. See *Post*, 30 December 1962, 29 March 1964, for two such accounts.

61. Coplan notes that the famous singer Puseletso Seema was kidnapped numerous times. *Cannibals*, 197.

62. *World*, 6 March 1962.

63. Coplan, *Cannibals*, 188.

64. A Lerashea woman was given a six-month suspended sentence for concealing a gun following a battle on the trains between rival Marashea groups on the East Rand in 1971. *World*, 22 July 1971.

65. Bonnin, "Claiming Spaces, Changing Places," 310.

CHAPTER 3

1. Guy and Thabane, "Ma-Rashea," 440.

2. Bonner, "Russians," 180.

3. More Marashea were involved in the illicit gold trade because of the numbers of Basotho miners on the gold mines. Most Marashea who dealt in diamonds acquired the stones in Lesotho and smuggled them into South Africa for sale.

4. Two Marashea interviewed for this study are recording artists.

5. 'Mè RB reports that Tsotsi Raliemere, the leader of Matsieng in Phiri, gave out "soft loans" to people in the community, and a long-time mineworker on Harmony Mine, near Virginia, mentioned that Marashea engaged in money lending within the compound.

6. I have uncovered twenty-nine newspaper reports that mention Russian involvement in robberies on the Rand (distinct from fights, assaults, public violence, and murder) from 1949 to 1970. Archival documents paint a similar picture. Free State Russians are mentioned in police and mining reports primarily for robbing mineworkers, and security at Harmony Mine stated that Russians were feared because they assaulted and robbed mineworkers off mine premises. For example, a 1972 report from Vaal Reefs characterized Russians as "thugs . . . who derive their income from illicit liquor selling, prostitution and robbery." CAD, KKD 2/1/8, file N1/9/2 (7), A. N. Shand, Manager, West Division, Vaal Reefs Exploration and Mining Company, to Bantu Affairs Commissioner, Klerksdorp, 19 February 1973.

7. OB and some fellow Marashea robbed a shebeen. In 1968 Michael Nhlapo was sentenced to hang for his role in the shooting death of a white merchant in

Johannesburg. Nhlapo reportedly fired the fatal shots during a robbery committed by five Russian gang members. *World*, 9 August 1968.

8. *World*, 24 May 1958.

9. Bonner, "Russians," 183. For example, in 1951 Corporal Molapo and Sergeant Majola allegedly intimidated witnesses who wanted to press complaints against Marashea. CAD, NTS 7921, file 520/400(12), L. I. Venables, Manager, Non-European Affairs Department, to Native Commissioner, Johannesburg, 25 June 1951.

10. A municipal police officer, along with nine other Marashea, was arrested for his part in a series of robberies and assaults said to have been committed by a Russian gang in Kliptown. *World*, 25 June 1970.

11. Informants supplied many accounts similar to this one.

12. Brewer, *Black and Blue*.

13. CAD, KKD 2/1/8, file N1/9/2(5), Bantu Commissioner, Klerksdorp, to Chief Bantu Affairs Commissioner, Mafikeng, 20 April 1970. This is one of a number of similar reports contained in police files. It seems that Marashea were quick to attack when they held a large numerical advantage, and police retreated and returned with reinforcements on numerous occasions. CAD, SAP 602, 532, and FSA, PNV 1302, contain several files detailing such incidents.

14. *World*, 27 August 1969.

15. FSA, PNV, file 1302, vol. 1/4, Captain Kruger, District Command, no. 23 District to Deputy Commissioner, SAP, Bloemfontein, 5 November 1956.

16. Bonner, "Russians," 184.

17. *World*, 6 March 1962.

18. CAD, NTS 7689, file 325/332, Deputy Commissioner, SAP, Commanding Witwatersrand Division, to Commissioner, SAP, Cape Town, 23 February 1950. Bonner's informants reported that Notnagel's genitals were hacked off and taken as a trophy. Bonner, "Russians," 184.

19. CAD, SAP 397, file 15/21/47, undated memo; CAD, NTS 7689, file 325/332.

20. Interview, BH; Bonner, "Russians," 184–85. Matsarapane escaped to Lesotho, but then made his way to the Free State, where he was informed upon by Matsieng, taken into custody, and hanged in Pretoria.

21. *World*, 25 October 1958.

22. Tsilo's story will be dealt with at length later in this chapter.

23. These stories are taken from Litabe, "Marashea."

24. Guy and Thabane, "Ma-Rashea," 450.

25. Bonner, "Russians," 178.

26. FSA, PNV, file 1302, vol. 1/27, Deputy Commissioner, Orange Free State to District Commander, SAP, Welkom, 2 January 1957. The practice of contributing to a communal legal fund was also reported in newspaper stories covering court cases. See, for example, *Post*, 12 June 1966.

27. Newspapers and police reports often listed the numbers of men arrested and announced those who were acquitted or released. On a number of occasions

all those arrested were discharged because of a lack of evidence. Michael Hodes, for example, successfully argued that none of the thirteen men he represented—who were arrested for public violence and culpable homicide following a street battle between rival factions in which two men were killed—could be proven to have taken part in the attack. His clients were subsequently acquitted. *Post*, 29 August 1965. Of the seventy-eight men charged with public violence following a fight between two Marashea factions and a subsequent conflict with the police in Benoni, only twenty-two were convicted. CAD, NTS 7689, file 325/332, 16 November 1950. There are many such examples.

28. This is in contrast to Leroy Vail, who attributes the invention of ethnicity in southern Africa to African intellectuals, European anthropologists, and missionaries. See Vail, "Ethnicity in Southern African History."

29. Only in more recent years has the Marashea provided a living for a significant portion of its membership.

30. Coplan, *Cannibals*, 143.

31. The identities of non-Basotho Marashea merit further investigation. Informants, including some Xhosa women, all claimed that non-Basotho Marashea were loyal to their groups when engaged in fights against ethnic rivals. Thus Mpondo and Shangaan members fought against ethnic compatriots whom their Marashea group engaged in battle. In such cases, organizational rather than ethnic identity seems to have taken precedence. Survival would likely have demanded such a course of action.

32. Guy and Thabane, "Basotho Miners, Oral History and Workers' Strategies," 239.

33. *Bantu World*, 4 September 1954.

34. Guy and Thabane, "Ma-Rashea," 443.

35. See also Bonner, "Russians," 165.

36. For more detail see *World*, 14, 15, 21 September 1957; *Rand Daily Mail*, 18 September 1957; South African Institute of Race Relations Files, AD 1646, Records of Unrest and Disturbances, file 3 (Rand Riots), University of the Witwatersrand; Report of the Riots Commission, Dube Hostel, 14–15 September by A. Van de Sandt Centlivres, March/April 1958; CAD, NTS 4573, file 51/313(1), Office of the District Commander, SAP, Newlands, to Deputy Commissioner, SAP, Johannesburg, re: Unrest in Western Native Areas, 17 September 1957.

37. *World*, 15 August 1959.

38. Ashton, *The Basuto*, 303. For example, Ashton lists the following uses for moriana: stock thieves use medicine for invisibility, students use it to prepare for examinations, aspirant mineworkers use it to ensure they pass the medical exam required for employment, and litigants use it to strengthen their cases over boundary disputes and other matters. Dating back to the time of Moshoeshoe, Basotho warriors have employed moriana to doctor themselves and their weapons prior to battle.

39. A group of rebel diamond diggers in Lesotho that rose against the government in 1970 also made extensive use of magical protection. Interestingly, some of these diggers were former Marashea. Thabane, *"Liphokojoe of Kao."*

40. Sitas, "Comrades," 637.

41. Adam and Moodley, "Political Violence," 507.

42. Lan, *Guns and Rain*, 209.

43. Glaser, "Youth Culture and Politics in Soweto, 1958–1976," 273. The Russians' role was not completely altruistic, as it seems some of them were paid from the fines exacted by the courts.

44. *World*, 23 January, 4 February 1963.

45. *World*, 12 April 1958.

46. *World*, 5 August 1970.

47. CAD, NTS 7921, file 520/400(12), Native Commissioner, Johannesburg, to Director of Native Labour, Johannesburg, 20 February 1951.

48. *Sunday Express*, 23 September 1951.

49. In 1952, for example, thirteen members of Matsieng leader Solomon Hlalele's gang were charged with extortion, including Hlalele himself. CAD, WRO 352/2, Deputy Commissioner, SAP, Johannesburg, to Manager, Non-European Affairs Department, 28 June 1952.

50. *World*, 22 August 1968.

51. *Rand Daily Mail*, 7 November 1975; *World*, 25 November 1975.

52. *Post*, 9 July 1967.

53. The Civilian Guard movements discussed in the following chapter were partly a response to Russian activities, and similar initiatives cropped up from time to time. Russians also clashed with Guards in a series of conflicts in Natalspruit in the mid-1950s.

54. *World*, 28 December 1957.

55. *World*, 1 November 1965.

56. *Post*, 19 March 1967.

57. *Sunday Times*, 20 July 1975.

58. Tsilo was never convicted but numerous Marashea, one of whom claims to have witnessed the act, confirm that he was the shooter (TB).

59. *World*, 14 December 1965.

60. *World*, 21 January 1966.

61. *Post*, 5 December 1965; *World*, 9 December 1965.

62. See also AT and WL.

63. *Post*, 29 January 1967.

64. *World*, 25 August 1967.

65. This is inexplicable, given that a number of papers covered the shootings—even the local paper, the Carletonville *Herald*, devoted no coverage to the trials.

66. *World*, 19 June 1967.

67. See especially interview with WL.

68. Bonner, Delius, and Posel, "Shaping of Apartheid," 15. The authors use this phrase in the context of spaces African women hollowed out for themselves, but the description is applicable for all Africans negotiating the constraints of urban life in apartheid South Africa.

CHAPTER 4

1. City of Johannesburg Non-European Affairs Department, *Survey of the Western Areas*, 1950, 27, 50, 63; City of Johannesburg Non-European Affairs Department, *Report on a Sample Survey of the Native Population Residing in the Western Areas of Johannesburg*, 1951 (issued 1955), 19, 183.

2. CAD, NTS 7674, file 90/332, undated notes of Gideon Pott, Agent for the High Commission Territories.

3. Interview, PL (Lesotho, 23–24 May 1998); Bonner, "Russians," 177; Guy and Thabane, "Ma-Rashea," 446.

4. Mopeli-Paulus and Lanham, *Blanket Boy's Moon*, 44.

5. CAD, NTS 7722, file 145/333, Grobler, Chief Inspector, SAP, Johannesburg, to Deputy Commissioner, SAP, Witwatersrand Division, 1 July 1949.

6. *Bantu World*, 12 September 1950.

7. *Bantu World*, 27 January 1951; CAD, NTS 7674, file 90/332, Deputy Commissioner, SAP, Commanding Witwatersrand Division, to Commissioner, SAP, Pretoria, 5 February 1951.

8. *Star*, 20 March 1951.

9. *Sunday Times*, 11 February 1951; *Bantu World*, 24 March 1951.

10. Goodhew, "Police Force."

11. Bantu World, 17 November 1951. It was assumed that those who resisted being searched were criminals, and therefore the language they would best understand was violence.

12. CAD, SAP 332, file 1/168/40/2, Deputy Commissioner, SAP, Johannesburg, to Commissioner, SAP, Pretoria, 17 May 1952; CAD, WRAD, file 352/2, Native Commissioner, Johannesburg, to Director of Native Labour, Johannesburg, 8 April 1952; *Star*, 14 June 1952; *Bantu World*, 5 March 1952.

13. Interview, MC; CAD, NTS 4573, file 51/313(1), Summary of the Riots in Newclare, Johannesburg, in which Basutos were involved, 23 September 1957.

14. Bonner, "Russians," 181.

15. The English press campaign against the Russians may have been partially inspired by anti–National Party sentiment among the liberal papers like the *Star* and the *Rand Daily Mail* that were eager to point out the government's failure to manage "relations with the Natives." For instance, in the midst of the squatter crisis the *Star* published an article complete with statistics claiming that racial disturbances were more common under the Nationalists than under United Party rule. *Star*, 5 December 1952. Influential figures such as Father Trevor Huddlestone, who claimed that the government refused to act against the Russians

because the conflict suited its political agenda, also contributed to an English media climate that vilified the Marashea.

16. *Bantu World*, 22 March 1952.

17. Bonner, "Russians," 181.

18. CAD, NTS 7674, file 90/332, Meeting of various Russians with K. B. Morgan, Native Commissioner, Johannesburg, 22 April 1952, and Hlalele affidavit given to Sergeant Papendorp, SAP, 19 July 1952; *Bantu World*, 9 February, 22 March 1952; *Star*, 3 April 1952.

19. Goodhew, "Police Force," 465.

20. CAD, SAP 332, file 1/168/40/2, Deputy Commissioner, SAP, Johannesburg, to Commissioner, SAP, Pretoria, 17 May 1952.

21. Bonner, "Russians," 182.

22. CAD, WRAD 352/2, Minutes at a Roundtable Talk Held in the Office of the Director of Native Labour, Johannesburg, on the Question of Disturbances at Newclare, 18 June 1952. The terms *civic* and *civilian* were interchangeable when referring to guard groups.

23. CAD, NTS 7674, file 90/332, Major Prinsloo, SAP, Johannesburg, to Commissioner, SAP, Pretoria, 28 July 1952. Police antagonism toward the Guards was not limited to Newclare. When Russians clashed with Guard groups in townships on the East Rand in the mid-1950s, police stressed the Guards' ties to the ANC, described them as a menace to white authority and held them responsible for "a reign of terror" in the townships. CAD, SAP 539, file 15/2/56, Assistant Commissioner, SAP, Witwatersrand Section, to Commissioner, SAP, Pretoria, and Officer in Charge, Security Branch, Johannesburg, 7 January 1956; CAD, MGT 2/3/1/355, file 42/7/2, Report of the Manager Non-European Affairs: Unrest Incidents in Natalspruit over Christmas and New Year Weekends, 10 January 1956; CAD, NTS 7690, file 352/332, Native Commissioner, Germiston, to Chief Native Commissioner, Johannesburg, 29 March 1956; *World*, 7 January, 31 March, 16 June 1956. Russian-Guard tension apparently surfaced wherever the two coexisted. SC, who was a mineworker near Springs in the 1950s, decided to visit his cousin in Kwa Thema over the Christmas period in 1956: "By 4 o'clock my cousin told us to leave because he was afraid that the Civic Guard would learn we were there, and if they found us inside would burn the house down because I was well known as Lerashea." As it turned out, SC was caught by the Guard after he left the house. He was badly beaten and had to be hospitalized.

24. CAD, NTS 7674 file 90/332, sworn statement of Joubert Nhlela at the office of the Native Commissioner, Johannesburg, 27 May 1952. See also, same file, Dhlamini affidavit to Native Commissioner, 28 May 1952; *Star*, 14 June 1952; *Bantu World*, 17 May 1952.

25. CAD, WRAD 158/15 vol. 1, Superintendent, Western Native Township, to Manager of Non-European Affairs Department, Johannesburg, 5 September 1952; CAD, NTS 7674, file 90/332, Native Commissioner, Johannesburg, to Director of Native Labour, Johannesburg, 4 June 1952.

26. See also CAD, WRAD 158/15, vol. 1, Report no. 22/1952 of Manager, Non-European Affairs Department, to Non-European Affairs Committee, 26 June 1952.

27. *Bantu World*, 24 May 1952.

28. CAD, NTS 7674, file 90/332, Native Commissioner, Johannesburg, to Director of Native Labour, 4 June 1953; CAD, WRAD 158/15 vol.1, Report of Manager, Non-European Affairs Department to Non-European Affairs Committee, 26 June 1952.

29. CAD, WRAD 158/15, vol. 1, Report of Manager, Non-European Affairs Department, to Non-European Affairs Committee, 26 June 1952; *Star*, 14 June 1952.

30. CAD, NTS 7674, file 90/332, undated affidavit by Dhlamini given to Sergeant Papendorp; Dhlamini affidavit, 28 May 1952; Native Commissioner, Johannesburg, to Director of Native Labour, Johannesburg, 4 June 1952; Major Prinsloo, SAP, to Commissioner, SAP, Pretoria, 28 July 1952; *Bantu World*, 15 July, 23 August 1952.

31. CAD, NTS 7674, file 90/332, Acting Town Clerk, Johannesburg, to Minister of Native Affairs, Pretoria, 11 July 1952; Director of Native Labour, Johannesburg, to Secretary of Native Affairs, Pretoria, 30 June 1952; *Umteteli wa Bantu*, 20 December 1952; *Star*, 14 June, 18 August 1952; *Egoli*, 1 June 1952; *Bantu World*, 24 May 1952.

32. CAD, NTS 7674, file 90/332, Major Prinsloo, SAP, to Commissioner, SAP, Pretoria, 28 July 1952.

33. CAD, NTS 7674, file 90/332, Native Affairs Department, undated memo. Newclare Squatters: police report.

34. Melamu, *Children of the Twilight*, 139.

35. Interview, PP; CAD, SAP 367, file 15/60/44, vol. 2, Deputy Commissioner, SAP, Witwatersrand, to Commissioner, SAP, Pretoria, 9 September 1956; CAD, WRAD 352/2, Native Commissioner, to Director of Native Labour, 9 April 1952; CAD, NTS 7674, file 90/332, Chief Commissioner Native Affairs, Witwatersrand, to Secretary of Native Affairs, Pretoria, 23 February 1957; *Rand Daily Mail*, 20 May 1952; *Bantu World*, September 2 1950, May 31 1951.

36. CAD, NTS 7674, file 90/332, Native Commissioner, Johannesburg, to Director of Native Labour, Johannesburg, 13 June 1952.

37. TEBA, Johannesburg, NRC files, A.9, pad 1, Assaults and Disturbances Files, Inspector, Native Recruiting Corporation, Ltd., Memorandum to Chief Inspector, 13 November 1951.

38. *Bantu World*, 24 May 1952.

39. *Bantu World*, 5 June 1954.

40. CAD, NTS 7674, file 90/332, Meeting of various Russians with Native Commissioner, Johannesburg, 22 April 1952; Hlalele affidavit, 19 July 1952; Bonner, "Russians," 182.

41. CAD, NTS 7674, file 90/332, sworn statement of Detective Sergeant Gerhardus Paulus van Papendorp, Special Branch, 20 July 1952.

42. CAD, NTS 7674, file 90/332, Under-Secretary Native Affairs to Secretary for Native Affairs, September 1952.

43. CAD, NTS 7674, file 90/332, Gratus Sacks and Bernard Melman, Solicitors, Notaries and Conveyancers, Johannesburg, to the Secretary of Justice, Pretoria, 21 August 1952.

44. CAD, NTS 7674, file 90/332, a series of statements collected by Pott along with his notes on same, February, March 1952.

45. CAD, WRAD 158/15, vol. 2, W. J. Carr to F. Lowenburg, 18 December 1952; W. J. Carr to Chairman, Non-European Affairs Committee, 27 October 1952; CAD, NTS 6472, file 51/3135(2), Chief Native Commissioner, Witwatersrand, to Native Commissioner, Johannesburg, 22 December 1952.

46. CAD, NTS 7674, file 90/332, interview between Dr. H. F. Verwoerd, the Honourable the Minister of Native Affairs and Advocate Mr. Lakier and Attorney Mr. Bernard Melman representing Gratus Sacks and Bernard Melman, 6 September 1952.

47. *Star*, 10 September 1952.

48. Van Tonder, "Gangs," 102.

49. *Star*, 10 September 1952.

50. *Bantu World*, 12 September 1953; Bonner, "Russians," 185. The expert legal counsel employed by the Russians (along with bribery) ensured that a high percentage of those charged still gained acquittals.

51. ST remembers that it was a shooting related to a leadership dispute that sparked the conflict, while MS reports that it was squabbles over women that split the two groups.

52. Interviews, HM, MK; CAD, NTS 4573, file 51/313(1), Chief Superintendent of Townships, Johannesburg, to Native Commissioner, Johannesburg, 8 November 1957.

53. *Bantu World*, 26 September 1953.

54. CAD, NTS 7674, file 90/332, Native Commissioner, Johannesburg to Director of Native Labour, Johannesburg, 18 December 1953.

55. Interviews, MC, PP, TT; see also CAD, NTS 7674, file 90/332, Native Commissioner, Johannesburg, to Director of Native Labour, Johannesburg, 7 May 1954.

56. CAD, SAP 367, file 15/60/44, vol. 2, Deputy Commissioner, SAP, Witwatersrand, to Commissioner, SAP, Pretoria, 9 September 1956. The report states that the police were forced to use machine guns to stop the fighting.

57. *Bantu World*, 17 July 1954.

58. Ibid., 2 October 1954.

59. *Bantu World*, 23 October 1954; *Star*, 21 January 1957.

60. CAD, SAP 367, file 15/60/44, vol. 2, District Commander, Newlands Station, to Deputy Commissioner, SAP, Johannesburg, 22, 24 January 1957.

61. Rantoa sheds some light on Russian attitudes toward the police. When asked why he engaged in a clash with the police, Rantoa responded, "We fought because we were protecting melamu. It was a way that they also—it was their standing in front of us—it was a way to make them afraid of us—they should not

treat us with contempt." Guy and Thabane, "Ma-Rashea," 453. See also interviews, NN, 13 May, TT.

62. CAD, NTS 7674, file 90/332, Affidavit of Gideon Daniel Pienaar, District Commander, Newlands Police District, 27 May 1957. For other accounts of Russian-police clashes in Newclare, see CAD, SAP 367, file 15/60/44, vol. 2, Deputy Commissioner, SAP, Witwatersrand, to Commissioner, SAP, Pretoria, 11 September 1956; and CAD, NTS 4573, file 51/313(1), Chief Commissioner Native Affairs, Johannesburg, to Minister of Native Affairs, Pretoria, Summary of the Riots in Newclare, Johannesburg, in which Basutos were involved, 23 September 1957.

63. CAD, NTS 7674 file 90/332, Chief Commissioner Native Affairs, Witwatersrand to the Secretary of Native Affairs, Pretoria, 23 February 1957; . CAD, NTS 4573, file 51/313(1), Chief Commissioner Native Affairs, Johannesburg, to Minister of Native Affairs, Pretoria, 15 May 1957.

64. CAD, NTS 7674, file 90/332, memo, Native Affairs Department, March 1957.

65. CAD, NTS 7674 file 90/332, affidavits of Sergeant James Swanepoel, 15 May 1957; Constable Samuel van Jaarsveld, 16 May 1957; Sergeant Johannes Makasela, 17 May 1957.

66. *World*, 9 July 1958.

67. Bonner, "Russians," 185.

68. Multiple interviews. See also, CAD, NTS 4573, file 51/313(1), Chief Commissioner Native Affairs, Johannesburg, to Minister of Native Affairs, Pretoria, Summary of the Riots in Newclare, Johannesburg, in which Basutos were involved, 23 September 1957.

69. CAD, NTS 7674, file 90/332, Director of Native Labour to Native Commissioner, Johannesburg, 4 June 1952.

70. *Star*, 14 June 1952.

71. *Bantu World*, 19 July 1952.

72. Bonner, "Russians," 186.

73. CAD, NTS 7674, file 90/332, Major Prinsloo, SAP, to Commissioner, SAP, Pretoria, 28 July 1952.

74. CAD, NTS 4573, file 51/313(1), Summary of the Riots in Newclare; CAD, WRAD 352/2, Native Commissioner to Director of Native Labour, 8 April 1952; CAD, NTS 7674, file 90/332, Agent for High Commission Territories to Native Commissioner, Johannesburg, 18 March 1952; *Drum*, December 1955, 31–32.

75. CAD, NTS 7674, file 90/332, Director of Native Labour to Native Commissioner, Johannesburg, 14 June 1952.

76. Report on a Sample Survey, 19.

77. *World*, 5 January 1957 and 31 May 1958.

78. Although the Russians controlled Newclare South, enjoyed a degree of popular support among Basotho migrants, and could call on reinforcements from the mines and other townships, they were ethnically, geographically, and to an extent politically isolated on the Rand.

79. *Bantu World*, 16 June 1951; *Sunday Express*, 23 September 1951; *Drum*, December 1955, 31–32; Bonner, "Russians," 166; Guy and Thabane, "Ma-Rashea," 455. A Mosotho resident of Siteketekeng told me that whenever the Marashea in Newclare were involved in a large-scale fight they would come and rouse non-members like himself to supplement their forces. Reporting on a Russian–Civilian Guard clash in which twelve people were killed, the *Bantu World* quoted a witness who claimed, "All male residents in the Russian sector, irrespective of who they were, were awakened and commandeered to join the Russian gang." *Bantu World*, 15 March 1951.

80. Carter-Karis Collection, University of the Witwatersrand, reel 14, 2:Z13/3/7, New Age, 9 August 1956.

81. See for example, CAD, SAP 518, file 15/29/54, Secretary and Chairman, Evaton Boycott Committee, to Secretary of Minister of Justice, Pretoria, 19 January 1956. Also, Ruth First, in *New Age*, accused the Evaton police of allowing, and even encouraging, the Russians to attack boycotters. Carter-Karis Collection, University of the Witwatersrand, reel 14, 2:Z13/3/7, 9 August 1956.

82. Lodge, *Black Politics*, 176–77.

83. CAD, SAP 518, file 15/29/54, Deputy Commissioner, Witwatersrand Division, to Commissioner, SAP, Pretoria, 20 March 1956.

84. CAD, SAP 518, file 15/29/54, affidavit of Sergeant Groenewald, 20 August 1956.

85. Guy and Thabane, "Ma-Rashea." 438.

86. *World*, 25 August 1956; Carter-Karis Collection, University of the Witwatersrand, reel 21B, 2:YE1, memo of Crown Evidence, part 1, Precis of Evidence, Evaton Bus Boycott, 12–15.

87. The transport manager of the EPS admitted hiring Ralekeke and his men over a one-year period to escort the buses. Carter-Karis Collection, University of the Witwatersrand, reel 21B, 2:YE1, memo of Crown Evidence, part 1, Précis of Evidence, Evaton Bus Boycott, 11–12.

88. CAD, SAP 518 file 15/29/54, Deputy Commissioner, SAP, Witwatersrand Division, to Commissioner, SAP, Pretoria, 20 March 1956; Commissioner, SAP, to Secretary of Native Affairs, memo: Removal of Natives from Evaton, 15 September 1956; affidavit of Head Constable Charles Kukard, 21 August 1956; affidavit of Detective Sergeant Gordon Polson, 23 August 1956; Colonel Grobler, Deputy Commissioner, SAP, Witwatersrand Division to Commissioner, SAP, Pretoria, 5 July 1956.

CHAPTER 5

1. Bonner, "Russians," 185; Coplan, *Cannibals*, 189.

2. Dunbar Moodie, *Going for Gold*, 198.

3. McNamara, "Inter-Group Violence among Black Employees on South African Gold Mines, 1974 to 1986," 29.

4. The real average wage of black mineworkers nearly tripled between 1974 and 1987. Steinberg, *Labour Markets*, 19.

5. *Rand Daily Mail*, 12 June 1956.

6. NT is a mine employee but not Lerashea.

7. CAD, K325, vol. 1, 1975 Commission on Mine Violence, F. J. Ferreira to Minister of Mining, 10 March 1975.

8. FSA, PNV 1/2, FS 1302, vol. 1/26, District Commander, Welkom, to Deputy Commissioner, SAP, Bloemfontein, 16 January 1957. Numerous other accounts of Marashea activities appear in these files (also PNV 1/3), primarily reports on Marashea-related violence either between rival factions or with other ethnic groups. See also SAP 517 for Marashea violence in Thabong Township (Welkom) during the 1950s.

9. *World*, 29 March, 16 August 1958.

10. Goldstone Commission, *Report of the Committee of Inquiry into the Violence during November 1991 at the President Steyn Gold Mine, Welkom*, 1992, 19.

11. For Russian recruiting of miners see, CAD, SAP 602, file 115/15/60, Commanding Officer, Kroonstad, to Commissioner, SAP, Pretoria, 7 March 1961.

12. TEBA, NRC files, A.9, pad 1, Inspector, Native Recruiting Corporation, Ltd., to Chief Inspector, 13 November 1951.

13. CAD, K325, file 7, vol. 5, An Inquiry into the Disturbances on Anglo-American Gold Mines, January 1975, 54.

14. CAD, KKD 2/1/8, file N1/9/2(7), Report on Disturbance Involving Tribal factions at No. 3 Compound, Vaal Reef West Division, 25–27 December 1972.

15. TEBALD, Lesotho "Russian" Gangs, March 1980. See also Chamber of Mines of South Africa Research Organisation, *A Human Resources Audit of Elandsrand Gold Mine Following the April 1979 Disturbances.*

16. TEBALD, Notes on Visit to Elandsrand Mine, 11 January 1979.

17. HF was not Lerashea.

18. RA was not Lerashea.

19. CAD, SAP 480, file 15/16/50, Deputy Commissioner, SAP, O.F.S. Division to Commissioner, SAP, Pretoria, 29 May 1953; CAD, BAO 2881, file 36/5/980, District Commander, Welkom, to Division Commander, Kroonstad, 25 February 1962; CAD, KKD 2/1/7, file 1/9/2, District Commandant, Klerksdorp, to Deputy Commissioner, SAP, Pretoria, 9 July 1960; CAD, SAP 664, file 15/21/62, Division Commissioner, Western Transvaal Division, to Commissioner, SAP, Pretoria, 18 June 1962; CAD, KKD 2/1/8, file N1/9/2(7); TEBALD, Disturbances Involving Basotho Mine Labour Effective from 26 December 1978, 25 March 1981; interview, R. de Boiz.

20. Although some informants reported that they kept their identity as Marashea hidden from management for fear they would be fired. Also, there are scattered references to Marashea having their contracts terminated following episodes of violence. During the Newclare conflicts it was noted, "Compound managers have taken to discharging as undesirable characters all Natives who are known to be

associated with either of these gangs [Russians and Japanese]." TEBA, NRC files, A.9, pad 1, Memorandum to General Manager–Native Criminal Organisations, 14 November 1951. And, in 1980, "the management of Welkom Gold Mine declared those employees (8) identified as members of 'Russian' gangs as undesirable to the industry." TEBALD, Lesotho "Russian" Gangs, March 1980.

21. See TEBALD, Unrest Files, Basotho Congress Party and Lesotho Liberation Army, 11 July 1980; interviews with Inspector K, Russian veterans.

22. TEBALD, Disturbances Involving Basotho Mine Labour Effective from 26 December 1978, 25 March 1981. See also, CAD, K325, vol. 2, file 7, Comments on Strike and Disturbances by Basotho Employees at Vaal Reefs South Hostel, 5–10 January 1975, 15 January 1975.

23. McNamara, "Black Worker Conflicts on South African Gold Mines, 1973–1982," 108–21; CAD, K325, file 2, vol. 1, Manager, Western Holdings, Ltd., to General Manager, Chamber of Mines, 1 April 1975; CAD, K325, volume 2, file 7, vol. 2, Comments on Strike and Disturbances by Basotho Employees at Vaal Reefs South Hostel from January 5th to 6th, 1975, by E. Schmid, Manager, South Division, 15 January 1975.

24. McNamara, "Black Worker Conflicts," 108–21; CAD, K325, file 7, vol. 2, Vaal Reefs Exploration and Mining Company, Ltd., Disturbances 5 January 1975, 9 January 1975.

25. Marashea cooperation with BOSS to support the BCP was consistent with Russian readiness to get into bed with any force that could advance its interests.

26. CAD, K325, file 7, vol. 5, An Inquiry into the Disturbances on Anglo-American Gold Mines, January 1975, 53–56.

27. Elandsrand Gold Mining Company, Note for the Record–Security Arrangements When the Riot Proceeded on 8 April 1979, 16 April 1979. This was the conclusion of the manager of the mine and apparently some TEBA officials, even though an internal report noted that workers had "widely held grievances" and were "genuinely dissatisfied." *Human Resources Audit of Elandsrand Gold Mine*, 5.

28. It was stressed, however, that no revenge was taken against the mineworkers because the dead Lerashea had acted on his own behalf, not as a representative of his group.

29. CAD, SAP 664 file 15/21/62, Division Commissioner, Potchefstroom, to Commissioner, SAP, 18 June 1962; CAD, KKD 2/1/7, file 1/9/2, District Commandant, Klerksdorp, to Deputy Commissioner, SAP, 9 July 1960; McNamara, "Black Worker Conflicts," 234–35; FSA, PNV 1/2, FS 1302, vol.1/39, Report on a Faction Fight: President Steyn Gold Mine, 25 February 1962.

30. At the four mines where polling took place all the men polled had heard of the Russians. The mineworkers at Kinross (77%), Winklehaak (63%), Leslie (59%), and Bracken (57%) mines identified the Russians as professional killers. Interestingly, only a small minority (12–25%) stated that miners feared the Russians. Intercontinental Marketing Services Africa, *Survey Report of a Study of the Labour*

Situation on Certain Gold Mines, Prepared for General Mining Corporation,
March 1988, tables 56, 57.

31. MW was not Lerashea.

32. Target workers went to the mines for one or two contracts for the purpose of attaining sufficient funds to buy specific goods, not necessarily to take up careers as miners.

33. Goldstone Commission Report, 13, 16, 19.

34. Bank, "QwaQwa 'Mafia'?" 83.

35. It is common knowledge in Lesotho, and the South African townships served by Majakathata, that Marashea are influential in the taxi association.

36. Bank, "Culture of Violence," 134.

37. Independent Board of Inquiry into Informal Repression, Monthly Reports, November 1990, University of the Witwatersrand, 10–11.

38. See *World*, 6 March 1962, 8 March 1965, 29 August 1965, 23 December 1965, 20 February 1968, 22 May 1970; 4 August 1970, 25 January 1971, 22 July 1971, 9 September 1974, 15 July 1975, 18 January 1977; *Post*, 19 October 1969, 22 March 1970.

39. *World*, 25 July 1973.

40. *World*, 19 March 1967, 25 June 1970.

41. *Rand Daily Mail*, 11 September 1971.

42. *World*, 13 March 1967.

43. The *World* in particular contains dozens of references to such Russian offenses in the 1960s and 1970s.

44. Bank, "QwaQwa 'Mafia'?" 84.

45. Bank, "Culture of Violence," 132.

46. Bank, "QwaQwa 'Mafia'?" 85.

CHAPTER 6

1. Bonner, "Russians," 180.

2. CAD, SAP 386, file 15/2/46, Duty Report of the Deputy Commissioner, SAP, Pretoria, 14 November 1950; CAD, SAP 517, file 15/4/54, District Commander, Welkom, to Commissioner, SAP, Pretoria, 26 October 1956; CAD, WRO 352/1, Assistant District Officer Jabavu to Manager, Non-European Affairs Department, Johannesburg, 30 June 1960.

3. Guy and Thabane, "Basotho Workers," 245.

4. *New Nation*, 12–18 February 1987. The *Weekly Mail* (20–26 February 1987) also carried stories discussing the alleged collaboration between Marashea and the Soweto Council.

5. Morris and Hindson, "South Africa," 51.

6. Nicholas Haysom, "Vigilantism and the Policing of African Townships: Manufacturing Violent Stability," 67.

7. Josette Cole, *Crossroads: The Politics of Reform and Repression, 1976–1986*, 131.

8. Indunas were appointed and empowered by mine management to keep order in the hostels in return for higher wages and other benefits. Each "tribal group" was represented by their indunas, who were typically older, more conservative men.

9. Anecdotal evidence from mine employees indicates that Basotho occupied the majority of such positions on Harmony. Moodie attributes Basotho dominance of senior positions on Free State mines to the 1963 legislation that forbade Basotho from working in South Africa except on the mines and as farm laborers. "Thus Sotho mine workers on the Free State mines worked longer contracts on the mines and returned more regularly building up seniority." Moodie, *Going for Gold*, 198.

10. NUM representative Jerry Majatladi provided newspapers with a similar account of the conflict, although he alleged that when the fighting started mine security intervened on the side of the Russians. *Weekly Mail*, 2–8 November 1990.

11. This account of the Harmony conflict was gleaned from a series of interviews with security personnel, hostel managers, and industrial relations officers.

12. For NUM accusations that mine security assisted the Marashea in the conflict, see *Weekly Mail*, 2–8 November, 9–15 November 1990.

13. MB was *morena* of a Matsekha group. The group alleged to have done most of the fighting was Matsieng, as they were the dominant group in Virginia at that time.

14. Moodie, *Going for Gold*, 178–79.

15. Ibid., 267.

16. Goldstone Commission Report, 17.

17. Moodie, *Going for Gold*, 203.

18. *Report of the Commission of Enquiry into Events at the Bafokeng North Mine During March 1992*, 27–31.

19. Satchwell Commission, *Commission of Enquiry into Violence at No. 8 Shaft, Vaal Reefs Mine on 28–29 January 1995*.

20. A few Marashea showed me their NUM membership cards.

21. Gencor Manpower Division, *Report on Faction Fighting at Bracken (1–3 May 1987) and Leslie (10–20 May 1987)*.

22. James Motlatsi, "The History of Violence in the Mining Industry of South Africa," 10; see also J. Leatt et al., "Reaping the Whirlwind," 24; *Weekly Mail*, 20–26 February 1987, 2–8 November 1990.

23. Goldstone Commission Report, 14–15.

24. Dunbar Moodie, "The Interplay of Race and Ethnicity in South African Social Movement Unionism: A Case Study of Struggles on Vaal Reefs Gold Mine in Early 1986," 22.

25. For a discussion of the different mining groups' attitudes toward, and treatment of, the NUM, see Jonathan Crush, Alan Jeeves, and David Yudelman, *South Africa's Labor Empire: A History of Black Migrancy to the Gold Mines*.

26. Bregman Report, vol. 4, *Report of the Commission of Enquiry into Violence at Vaal Reefs Mine, No. 1 Shaft Hostel during 1986*, 533.

27. Report of the Commission (Bafokeng North), 27–32, 37.

28. McNamara, "Inter-group Violence," 35.

29. Ibid.

30. Conversation with Buffelsfontein mine security, May 1999. My informant was sure that the Russians were guilty despite the acquittal.

31. For a discussion of hostility between NUM members and subcontracted miners, see Jonathan Crush, Theresa Ulicki, et al., *Undermining Labour: Migrancy and Sub-contracting in the South African Gold Mining Industry*, 56–57.

32. Campbell, "Learning to Kill?" 622, 621.

33. *City Press*, 21 December 1986. See also *Sunday Times*, 21 December 1986; *Sowetan*, 19, 30 December 1986; *Star*, 31 December 1986.

34. University of Natal Indicator Project South Africa, *Political Conflict in South Africa: Data Trends 1984–1988*, 1988, 196.

35. Wilson, *Politics of Truth*, 186–91. Umkhonto we Sizwe is the military wing of the ANC.

EPILOGUE

1. Of course Basotho were familiar with firearms; after all, the Gun War of 1880–81 stemmed from their refusal to surrender their guns and other weapons to colonial authorities. That said, the consolidation of colonial control meant that guns were not commonly available in Lesotho in the 1940s and 1950s. Informants (with the exception of those who served in the military) insist they had no experience with firearms until they arrived in South Africa.

2. Since 1987, when 116,345 Basotho mineworkers were employed, Basotho have experienced a 48 percent decline in jobs on gold, coal, copper, and platinum mines, so that in 1999 there were approximately 60,600 Basotho working on South African mines. Chris Hechter, regional TEBA manager, Lesotho/Free State, pers. comm., 6 May 1999. See also G. Standing, J. Sender, and J. Weeks, *Restructuring the Labour Market: The South African Challenge*. While the number of jobs lost differs from one study to another, the downward trend is consistently acknowledged.

3. Retrenched Basotho who return to Lesotho face even bleaker economic prospects than those who remain in South Africa. Gay Seidman, "Shafted: The Social Impact of Down-Scaling in the OFS Goldfields."

4. Theresa Ulicki and Jonathan Crush, "Poverty and Women's Migrancy: Lesotho Farmworkers in the Eastern Free State."

5. For example, a recent survey conducted in the Carletonville area found that 25 percent of mineworkers and 69 percent of sex workers tested were HIV positive. Brian Williams, Catherine Campbell, and Catherine MacPhail, "The Carletonville Pilot Survey."

6. For a discussion of mineworkers' masculine identities and attitudes toward condom use, see Campbell, "Going Underground and Going After Women: Masculinity and HIV Transmission amongst Black Workers on the Gold Mines."

7. Catherine Campbell and Zodwa Mzaidume, "Grassroots Participation, Peer Evaluation, and HIV Prevention by Sex Workers in South Africa."

Glossary

Marashea: the society as a whole; group members (plural form).

Lerashea: an individual group member.

Borashea: refers to the culture of Marashea and might best be translated as Russianism.

Marashea Factions

Makaota: see *Matsieng*.

Masupha: faction from northern Lesotho.

Matsekha: collective name for the Molapo and Masupha factions.

Matsieng: faction from southern Lesotho.

Molapo: main faction from northern Lesotho.

NATIONAL DESIGNATIONS

Lesotho: the country.

Sesotho: the language and culture.

Basotho: the people of Lesotho.

Mosotho: an individual from Lesotho.

SESOTHO TERMS

joala: beer, usually home brew.

koma: secret male society.

lekhotla: council; can also refer to a particular group.

lingaka: see *ngaka*.

linyatsi: see *nyatsi*.

makhotla (also Makgotla): traditional courts that disciplined suspected criminals.

malofa: unemployed Marashea; lit., loafers.

marabele: fighters; term for Marashea rank and file.

marena: see *morena*.

masole: soldiers; term for Marashea rank and file.

'Mè: term of address for an adult female, lit. "mother."

mekhukhu: shack settlement.

molamu (pl., melamu): fighting stick.

morena (pl., marena): chief, faction leader.

moriana: traditional medicine imparting special powers or protection.

ngaka (pl., lingaka): traditional doctor.

Ntate: term of address for an adult male, lit. "father."

nyatsi (pl., linyatsi): lover, concubine.

GENERIC SOUTH AFRICAN TERMS

blackjacks: African municipal police.

comrade: ANC-affiliated activist, usually a youth.

comtsotsi: comrade who engaged in criminal activities.

dagga: marijuana.

muti: traditional medicine.

shebeen: unlicensed drinking establishment.

stokvel: gathering where food or liquor is sold, with proceeds going to a
Marashea group or a specific group member.

tsotsi: young urban thug, often a gang member.

Bibliography

ARCHIVES

CAD Central Archives Depot, Pretoria

BAO	Department of Bantu Affairs
JUS	Department of Justice
K325	Commission Evidence
KKD	Native Affairs Commissioner, Klerksdorp
MGT	Town Clerk, Germiston
NTS	Native Affairs Department
SAP	South African Police
WRAD, WRO	West Rand Administration Department

FSA Free State Archives, Bloemfontein

CO	Colonial Secretary
PNV	Divisional Commissioner, South African Police, Welkom

Special Collections, University of the Witwatersrand, Johannesburg

Carter-Karis Collection. Independent Board of Inquiry into Informal Repression, Monthly Reports.

TEBA The Employment Bureau of Africa Archives, Johannesburg

NRC	Native Recruiting Corporation
TEBALD	The Employment Bureau of Africa, Liaison Division

COMMISSIONS AND INQUIRIES

Bregman Report. Vol. 4, *Report of the Commission of Enquiry into Violence at Vaal Reefs Mine, no. 1 Shaft Hostel during 1986.*

Chamber of Mines of South Africa Research Organisation. *A Human Resources Audit of Elandsrand Gold Mine Following the April 1979 Disturbances*, Project no. GH2Co6, Internal Report no. 5.

City of Johannesburg. Non-European Affairs Department. *Report on a Sample Survey of the Native Population Residing in the Western Areas of Johannesburg, 1951* (1955).

———. *Survey of the Western Areas, 1950.*

Gencor Manpower Division. *Report on Faction Fighting at Bracken (1–3 May 1987) and Leslie (10–20 May 1987).*

Goldstone Commission. *Report of the Committee of Inquiry into the Violence during November 1991 at the President Steyn Gold Mine, Welkom* (1992).

Intercontinental Marketing Services Africa. *Survey Study of a Report of the Labour Situation on Certain Gold Mines Prepared for the Gencor Mining Corporation* (March 1988),

Kroon Commission. *Report of the Commission Appointed to Inquire into the Tsolo Violence and Related Matters* (1995).

Moseneke Commission. *Commission of Inquiry into Violence at 9 Village Vaal Reefs East Mine on 1st and 9th April 1995* (1995).

Report of the Commission of Enquiry into Events at the Bafokeng North Mine during March 1992.

Satchwell Commission. *Commission of Enquiry into Violence at No. 8 Shaft, Vaal Reefs Mine, on 28–29 January 1995.*

University of Natal Indicator Project South Africa. *Political Conflict in South Africa: Data Trends 1984–1988* (1988).

PERIODICALS

All periodicals are published in Johannesburg unless otherwise noted.

Bantu World. Weekly.
Business Day. Daily.
City Press. Daily.
Drum. Monthly.
Egoli.
Email and Guardian. Daily.
Golden City Post. Weekly.
Mail and Guardian. Weekly.
New Nation. Weekly.
Post. Daily.
Rand Daily Mail.
Servamus (Pretoria). Monthly.
Sowetan. Daily.
Star. Daily.
Sunday Express.

Sunday Times.
Umteteli wa Bantu. Weekly.
Weekly Mail.
Weekly Mail and Guardian.
World. Daily.

BOOKS AND ARTICLES

Adam, H., and K. Moodley. "Political Violence, 'Tribalism,' and Inkatha." *Journal of Modern African Studies* 30, no. 3 (1992): 485–510.

Ashton, H. *The Basuto: A Social Study of Traditional and Modern Lesotho.* London: Oxford University Press, 1967.

Austen, R. "Social Bandits and Other Heroic Criminals: Western Models of Resistance and Their Relevance for Africa." In *Banditry, Rebellion and Social Protest in Africa*, ed. D. Crummey, 89–108. London: James Currey, 1986.

Bank, L. "A Culture of Violence: The Migrant Taxi Trade in QwaQwa, 1980–1990." In *South Africa's Informal Economy*, ed. E. Preston-Whyte and C. Rogerson, 124–41. Cape Town: Oxford University Press, 1991.

———. "The Making of the QwaQwa 'Mafia'? Patronage and Protection in the Migrant Taxi Business." *African Studies* 49, no. 1 (1990): 71–93.

———. "Men with Cookers: Transformations in Migrant Culture, Domesticity and Identity in Duncan Village, East London." *Journal of Southern African Studies* 25, no. 3 (1999): 393–416.

Barnes, T. *"We Women Worked So Hard": Gender, Urbanization, and Social Reproduction in Colonial Harare, Zimbabwe, 1930–1956.* Portsmouth: Heinemann, 1999.

Beach, D. *War and Politics in Zimbabwe, 1840–1900.* Gweru: Mambo Press, 1986.

Beinart, W. "Conflict in Qumbu: Rural Consciousness, Ethnicity and Violence in the Colonial Transkei." In *Hidden Struggles in Rural South Africa*, ed. W. Beinart and C. Bundy, 106–37. Johannesburg: Ravan Press, 1987.

———. "The Origins of the *Indlavini*: Male Associations and Migrant Labour in the Transkei." *African Studies* 50, nos. 1–2 (1991): 103–28.

———. "Political and Collective Violence in Southern African Historiography." *Journal of Southern African Studies* 18, no. 3 (1992): 455–86.

Berman, B., and J. Lonsdale. *Unhappy Valley: Conflict in Kenya and Africa.* London: James Currey, 1992.

Bhebe, N., and T. Ranger, eds. *Soldiers in Zimbabwe's Liberation War.* Portsmouth: Heinemann, 1995.

Blee, K. "Evidence, Empathy and Ethics: Lessons from Oral Histories of the Klan." In *The Oral History Reader*, ed. R. Perks and A. Thomson, 333–43. London: Routledge, 1998.

Bonner, P. "African Urbanisation on the Rand between the 1930s and 1960s: Its Social Character and Political Consequences." *Journal of Southern African Studies* 21, no. 1 (1995): 115–29.

———. "Desirable or Undesirable Basotho Women: Liquor, Prostitution and the Migration of Basotho Women to the Rand, 1920–1945." In *Women and Gender in Southern Africa to 1945*, ed. C. Walker, 221–50. Cape Town: David Philip, 1990.

———. "Family, Crime and Political Consciousness on the East Rand, 1939–1955." *Journal of Southern African Studies* 14, no. 3 (1988): 393–420.

———. "The Politics of Black Squatter Movements on the Rand, 1944–1952." *Radical History Review* 47, no. 7 (1990): 89–116.

———. "The Russians on the Reef, 1947–57: Urbanisation, Gang Warfare and Ethnic Mobilisation." In *Apartheid's Genesis, 1935–1962*, ed. P. Bonner, P. Delius, and D. Posel, 160–94. Johannesburg: Ravan Press, 1993.

Bonner, P., P. Delius, and D. Posel. "The Shaping of Apartheid: Contradiction, Continuity and Popular Struggle." In *Apartheid's Genesis, 1935–1962*, ed. P. Bonner, P. Delius, and D. Posel, 1–24. Johannesburg: Ravan Press, 1993.

Bonner, P., and L. Segal. *Soweto: A History*. Cape Town: Maskew Miller Longman, 1998.

Bonnin, D. "Claiming Spaces, Changing Places: Political Violence and Women's Protests in KwaZulu-Natal." *Journal of Southern African Studies* 26, no. 2 (2000): 301–16.

Bozzoli, B., with M. Nkotsoe. *Women of Phokeng*. Johannesburg: Ravan Press, 1991.

Breckenridge, K. "The Allure of Violence: Men, Race and Masculinity on the South African Goldmines, 1900–1950." *Journal of Southern African Studies* 24, no. 4 (1998): 669–93.

———. "Migrancy, Crime and Faction Fighting: The Role of the Isitshozi in the Development of Ethnic Organisations in the Compounds." *Journal of Southern African Studies* 16, no. 1 (1990): 55–78.

Brewer, J. *Black and Blue: Policing in South Africa*. Oxford: Oxford University Press, 1994.

Burton, A. "Urchins, Loafers and the Cult of the Cowboy: Urbanization and Delinquency in Dar es Salaam, 1919–61." *Journal of African History* 42, no. 2 (2001): 199–216.

Campbell, Catherine. "Going Underground and Going After Women: Masculinity and HIV Transmission amongst Black Workers on the Gold Mines." In *Changing Men in Southern Africa*, ed. Robert Morrell. Pietermaritzburg: University of Natal Press, 2001.

———. "Learning to Kill? Masculinity, the Family and Violence in Natal." *Journal of Southern African Studies* 18, no. 1 (1992): 614–28.

Campbell, Catherine, and Zodwa Mzaidume. "Grassroots Participation, Peer Evaluation, and HIV Prevention by Sex Workers in South Africa." *American Journal of Public Health* 91, no. 12 (2001): 1978–87.

Chobokoane, C. *Ke lesheshele leo a iphehletseng lona*. Maseru: Macmillan Boleswa, 1995.

Clegg, J. "*Ukubuyisa isidumbu* — 'Bringing Back the Body': An Examination into the Ideology of Vengeance in the Msinga and Mpofana Rural Locations,

1882–1944." In *Working Papers in Southern African Studies*, ed. P. Bonner, 2:164–98. Johannesburg: Ravan Press, 1981.

Cole, J. *Crossroads: The Politics of Reform and Repression, 1976–1986*. Johannesburg: Ravan Press, 1987.

Cooper, F. "Conflict and Connection: Rethinking Colonial African History." *American Historical Review* 99, no. 5 (1994): 1516–45.

Coplan, D. *In the Time of Cannibals: The Word Music of South Africa's Basotho Migrants*. Chicago: University of Chicago Press, 1994.

———. *In Township Tonight*. London: Longman, 1985.

Crush, J., A. Jeeves, and D. Yudelman. *South Africa's Labor Empire: A History of Black Migrancy to the Gold Mines*. Boulder: Westview, 1991.

Crush, J., T. Ulicki, T. Tseane, and E. Jansen Van Vuuren. *Undermining Labour: Migrancy and Sub-contracting in the South African Gold Mining Industry*, Southern African Migration Project, Migration Policy Series, no. 15. Cape Town: IDASA, 1999.

Delius, P. *A Lion amongst the Cattle*. Portsmouth: Heinemann, 1996.

Ellis, S. "The Historical Significance of South Africa's Third Force." *Journal of Southern African Studies* 24, no. 2 (1998): 261–99.

Epprecht, M. "Women, Class and Politics in Colonial Lesotho, 1930–1965." PhD diss., Dalhousie University, 1992.

Fanon, F. *The Wretched of the Earth*. New York: Grove Press, 1963.

Furedi, F. "The African Crowd in Nairobi: Popular Movements and Elite Politics." *Journal of African History* 14, no. 2 (1973): 275–90.

Gay, J. "Wage Employment of Rural Basotho Women: A Case Study." *South African Labour Bulletin* 6, no. 4 (1980): 40–53.

Glaser, C. *Bo-Tsotsi: The Youth Gangs of Soweto, 1935–1976*. Portsmouth: Heinemann, 2000.

———. "The Mark of Zorro: Sexuality and Gender Relations in the Tsotsi Subculture on the Witwatersrand." *African Studies* 51, no. 1 (1992): 47–67.

———. "Youth Culture and Politics in Soweto, 1958–1976." PhD diss., Cambridge University, 1994.

Goodhew, D. "The People's Police Force: Communal Policing Initiatives in the Western Areas of Johannesburg, circa 1930–1962." *Journal of Southern African Studies* 19 (1993): 447–70.

Greenstein, R. "The Future of the South African Past." *Journal of Southern African Studies* 22, no. 2 (1996): 325–31.

———. "The Study of South African Society: Towards a New Agenda for Comparative Historical Inquiry." *Journal of Southern African Studies* 20, no. 4 (1994): 641–61.

Guttenplan, D. D. "Holocaust on Trial." *Atlantic Monthly*, February 2000.

Guy, J., and M. Thabane. "Basotho Miners, Oral History and Workers' Strategies." In *Cultural Struggle and Development in Southern Africa*, ed. P. Kaarsholm, 239–58. Harare: Baobab, 1991.

——. "The Ma-Rashea: A Participant's Perspective." In *Class, Community and Conflict*, ed. B. Bozzoli, 436–55. Johannesburg: Ravan Press, 1987.

——. "Technology, Ethnicity and Ideology: Basotho Miners and Shaft-Sinking on the South African Gold Mines." *Journal of Southern African Studies* 14, no. 2 (1988): 257–78.

Harries, P. *Work, Culture and Identity: Migrant Laborers in Mozambique and South Africa, c. 1860–1910*. Portsmouth: Heinemann, 1994.

Haysom, N. "Vigilantism and the Policing of African Townships: Manufacturing Violent Stability." In *Towards Justice? Crime and State Control in South Africa*, ed. D. Hansson and D. Van Zyl Smit, 63–84. Cape Town: Oxford University Press, 1990.

Huddlestone, T. *Naught for Your Comfort*. London: Collins, 1956.

Hunt, N. R. Introduction to *Gender and History* 8, no. 3 (1996): 323–37.

Jeffrey, A. *The Natal Story: Sixteen Years of Conflict*. Johannesburg: South African Institute for Race Relations, 1997.

Kynoch, Gary. "Friend or Foe? A *World* View of Community-Police Relations in Gauteng Townships, 1947–77." *Canadian Journal of African Studies* 37, nos. 2–3 (2003).

——. "From the Ninevites to the Hard Livings Gang: Township Gangsters and Urban Violence in Twentieth-Century South Africa." *African Studies* 58, no. 1 (1999): 55–85.

——. "A Man among Men: Gender, Identity, and Power in South Africa's Marashea Gangs." *Gender and History* 13, no. 2 (2001): 249–72.

——. "Marashea on the Mines: Economic, Social, and Criminal Networks on the South African Gold Fields, 1947–1999." *Journal of Southern African Studies* 26, no. 1 (2000): 79–103.

——. "Politics and Violence in the Russian Zone: Conflict in Newclare South, 1950–1957." *Journal of African History* 41, no. 2 (2000): 267–90.

La Hausse, P. "The Cows of Nongoloza: Youth, Crime and Amalaita Gangs in Durban, 1900–1936." *Journal of Southern African Studies* 16, no. 1 (1990): 79–111.

Lan, D. *Guns and Rain: Guerrillas and Spirit Mediums in Zimbabwe*. London: James Currey, 1985.

Leatt, J., et al. "Reaping the Whirlwind." Report on a joint study by the National Union of Mineworkers and Anglo American Gold Division on the causes of mine violence, 1986.

Litabe, M. "Marashea: A Participant's Experiences as a Leader of Molapo-Masupha Faction versus the Matsieng Faction, Zulu, Tsotsis and the Police." B.A., B.Ed. paper, Department of History, National University of Lesotho, 1986.

Little, K. *West African Urbanization: A Study of Voluntary Associations in Social Change*. London: Cambridge University Press, 1965.

Lodge, T. *Black Politics in South Africa since 1945*. London: Longman, 1983.

Majara, S. *Liakhela*. Maseru: Mazenod Books, 1972.

Maloka, T. "*Khoma lia oela*: Canteens, Brothels and Labour Migrancy in Colonial Lesotho, 1900–1940." *Journal of African History* 38, no. 1 (1997): 101–22.

Marks, M. *Young Warriors: Youth Politics, Identity and Violence in South Africa.* Johannesburg: University of the Witwatersrand Press, 2001.

Martin, P. *Leisure and Society in Colonial Brazzaville.* Cambridge: Cambridge University Press, 1995.

Mathabane, M. *Kaffir Boy.* New York: Macmillan, 1986.

Mattera, D. *Gone with the Twilight: A Story of Sophiatown.* London: Zed Books, 1987.

McNamara, J. K. "Black Worker Conflicts on South African Gold Mines, 1973–1982." PhD diss., University of the Witwatersrand, 1985.

———. "Inter-Group Violence among Black Employees on South African Gold Mines, 1974 to 1986." *Industrial Relations Journal of South Africa* 9 (1989).

Melamu, M. *Children of the Twilight.* London: Skotaville, 1987.

Minaar, A., ed. *Patterns of Violence: Case Studies of Conflict in Natal.* Pretoria: Human Sciences Research Council, 1992.

Mokwena, S. "The Era of the Jackrollers: Contextualising the Rise of Youth Gangs in Soweto." Seminar no. 7, Centre for the Study of Violence and Reconciliation, Johannesburg, 1991.

Moodie, Dunbar. *Going for Gold: Men, Mines, and Migration.* Berkeley: University of California Press, 1994.

———. "The Interplay of Race and Ethnicity in South African Social Movement Unionism: A Case Study of Struggles on Vaal Reefs Gold Mine in Early 1986." Paper presented at the North Eastern Workshop on Southern Africa, Burlington, Vermont, April 2002.

Mopeli-Paulus, A. S., and P. Lanham. *Blanket Boy's Moon.* Cape Town: David Philip, 1953.

Morrell, R. "Of Boys and Men: Masculinity and Gender in Southern African Studies." *Journal of Southern African Studies* 24, no. 4 (1998): 605–30.

Morris, M., and D. Hindson. "South Africa: Political Violence, Reform and Reconstruction." *Review of African Political Economy* 53 (1992): 43–59.

Motlatsi, J. "The History of Violence in the Mining Industry of South Africa." Paper presented to the National Executive Committee Meeting of the National Union of Mineworkers, 25 August 1995.

Mphahlele, E. *Down Second Avenue.* London: Farber & Farber Ltd., 1959.

Nicol, M. *A Good Looking Corpse.* London: Secker and Warburg, 1991.

O'Meara, D. *Forty Lost Years: The Apartheid State and the Politics of the National Party, 1948–1994.* Johannesburg: Ravan Press, 1996.

Nuttall, T., and J. Wright. "Exploring History with a Capital 'H.'" *Current Writing* 10, no. 2 (1998): 38–61.

Ortner, S. "Resistance and the Problem of Ethnographic Refusal." *Comparative Studies in Society and History* 37, no. 1 (1995): 173–93.

Parpart, J. "Sexuality and Power on the Zambian Copperbelt: 1926–1964." In *Patriarchy and Class*, ed. J. Parpart and S. Stichter, 115–38. Boulder: Westview, 1988.

Parry, R. "The Durban System and the Limits of Colonial Power in Salisbury, 1890–1935." In *Liquor and Labor in Southern Africa*, ed. J. Crush and C. Ambler, 115–38. Pietermaritzburg: University of Natal Press, 1992.

Penvenne, J. *African Workers and Colonial Racism*. Portsmouth: Heinemann, 1995.

Perks, R., and A. Thomson, eds. *The Oral History Reader*. London: Routledge, 1998.

Pinnock, D. *The Brotherhoods: Street Gangs and State Control in Cape Town*. London: David Philip, 1984.

———. "Stone's Boys and the Making of a Cape Flats Mafia." In *Class, Community and Conflict*, ed. B. Bozzoli, 418–35. Johannesburg: Ravan Press, 1987.

Portelli, A. "What Makes Oral History Different." In *The Oral History Reader*, ed. R. Perks and A. Thomson, 63–74. London: Routledge, 1998.

Posel, D. *The Making of Apartheid, 1948–1961*. Oxford: Oxford University Press, 1991.

Ranger, T. *Dance and Society in Eastern Africa*. Berkeley: University of California Press, 1975.

Sampson, A. *Drum: A Venture into the New Africa*. London: Collins, 1956.

Samuels, R. "Perils of the Transcript." In *The Oral History Reader*, ed. R. Perks and A. Thomson, 389–92. London: Routledge, 1998.

Seal, G. *The Outlaw Legend: A Cultural Tradition in Britain, America and Australia*. Cambridge: Cambridge University Press, 1996.

Segal, L. "The Human Face of Violence: Hostel Dwellers Speak." *Journal of Southern African Studies* 18, no. 1 (1991): 190–231.

Segal, L., J. Pelo, and P. Rampa. "Into the Heart of Darkness: Journeys of the Amagents in Crime, Violence, and Death." In *Crime World: The South African Underworld and Its Foes*, ed. J. Steinberg, 95–114. Johannesburg: Witwatersrand University Press, 2001.

Seidman, Gay. "Shafted: The Social Impact of Down-Scaling in the OFS Goldfields." In *Crossing Boundaries: Mine Migrancy in a Democratic South Africa*, ed. J. Crush and W. James. Cape Town: Institute for Democracy in South Africa, 1995.

Serote, M. *To Every Birth Its Blood*. Johannesburg: Ravan Press, 1981.

Shaw, M. "Organised Crime in Post-Apartheid South Africa." Institute for Security Studies paper no. 17, Pretoria, 1998.

Simpson, Graeme. "Shock Troops and Bandits: Youth, Crime and Politics." In *Crime Wave*, ed. Jonny Steinberg. Johannesburg: Witwatersrand University Press, 2001.

Sitas, A. "The Making of the Comrades Movement in Natal, 1985–1991." *Journal of Southern African Studies* 18, no. 3 (1992): 629–41.

———. "The New Tribalism: Hostels and Violence." *Journal of Southern African Studies* 22, no. 2 (1996): 235–48.

Standing, G., J. Sender, and J. Weeks. *Restructuring the Labour Market: The South African Challenge*. Geneva: International Labour Office, 1996.

Steinberg, J., with G. Seidman. *Gold Mining's Labour Markets: Legacies of the Past, Challenges of the Present*. Labour Studies Research Report 6, Sociology of Work Unit, University of the Witwatersrand, Johannesburg, 1995.

Stoler, A., and F. Cooper. "Between Metropole and Colony: Rethinking a Research Agenda." In *Tensions of Empire*, ed. Stoler and Cooper, 1997.

———, eds. *Tensions of Empire: Colonial Cultures in a Bourgeois World*. Berkeley: University of California Press, 1997.

Taylor, Rupert. "Justice Denied: Political Violence in KwaZulu-Natal after 1994." *African Affairs* 101, no. 405 (2002): 473–508.

Thabane, M. "*Liphokojoe of Kao*: A Study of a Diamond Digger Rebel Group in the Lesotho Highlands." *Journal of Southern African Studies* 26, no. 1 (2000): 105–22.

Thomson, A. "Anzac Memories: Putting Popular Memory Theory into Practice in Australia." In *The Oral History Reader*, ed. R. Perks and A. Thomson, 300–10. London: Routledge, 1998.

Ulicki, Theresa, and J. Crush. "Poverty and Women's Migrancy: Lesotho Farmworkers in the Eastern Free State." In *Borderline Farming: Foreign Migrants in South African Commercial Agriculture*, ed. J. Crush and C. Mather. Southern African Migration Project, Migration Policy Series, no. 16. Cape Town: IDASA, 2000.

———. *Undermining Labour: Migrancy and Sub-contracting in the South African Gold Mining Industry*. Southern African Migration Policy Series, no. 15. Cape Town: IDASA, 1999.

Vail, L. "Ethnicity in Southern African History." In *The Creation of Tribalism in Southern Africa*, ed. L. Vail, 1–18. London: James Currey, 1989.

Van Onselen, C. *New Babylon*. Vol. 1 of *Studies in the Social and Economic History of the Witwatersrand, 1886-1914*. Johannesburg: Ravan Press, 1982.

———. *New Nineveh*. Vol. 2 of *Studies in the Social and Economic History of the Witwatersrand, 1886-1914*. Johannesburg: Ravan Press, 1982.

———. *The Seed Is Mine*. New York: Hill and Wang, 1996.

Van Tonder, D. "Gangs, Councillors and the Apartheid State: The Newclare Squatters' Movement of 1952." *South African Historical Journal* 22 (1990): 82–107.

Williams, Brian, Catherine Campbell, and Catherine MacPhail. "The Carletonville Pilot Survey." In *Managing HIV/AIDS in South Africa: Lessons from Industrial Settings*, ed. B. Williams, C. Campbell, and C. McPhail. Johannesburg: CSIR, 1999.

Williams, J., ed. *From the South African Past: Narratives, Documents, and Debates*. Boston: Houghton Mifflin, 1997.

Wilson, R. *The Politics of Truth and Reconciliation in South Africa: Legitimizing the Post-Apartheid State*. Cambridge: Cambridge University Press, 2001.

Index

Daveyton, 82, 106
deferred pay, 123–24, 147
Delius, Peter, 6
de Villiers, Captain, 106
Dhlamini, Mamalinyane December
   assassination of, 27, 33
   conflict in Newclare, 98–100, 102–3,
     105, 110
diamonds, 59
dice. *See* gambling
District Six, 5
dompass, 17
Dube Hostel conflicts, x, xi, 70, 71

Employment Bureau of Africa, The
   (TEBA), ix, 120, 123, 128, 142, 145
Evander, 125, 144
Evaton, 64–65
   bus boycott, 92, 112–14
Evaton Passenger Service (EPS), 112, 113
Evaton People's Transport Council
   (EPTC), 112
extortion. *See* protection fees

faction fights, viii, 71, 83, 122, 125, 144, 145
famo, 39, 40, 54
Ficksburg, 18, 129
firearms, 33, 34, 40, 62, 70, 74, 87, 89, 91,
     101, 105–6, 129, 142, 154
   acquisition of, 58, 88, 101–2
   at funerals, 19
   and women, 54, 66
funerals, 16, 24, 28, 34, 38, 47, 55, 94,
     134
   in Lesotho, 18, 19, 34, 39
   violence at, 34–35, 43, 71

gambling, 61, 63, 72, 86, 118
Gay, Judy, 22
Germiston, 17, 51, 71, 80, 111, 130, 132–34
Glaser, Clive, 5, 42, 78
Goldstone Commission, 117, 126–27, 143,
   146
gold theft, 59, 155
guns. *See* firearms
Guy, Jeff, and Motlatsi Thabane, 9, 10,
    32, 42, 57, 66, 69, 113, 138

Hard Livings Gang, 5
Hazels gang, 5
Hlalele, Solomon, 24–25, 96–100, 102,
    104–5, 109, 119
Hlubi, 15, 33, 98–105, 109–11, 114
Hunt, Nancy Rose, 7

indlavini, 42
influx controls. *See* pass laws
Inkatha Freedom Party (IFP), 1–2, 11, 68,
    75, 137, 140, 149–50
Isitshozi, 4, 14

jackrollers, 5, 42
joala (beer), 16, 26, 36, 119
Jonathan, Leabua, 122–24

Kenosi, Ben, 97, 103
Khabutlane, 112–13
Khoeli, Maliehe, 16, 66, 95, 113
Khutsong, 17, 27, 36, 51, 76, 83
kidnapping, 16, 23, 35–36, 42, 45–47,
    49–53, 55, 133
Kimberley. *See* Mokhemele
Klerksdorp, viii, 25, 30, 38, 128, 147
Kloof, 27, 36
kola (fatal beating), 48
koma (secret male society), 43
Kroonstad, 64–65

Lan, David, 75
lawyers. *See* legal counsel
legal counsel, ix, 30, 43, 66–68, 74, 78,
    98–99, 103–4, 133
Lenkoane, 75
   assassination of, 25, 27, 38, 76
Leribe, 15, 31, 38, 85, 105, 112, 127
Leshoailane, 105
Lesotho
   sanctuary in, 83–84
Lesotho Liberation Army (LLA), 122–24
Letsie I, 30
lingaka (traditional doctors), 16, 28, 45,
    58, 73–77, 154
linyatsi (lovers or concubines), 17,
    40–41, 45–47, 58, 119
   conflict over, 28, 51
   punishment of, 48
Lipstadt, Deborah, x
Lodge, Tom, 112

magic. *See moriana*
Majakathata Taxi Association, 59, 129,
    132–33
Majapane, 15
Majoro, Teboho, 38
makhotla (traditional courts), 78–79
malofa (loafers), 15, 22, 57–61, 118, 126,
    128
Maloka, Tshidiso, 22
Malunga Hotel, 18